# THE
# HONEST
# HISTORY
## BOOK

'The Honest History group announced its arrival in 2013 with a clear, urgent purpose: to challenge the dominance of the Anzac legend in Australian popular memory. As the centenary of World War I approached, it seemed more important than ever to remind Australians not just of heroism and sacrifice, but of the social and political costs of war. Mythbusting and questioning, this book will challenge readers to think not only about the ways our national stories are told, but who funds them and for what purpose.' – **Michelle Arrow**

'This book not only offers a vital corrective to the flimflams and taradiddles of Anzackery, but also gives us a new collection of fascinating essays on Australian history. Complex, inclusive, balanced, disruptive and – crucially – evidence-based, *The Honest History Book* is destined to provide a much-needed talking point for teachers, journalists, general readers and, with any luck, politicians and policy makers. A timely reminder that there is no such thing as post-truth history.' – **Clare Wright**

'An important book, both timely and compelling: timely because it provides a powerful and much needed riposte to the current practice of elevating military history above all other aspects of the nation's past.' – **Henry Reynolds**

'Mark Twain once said that Australia's history read like "the most beautiful lies". *The Honest History Book* introduces some inconvenient truths. With so many contemporary debates involving appeals to history, the book concerns the present and future as well as the past, and invites the kind of contention that a confident country should welcome.' – **Gideon Haigh**

'For the past 30 years Australians have been enchanted by the story of the heroic landing of our soldiers at Gallipoli and by a highly romanticised version of the century-long Anzac military tradition. The fascinating and vital question this outstanding and highly readable collection poses is whether an honest version of history can displace or modify the comforts and dangers of state-cultivated and politically motivated myth. The book would be excellent for high school students and undergraduates.' – **Robert Manne**

'This is collective history at its finest. In promoting non-khaki stories of our history, *The Honest History Book* provides us with an invaluable perspective and a balanced approach to the past. Highly recommended.'
– **Melanie Oppenheimer**

'Fake history is as dangerous as fake news … This has never been more apparent in Australia than during the Anzac revival, where the relentless focus on Australian military history has overshadowed the past contributions and experiences of other Australians. Honest history – and *The Honest History Book* – demands better.' – **Martin Crotty**

'*The Honest History Book* delves into issues that are pertinent, painful and part of our wider story. It demands that we activate our critical thinking, not dull it down and accept what is written. I would be happy to recommend this book to any of my students, which is the greatest praise I can give.' – **Matthew Esterman**

'*The Honest History Book* is an inspiration to think more broadly, to challenge preconceptions and serially authorised misrepresentations of our past. This is vital work as Australia rattles around trying to define some agreed notion of national self. It's a must-read for thinking Australians, for the great truth is that until we acknowledge, understand and face up to our past, we'll all be living a bit of a lie.'
– **Jonathan Green**

'Being honest about our own country is essential so that we can properly assess both our achievements and our shortcomings, our strengths and weaknesses. We cannot be a harmonious, confident Australia unless we are honest with ourselves about our history.'
– **John Menadue**

'For some years now the Honest History website has been doing historians a great service by presenting alternative views and encouraging debate about many aspects of Australian history that become obfuscated by myths and half-truths. The publication of *The Honest History Book* is timely during both the centenary of World War I and debates about the appropriateness of celebrating "Australia Day". Here is a book that should be on the reading list in every tertiary Australian History course.' – **Bobbie Oliver**

'What really matters in Australian history? Why has Anzac wielded such influence in our national conversation about the past? This book puts Anzac in its place, and offers stories and analysis that account for so much of Australian history that the "Anzac spirit" cannot explain.' – **Christina Twomey**

# THE HONEST HISTORY BOOK

EDITED BY
**DAVID STEPHENS & ALISON BROINOWSKI**

NEWSOUTH

**A NewSouth book**

*Published by*
NewSouth Publishing
University of New South Wales Press Ltd
University of New South Wales
Sydney NSW 2052
AUSTRALIA
newsouthpublishing.com

National Library of Australia
Cataloguing-in-Publication entry

Title: The Honest History Book / edited by David Stephens & Alison Broinowski.
ISBN: 9781742235264 (paperback)
       9781742242781 (ebook)
       9781742248257 (ePDF)
Subjects: Australia – History.
   Historiography – Australia.
   Militarism – Australia – History.
   World War, 1914–1918.
Other Creators/Contributors: Stephens, David H. editor.
   Broinowski, Alison, 1941– editor.

*Design* Avril Makula
*Cover design* Blue Cork
*Cover images* (top line) Vietnam moratorium march (SLSA); World War I soldier M. Donlan and his wife, 1914 (SLQ); Australian soldiers in field kitchen, World War I (SLV); Australian soldiers embarking, World War I (SLV); Aboriginal land rights demonstration, 1982 (SLQ); (bottom line) Children and horse on unidentified farm (SLV); Vita Goldstein (NLA); woman and child, 1940s (SLV); Judith Wright, c. 1946 (NLA); Nurmurkah floods, Victoria, 1917 (SLV); May and Sidney Louey Gung with grandchildren, Melbourne, c. 1949 (Museums Victoria).
*Printer* Griffin Press

# Contents

# Contributors

**Vicken Babkenian** is an independent researcher for the Australian Institute for Holocaust and Genocide Studies. He has written for peer-reviewed history journals, including the *Journal of the Royal Australian Historical Society*, and is the co-author with Peter Stanley of *Armenia, Australia & the Great War* (2016).

**Larissa Behrendt** is a Eualeyai-Kamillaroi woman and holds the Chair of Indigenous Research at the University of Technology, Sydney. She is a broadcaster, award-winning novelist and Walkley-nominated film-maker. Her most recent book is *Finding Eliza: Power and Colonial Storytelling* (2016).

**Frank Bongiorno** is a historian at the Australian National University and has worked at King's College London and the University of New England. He wrote *The Sex Lives of Australians: A History*, and *The Eighties: The Decade that Transformed Australia*, both of which won ACT Book of the Year. He is president of the Honest History association.

**Alison Broinowski**, formerly an Australian diplomat, is vice president of the Honest History association and of Australians for War Powers Reform. Her PhD is in Asian Studies from the Australian National University. Her books include *Howard's War* (2003) and *Allied and Addicted* (2007).

**Burçin Çakır** has a PhD in History from Istanbul University and is now a post-doctoral fellow at Glasgow Caledonian University. She researches war, gender, memory and nationalism, with a recent focus on aspects of World War I in the Middle East. She has received research grants at Trinity College, Dublin, and the Georg Eckert Institute in Germany.

**Judith Crispin** is active in music, poetry, photography and cultural heritage. She is leading a virtual heritage project at the Australian Catholic University, and preparing for overseas exhibitions of her photographs and scans of monuments from Northern Iran and Armenia. She recently represented Australia in a poetry festival in Colombia, reading from her book *The Lumen Seed*.

**Paul Daley** is an author, journalist and playwright who writes the 'Postcolonial' column for *The Guardian*. He has won numerous prizes, including two Walkley Awards, the Paul Lyneham Award for political journalism and two Kennedy Awards. His most recent book is the political novel *Challenge*.

**Joy Damousi** is Professor of History and ARC Laureate Fellow at the University of Melbourne. Her latest book is *Memory and Migration in the Shadow of War: Australia's Greek Immigrants after World War II and the Greek Civil War* (2015), which was shortlisted for the 2016 Ernest Scott Prize.

**Mark Dapin** is an award-winning author and journalist. His first military history, *The Nashos' War* (2014), won an Alex Buzo Shortlist Prize and the People's Choice Prize at the Nib Waverley Library Awards, and was shortlisted for the New South Wales

Premier's Award for Non-fiction. He is a PhD candidate in military history at UNSW Canberra.

**Carolyn Holbrook** is Alfred Deakin Research Fellow at Deakin University. Her book *Anzac: The Unauthorised Biography* (2014) won the New South Wales Premier's History Award and the Queensland Premier's Literary Award. She is working with James Walter on a history of policy-making in Australia from the 1940s. She is a member of the Honest History committee.

**Rebecca Jones** is an environmental and Australian historian in the School of History and Centre for Environmental History at the Australian National University. She wrote *Slow Catastrophes: Living with Drought in Australia* (forthcoming, 2017) and *Green Harvest: A History of Organic Farming and Gardening in Australia* (2010).

**Carmen Lawrence** entered politics in 1986 and was the first woman Premier and Treasurer of a state government. Shifting to federal politics in 1994, she held several portfolios and was national president of the Labor Party. She is now in the School of Psychology at the University of Western Australia.

**Stuart Macintyre** is a professorial fellow of the School of Historical and Philosophical Studies at the University of Melbourne. A former president of the Academy of Social Sciences in Australia, he has written widely on aspects of Australian history. In 2015 he published *Australia's Boldest Experiment: War and Reconstruction in the 1940s,* which won the NSW Premier's Australian History Prize.

**Mark McKenna** is Professor of History at the University of Sydney. He has published widely on Australian political history, Anzac mythology, biography and Indigenous history. His most recent book is *From the Edge: Australia's Lost Histories* (2016).

**Douglas Newton** taught European history at Macquarie University, Victoria University of Wellington and Western Sydney University until his retirement in 2008. He is the author of *The Darkest Days: The Truth behind Britain's Rush to War, 1914* (2014) and *Hell-bent: Australia's Leap into the Great War* (2014).

**Michael Piggott** was a 2016 National Library Fellow and is deputy chair of the Territory Records Advisory Council, and president of the Friends of the Noel Butlin Archives Centre at the Australian National University. He wrote *Archives and Societal Provenance: Australian Essays* (2012). He has worked at national cultural institutions and the University of Melbourne. He is treasurer of the Honest History association.

**Julianne Schultz** is founding editor of *Griffith Review,* chair of the Australian Film, Television and Radio School, and a member of the Griffith Centre for Creative Arts Research, the editorial board of *The Conversation*, and the pool of peers of the Australia Council for the Arts. She has served on a number of other boards, including those of the ABC and the Grattan Institute, and written several books and opera libretti.

**Peter Stanley** is Research Professor at UNSW Canberra. Formerly principal historian at the Australian War Memorial, he has published more than 30 books, most recently *The Crying Years: Australia's Great War.* His *Bad Characters: Sex, Crime, Mutiny, Murder and the Australian Imperial Force* jointly won the Prime Minister's Prize for Australian History in 2011. He is past president of the Honest History association.

**David Stephens** is secretary of the Honest History association and editor of its website. He has postgraduate degrees from Monash University and the Australian National University, and has published a number of articles, many of them on the Honest History site, and a novel.

**Gwenda Tavan** is Associate Professor and head of the Department of Politics and Philosophy at La Trobe University. She has written the prize-winning book *The Long, Slow Death of White Australia* (2005) and many articles for journals. She has edited two collections of articles and is completing a biography of Arthur Calwell, Australia's first Immigration Minister.

# Foreword

JULIANNE SCHULTZ

Wars change people and they change countries – profoundly and intimately. Wars can be slow to build but quick to erupt, turning once peaceful neighbourhoods into fear-ridden battle zones. The impact is immediate, but produces legacies that endure to shape personal relations, political systems, social orders and economic structures. Framing the experience, interrogating the events, the characters and the sometimes invisible forces at play are all crucial to identifying and making sense of the legacies. These are essential if we are to find a thread that connects the past with the present and helps inform the future.

For eons war has been understood through the prism of battle: winners and losers, brilliant and flawed leaders, blood-soaked battlegrounds, body counts, armaments, strategy, devastation and triumph. The madness that can descend to destroy the lives of those who survive is brushed aside, the political and economic transformations that follow are too often assumed to be a given rather than a response shaped by what came before.

Interrogating the past – honestly, critically, avoiding the traps of ahistoricism and sentimentality – is essential. In a country like Australia, with the eyes of each new set of arrivals set firmly on the future horizon, it is particularly challenging to find the language and stories that shift perspectives and allow the past to be animated. The political response is generally to repeat the time-honoured national myths, to celebrate the heroics, to ignore the complicating details and counter-narratives and move on. In *Enduring Legacies*, the edition of *Griffith Review* published in April 2015, Peter Cochrane and I invited a diverse group of historians, some of whom have also written for this collection, to address the process of complicating what was thought to be simple and settled.

*The Honest History Book* takes the next step. It sets out the complications arising from the many threads of our national history that we need to know about and try to understand – the environment, immigration and multiculturalism, the economy, inequality, the role of women, settler-Indigenous relations, and our lingering ties to the monarchy and to large countries in the northern hemisphere. The book also deals trenchantly with some myths – some of them to do with war and Anzac, some not – that we should not have let ourselves become comfortable with. The chapters of the book present compelling evidence that our history is complex, even messy, a work in progress.

Evidence is, of course, the currency of history. One of the great public history initiatives taken in Australia in recent years has been the decision to digitise and make available the records of those who served in wars – the records of their engagement, where they were sent, the battles they fought in, the injuries and illnesses they contracted, death notices, attempts to repatriate personal effects and secure pensions. The heartbreaking stories of bravery and victory, loss and tragedy, once captured in the copperplate handwriting on yellowing official forms, now available on a screen near you.

This has been a remarkable project, and has given countless Australians some insight into the lives of their forebears, or those who once lived in their neighbourhoods, attended their schools, worked in their offices. At best it has explained a backstory that would otherwise not have been told (in a land where the prevailing ethos is not to talk too much about yourself), provided an important building block in national empathy. At worst it has fostered sentimentality, weeping in a field in western France over the presumed grave of great-great uncle Ralph, who died at twenty without a trace.

But, in a country where the only wars on our own soil have been with the Indigenous peoples, this digital investment skews our understanding of history and who we are. We need a similar project to animate the records of the Frontier Wars, the battles, the leaders, families, collaboration, betrayal, court cases and punishment. This is a matter of public record, records that languish in archives and libraries awaiting liberation. This is the evidence we need to set free and use.

There is evidence about immigration and multiculturalism, too. Apart from Indigenous Australians, we are a country of people who have arrived from elsewhere, many escaping from impending wars or fleeing in their aftermath, bringing with them memory and trauma and often a desire to forget and move on. These people's stories are captured in the official records of arrival and settlement, but they too languish in archives and libraries, kept alive only by the thread of family storytelling.

Imagine, though, a project that animated the records of the Frontier Wars and the management of Indigenous people, and a project that also made easily accessible the records of those who have been arriving by boat and plane for two centuries. All of these stories are matters of public record and go further than the experiences of soldiers in remote battles in making sense of who we are and where we have come from and how Australian norms and values were created and shaped. The skills developed in making war records available should in the name of honest and full history be applied to these other two defining matters of public record.

If countries and people are shaped and changed by war we need to be willing to fully examine that transformation – not just through the records of the men and women who fought on foreign soil, but those who fought *here*, and those who sought refuge *here*. History is complicated, nuanced, provisional. Making sense of it requires more work, more stories, more thinking and, for it to be honest, it demands a bigger frame. The collection in *The Honest History Book* continues to take us on that journey.

# 1

# Introduction

DAVID STEPHENS & ALISON BROINOWSKI

'History means interpretation', said EH Carr, and he was right.[1] The discipline of history is a contest between interpretations. Honest history – the concept – is interpretation robustly supported by evidence. History is distinguished from myth by the strength of the evidence supporting the interpretation. Dishonest history is characterised by tendentious interpretation or inadequate evidence. All historians select evidence. It is *how* they select it that matters, not the fact that they do.

The study of history involves choosing not just evidence but also subject matter. Recently in Australia there has been a sharp focus on military history, specifically the centenary of the Gallipoli landing – the invasion of the Ottoman Empire – in 1915 and of World War I as a whole. The Anzac centenary has been expensive: the commemoration industry has become shy about publicising figures but an overall amount of $A600 million seems about right.[2] Yet many Australians and some people overseas have been puzzled by our fixation on military exploits. The novelist and historian Thomas Keneally said in 2014 that 'there needs to be a certain amount of de-mythologising' about Gallipoli and associated events.[3] One way of doing this would be to attack the 'Anzac legend' head on. There are, however, more intelligent and inclusive options. The Honest History coalition has always recognised that war is important in our history – not so much because of what Australians have done in war but because of what war has done to Australia, to Australians and to others – but so are many other events and influences. Our mantra has been 'Not only Anzac but also' – the 'also' being shorthand for all the non-Anzac influences.

Some people believe the Australian nation was born on the beaches of Gallipoli in 1915. But focusing on that single foundation moment oversimplifies Australia's history and constrains its identity. Honest History – the coalition – has argued instead for a rebalanced view of Australian history, where Anzac is reduced to a proportionate place and other influences are recognised. Downsizing Anzac need not mean doing away with Anzac altogether (as we shall see in chapter 9 of this book), but does mean winding back its excesses. Geoffrey Serle, historian and biographer of Sir John Monash, coined the term 'Anzackery' in 1967 to apply to the sentimental, jingoistic commemoration of Anzac.[4] When Serle wrote, Anzackery seemed to be fading away, but it has come back, stronger, more sentimental and just as jingoistic, in the last 25 years. Finally, in 2016 the word 'Anzackery' appeared in a dictionary: the second edition of the *Australian National Dictionary* defines it as '[t]he promotion of the Anzac legend in ways that are perceived to be excessive or misguided'.[5] The definition is significant because it marks an analytical rather than a sacralised take on the Anzac legend.

Despite the recognition of Anzackery – the extreme version of the legend – there has still been considerable wariness about criticising Anzac itself. The Honest History coalition has responded by pointing to the words on the King's Penny (or Dead Man's Penny) a grateful King George V sent to bereaved families after World War I: 'He Died for Freedom and Honour'. Honest History has always felt this included the freedom to have dissenting views about Anzac, and that exercising this freedom was not unpatriotic. Still, as historian Peter Cochrane wrote in 2015, 'never has the Anzac tradition been more popular and yet never have its defenders been more chauvinistic, bellicose and intolerant of other viewpoints'.[6]

Some people blame governments for imposing a particular view of Anzac. Yet this top-down version of how historical myth takes hold is too simple. Asked in 2013 why the Australian government was putting so much effort into military commemoration, a senior official responded, 'It's what the bogans want'. Governments were simply responding to public demand, triggered by nostalgia or pseudo-spiritual longing or simply a desire for entertainment. One could add to this two-way explanation a version of Parkinson's law: interpretations of history, some of them dishonest because they lack or misuse evidence – they are really just myths – expand to fill the space available, particularly if there is no contest from alternative interpretations.

When a single thread of our nation's story is teased out to excess, it strangles the other threads. Australian history is social and cultural, political and economic, religious and anthropological, archaeological and scientific, as well as military. It is made by women, men, individuals, families, artists, philosophers, scientists, businesspeople, public servants, soldiers and politicians. We carry the imprint of the First Australians; the builders of the CSIRO, the Sydney Opera House and the Snowy scheme; the pioneers of the bush frontier in the 19th century and the urban frontier in the 1950s and 1960s; and 'boat people', whether convicts, post-war 'ten pound Poms' and 'New Australians' or asylum seekers. Australian history is to the credit – and discredit – of all of us, not just our Diggers.

We established the Honest History coalition and website (honesthistory.net.au) in 2013 because we were concerned that the forthcoming Anzac centenary would unbalance Australians' appreciation of their history, emphasising the military parts at the expense of the rest. It was just as important to us in the coalition to highlight other strands of Australian history as it was to critique the received view of Anzac. The 'Themes' list on our website makes this clear.[7] There is 'Anzac analysed' and 'Australia's war history', but there are also in our database hundreds of collected and commissioned items tagged 'The land we live in' (environmental history), 'People like us' (social history), 'Ruling ourselves' (political history), 'The sweat of our brows' (economic history), 'Learning and improving' (education, science and technology), 'Expressing ourselves' (cultural history) and 'Getting on with the world' (defence and international relations), as well as material on 'Using and abusing history' and 'Teaching history'. Honest History believes the best way of coming to terms with Anzac – and of countering its extreme version, Anzackery – is to display the richness of our broad national tapestry, of which khaki is but one strand.

Inevitably, this book (and our website) analyses the work of the commemoration industry located in such institutions as the Australian War Memorial, the Commonwealth Department of Veterans' Affairs (DVA) and their state equivalents.[8] We do not personally attack the people who work in these places. They are often very good at what they do. Yet with some exceptions, such as the *Love and Sorrow* exhibition at the Melbourne Museum and the new work on the World War I repatriation files, commemoration in 2016–17 focuses on much the same stories as it has for the last century.[9] Politicians and senior officials do this, too. It is surely a sign of arrested development in a nation that its prime minister – talking of 'the glorious dead' – and the head of its premier commemorative institution – saying all our soldiers have fought for 'righteousness and liberty' – can still spout the same glib commemoration-speak that was common for warmongering politicians and bloodthirsty clergymen a century ago.[10]

## The Honest History coalition and the politics of history

The Honest History coalition has flourished as commemoration of the Anzac centenary has peaked and faded since 2014. We have gathered distinguished supporters including leading historians, Twitter followers, Facebook 'likes', newsletter recipients and thousands of visitors to our website. (Of course, our supporters do not agree on every point, nor do the authors of this book. All our supporters and all our authors are responsible for their own views.) We have spoken to many groups and schools, and made media appearances. *Honest History's Alternative Guide to the Australian War Memorial* has been downloaded more than 1700 times.[11] Those who hold alternative views of history – like 'Not only Anzac but also' – need to speak up if they are to have an impact. There is a politics of history as well as a history of politics. People who differ from the Anzac-weighted received view have sometimes let themselves be shouted down. 'We agree with what you're saying', we have been told occasionally, 'but we've been afraid of being thought disloyal or unpatriotic'. So Honest History has been an advocacy group – for contestability in history, for balance and for honesty, and against cant, humbug and spin. As author Don Watson wrote in 2016, 'That's the thing about spin – or what goes under the banner today of "communications" – you begin to believe your own bullshit. Spin is the stuff that myths are made of'.[12] Bullshit flows relentlessly to fill the space available. Myths build Anzac into Anzackery, overshadowing the many other parts of our history that deserve examination and, sometimes, celebration.

Do we still have in 2016–17 the degree of bellicosity, chauvinism and intolerance Peter Cochrane detected in 2015? There is some evidence of the passing of 'Peak Anzac' in the falling numbers at 'marquee' events such as the Anzac services in Canberra and at Anzac Cove, the half-hearted efforts of the commemoration industry to promote variations such as 'the century of [defence force] service', dwindling audiences for much-hyped television shows, the low-key centenary of the horror of Fromelles-Pozières, and the rather shambolic events in August 2016 marking Australia's Vietnam involvement.[13] DVA has told travel agents about official arrangements for overseas commemoration in 2017–18 but there are far fewer ceremonies planned than appeared likely in the centenary scoping studies back in 2010–12.[14]

This tailing-off indicates that nothing else quite measures up to the centenary of Australians and New Zealanders splashing ashore on 25 April 1915. It also provides an opening for the more balanced version of Australian history that Honest History advocates, one that gives appropriate weight to our war history but also to the other influences that make Australia what it is. 'Commemoration fatigue' about the Great War need not mean ditching Australian history altogether until the next big military history show, 2020, the 75th anniversary of the end of World War II. Rather, it gives Australians some breathing space to get military things in perspective, to appreciate not just Anzac but also lots of other strands of our history, khaki and all the colours of the rainbow. We might even be able to inoculate ourselves and our children against making 2020 too big an extravaganza. War commemoration, like war itself, has lessons for those who are prepared to learn them. One of the contributors to this book, journalist and author Paul Daley, has predicted that 'with the end of the centenary celebrations of the first world war in 2018 … Anzac could assume a more low-key, contextual place in popular Australian consciousness'.[15] We hope Daley's prediction comes to pass and we hope this book helps that happen.

## Honest History: this book

This book downsizes Anzac by giving it context. It makes Anzac relatively less important by deflating it and by making other strands of our history more important. Honest History's mantra,

'Not only Anzac but also', leads us to criticise the Anzac-centric received view of Australian history – particularly when it spills over into Anzackery – while leaving room for a quieter, more useful version of Anzac. The book explores some non-khaki strands of Australian history – the influences that have helped produce modern Australia – as well as some influences that have not been as prominent as they should have been.

Chapters 2 to 9 form Part 1 of the book, under the heading 'Putting Anzac in its place'. Chapters 2 and 3 show in different ways how parochial and Australia-centric has been our appreciation of war, with World War I as an example. Chapter 2 by Douglas Newton puts Australia's Great War into perspective, using evidence of the war's global dimensions and effects. It also looks at the secret deals struck during the war by the Allied Powers – deals that prolonged the war. Chapter 3 from Vicken Babkenian and Judith Crispin tells the story of the Armenians, a people caught up in the Great War, the evidence of whose fate was known at the time by some Australians – who gave humanitarian assistance to displaced Armenians – but has been largely ignored since.

The next six chapters deal in different ways with the myths and misperceptions surrounding Anzac. Carolyn Holbrook's chapter 4 shows how the place of the Anzac legend in Australian identity has not been constant – as many of today's Australians assume – but has waxed and waned over a century. The legend's future depends on the capacity of our children for critical thinking. Chapter 5 from Michael Piggott looks at a founder of the Anzac legend, Charles Bean, and his continuing influence on how Anzac is presented, particularly by the Australian War Memorial. Piggott finds that the 'received Bean' distorts the man's views and glosses over the roles played by others.

Another Anzac-related myth is that soldiers who went to Vietnam were widely ostracised by the Returned and Services League when they came home, and were ill-served by governments. Chapter 6 by Mark Dapin shows the picture is more complicated than this and considers what the Anzac legend meant for these men. Chapter 7 from David Stephens and Burçin Çakır is about a myth Australia shares with Turkey. The history of the supposed Atatürk words of 1934 ('Those heroes that shed their blood ...') shows how myth becomes mistaken for history. There is no firm evidence that Atatürk ever said or wrote the words.

Bipartisanship about Anzac has helped preserve the myth. Frank Bongiorno's chapter 8 discusses how and why politicians have become so fond of the Anzac legend, whether they can escape its influence, and the political benefits and costs of Anzac. David Stephens' chapter 9 looks at Anzackery, the extreme version of Anzac, one often promoted by politicians. The chapter compares Anzackery with a quieter, more contemplative Anzac ideal, and asks whether a useful Anzac can and should survive.

Putting Anzac in its place also requires telling evidence-based stories about other parts of our history. Downsizing Anzac requires upsizing non-Anzac. Rather than overemphasise single factors, we need to look for a larger, often messier set of influences on our history, a mix that reflects the complexity of Australia today. Chapters 10 to 19 come under the heading 'Australian stories and silences'. These chapters are about the non-war influences on Australian history, some more discrepancies between myth and reality, and the stories of which we do not hear enough.

In chapter 10, Rebecca Jones looks at climate, the environment and natural disasters. She shows how natural events are not just backdrops but players, shaping us as we shape them. Then, in chapter 11, Gwenda Tavan discusses how understating immigration in our national story has reinforced the dominance of a narrow, Anglo-nativist view of Australia in which the so-called 'Anzac legend' is central. This has perpetuated a tension between Australian nationalist ideals and our multicultural, settler-state reality. In chapter 12, Stuart Macintyre reminds us of the influence of bust and boom – depression and prosperity – on Australia. The boom of the last quarter-century has made us wary of economic reform, even though the benefits of the boom have not been spread equitably. (These issues have been among those highlighted during 2016 by the return of Pauline Hanson, the Brexit vote and related movements in Europe, and the election of Donald Trump to the US presidency.)[16]

Carmen Lawrence's chapter 13 and Peter Stanley's chapter 14 then consider the divergence between Australia's egalitarian ideal and recent reality. Lawrence finds that Australian attitudes to equality are pretty much the same as the rest of the world's, and that, like the rest of the world, we are actually becoming less and less equal on key measures. Stanley compares the long-standing Australian military version of equality, built around 'mateship', with our more recent lionising of recipients of the Victoria Cross and of celebrity general Sir John Monash.

Chapters 15 to 17 are about two 'silences' in Australian history: the less than proportionate role of women in leadership, and the failure to confront the dispossession of the First Australians and its continuing effects. Chapter 15 from Joy Damousi tells of Cecilia John and Jessie Webb, two leaders during and after the Great War, whose work has tended to be overshadowed by the focus on military matters. Damousi concludes: 'Understanding and valuing the leadership contributions of women is something Australia has not done well and should do better'. Chapter 16 from Larissa Behrendt considers the colonisation of Indigenous Australia from 1788 to the present day. The story the nation tells itself has still not dealt with the invasion moment and its consequences. Paul Daley's chapter 17 then asks why frontier conflict between Indigenous Australians and settlers has been glossed over in our primarily Anglo-Celtic presentation of history. What does this say about mainstream Australian attitudes and our willingness to confront unpleasant realities?

The next two chapters are about changes that have not occurred. Mark McKenna's chapter 18 considers the connection between the Anzac legend and Australia's loyalty to the British monarchy. Does Anzac, with its inbuilt monarchical element – 'King and Country' – threaten our capacity to ever be a republic? This failure to become at last independent of the British monarchy is related to our historic lack of independence in foreign and defence policy. Will the advent of Trump force us to change? Alison Broinowski's chapter 19 looks at how Australia has entered overseas wars in the past, and how we could better assess the necessity and legality of future conflicts.

Chapter 20 concludes the book, bringing together some key themes. It also includes a modest list of policy options that would help shift the balance – in terms of Honest History's mantra – from 'Anzac' back towards 'also' or non-Anzac.

## Why it matters

Why is it important that Australians' grasp of their history balance the military and the non-military? First, because today's complex, kaleidoscopic Australia speaks of much more than military adventures on foreign shores. We are a much more interesting and fascinating country than one that believes 'our story' is the one depicted within the looming sandstone walls of the Australian War Memorial.[17] Many of us have always known that there is more to Australia than Anzac, but the Anzac legend has pushed other stories aside. Some of us have been content with this: because war stories are at once exciting and sad, and the myths that have grown up around them have been comforting; the commemoration industry, the media and politicians have even used the word 'sacred' about them.

Secondly, 'Not only Anzac but also' matters because *too much* Anzac – or Anzac without analysis or context – is dangerous. In 2008 the historian Anna Clark wrote about how Australian adolescents found war history attractive because of its colour and movement, and a feeling that Australian values like mateship were nurtured at Gallipoli and other battlefields. She wondered, however, whether the attitude to Anzac 'was more like a form of national spiritualism than historical understanding' and that there was developing 'a pride in our national past that's automatic rather than analysed'. Clark was also surprised by the number of students who assumed a 'militarised national identity' was 'intrinsically Australian'.[18] Nearly a decade later, with the Anzac centenary and the proliferation of Anzac prizes for students in most jurisdictions and the Commonwealth, these attitudes might be even more prevalent.

Practitioners of Anzackery, the extreme version of Anzac, often talk about passing the torch of remembrance down the generations.[19] They refer to 'legacies'. A far better legacy would be an Australia where we are aware of, understand and accept *all* of our history, where our wars are considered from all angles, not just the military, where Anzac is downsized, and which is entirely free of Anzackery. That sort of Australia is what this book is about.

# PART 1
# PUTTING ANZAC IN ITS PLACE

# 2

# Other people's war: The Great War in a world context

DOUGLAS NEWTON

n November 1916 President Woodrow Wilson composed a long note to himself, describing the Great War as 'this vast, gruesome contest of systematized destruction'. There were 'no brilliant battles' and 'no particular glory' to eclipse the horror. It was a war, Wilson wrote, 'wherein the big striking thing to respond to was the untold human suffering'.[1] While Europeans have generally marked the centenary of the war in that spirit, the attitude in Australia has been different. Rather than widening the Australian people's understanding of the Great War as a world tragedy, the Anzac centenary has often served to narrow it. The centenary has been marketed as a moment of national awakening. The battle honours of the Australian Imperial Force (AIF) loom large. New memorials and commemorative pageants place Australian military achievement at the heart of the centenary. Should a mature people really be persuaded that the single most important thing to take from the Great War is that Australians fought well? If so, we risk a profound loss of perspective.

## Our war and the war of other people

Formal speeches and popular books about Anzac heap praise on the AIF. Statistics show the numbers of prisoners taken, guns captured and square miles of territory liberated by the AIF by 1918. The point is drummed home: these gains were far beyond what might have been expected from a force of five divisions forming just eight per cent of the British Army. And military achievement there certainly was – at great cost. The total of Australian war deaths – counting the 550 post-war suicides and the 8000 war-related deaths – was probably 72 500. Of all Australian soldiers deployed to the front, 20 per cent were killed outright, a higher percentage than in any other army.

Other statistics are still more horrific. They emerge from the realities of a vast imperial war. Estimates of the total number of people killed across the globe vary widely, but there were at least ten million military deaths, probably a total of 17.8 million people killed, and the dying in Europe did not stop on 11 November 1918. In Germany, more than 760 000 civilians had already died in the food crisis created by the British-led economic blockade. This was cruelly worsened by the victors' decision to prolong the blockade after the Armistice. More German civilian deaths added to the two million military deaths. Far beyond Germany, a wave of civil and ethnic wars continued from Finland to Central Europe and across much of Russia and the Middle East, so that the killing went on for years.

## An imperial war

The Great War was undoubtedly the climax of the age of New Imperialism. Many rivalries, ancient and new, fuelled the sprawling catastrophe. Rival imperial fantasies were vital to prolonging the war, but this reality was shielded from British eyes. Most Britons accepted the tale that they were at war for one reason: the German decision to invade Belgium on 4 August 1914. British leaders depicted this as the essential justification for Britain's war. The subsequent 'war map' hypnotised the British, but the map was often restricted to the Western Front, where the German aggressor stood starkly revealed. In fact, all sides began military adventures and offered preposterous justifications for them. The Germans invaded Belgium and northern France – to save Germany. Russia invaded East Prussia – to save Serbia. Japan invaded German concessions in China – to help save Belgium. France, Britain and her dominions seized every German colony – to help save Belgium.

Britain's own seizures of imperial territory were all supposedly forgivable. In this moral wonderland, she had embarked upon the war as a national act of philanthropy – all to save Belgium. German guilt became the bleach to whiten our own sepulchres. A wave of books appeared suggesting the war was a clash of civilisations and that 'Prussianism' was a singular evil force in world history. This veiled the failures of the global system. Meanwhile, Britain's own imperial aims came into play very swiftly. Within a few months, most of the German Empire was swallowed up by British, dominion, French and Japanese forces, with the seizure of Togo and Cameroon in Africa, various German-held Pacific islands, New Guinea and Tsingtao (Qingdao) in China. German South-West Africa (now Namibia) was conquered in mid-1915. The dreadful campaign in German East Africa (now Burundi, Rwanda and Tanzania) lingered into 1918.

The jostling imperial powers exhibited from the first their double standards when at war. While Britain rightly condemned Germany's violation of Belgian neutrality, in October–November 1914 Japanese troops (supported by a small British force) repeatedly violated Chinese neutrality to seize the German port Tsingtao. In February 1915, British marines, preparing for the Dardanelles campaign, seized the island of Lemnos, violating Greek neutrality. Many more violations followed until Greece was sucked into the war in June 1917. Britain violated neutral rights and international law, as American jurists loudly complained, by imposing her blockade in the Atlantic and the North Sea to try to starve the Central Powers. All commerce across the Atlantic to Europe, including food, was subject to British interdiction. Even the neutral states were 'rationed' by Britain. There were food riots not only in Germany and Austria but also in neutral Sweden by 1917.

Imperial ambition also helped ignite war in the Middle East in November 1914. Loyally following Russia's lead, Britain and France declared war on the Ottoman Empire (whose territories included the Gallipoli peninsula), and Britain swiftly announced the outright annexations of Ottoman Egypt and Cyprus. Troops of the Indian Army, stationed in southern Persia, soon invaded Mesopotamia (now Iraq), moving north from the Persian Gulf to seize Basra. A long and costly campaign had begun.

The reach of the war was stunning. It is estimated that military casualties, forced labour, starvation and disease resulting from the campaigns to capture Germany's colonies cost the lives of one million Africans. Deaths among African porters in German East Africa reached over 100 000 on the German side and possibly 250 000 on the British side, among vast numbers of troops and labourers caught up in the war. Some four million Africans, Indians, Asians and Pacific Islanders served in Europe and beyond.

## The escalation of war aims

The imperial nature of the war can be seen in the steady enlargement of war aims on all sides. The German government in 1914 claimed to be fighting to defend German soil, but Chancellor Bethmann Hollweg, a moderate conservative, soon found himself under pressure from the Left to hold fast to defensive war and from the Right to go boldly for annexations in both east and west. The 'September memorandum', approved by Bethmann Hollweg in September 1914, called for the weakening of France and the throwing back of Russia, for the 'security' of Germany. The memorandum outlined territorial gains from France in the west and the imposition of a war indemnity. A commercial treaty would make France 'economically dependent on Germany'. Belgium would be 'reduced to a vassal state' that was 'economically a German province'. French Flanders and the Channel Ports would be incorporated in Belgium. Luxembourg would become 'a German federal state'. There was to be 'a central European economic association', assuring 'Germany's economic dominance over *Mitteleuropa*', as well as 'the creation of a Central African colonial empire'.[2]

By May 1915 a noisy quarrel had erupted in Germany. The representatives of the industrial, financial and commercial elites wanted territorial grabs that would 'bring us better security for our frontiers in East and West', but leading dissident socialists of the German Social Democratic Party (SPD) lashed out at annexation-ism. Bethmann Hollweg banned public discussion of war aims, but the men of property and the men of military might persisted. In April–August 1917 the High Command urged a sweeping program of annexations. The generals insisted that Germany and Austria expand into Russian Poland and gain military control over Russian territories in the Baltic, White Russia (now Belarus) and the Ukraine. Reactionary German nationalists hoped that annexations would give prestige to 'Kaiserism', undercut the liber-als and socialists, and distract the people. As suffering intensified, however, support for war crumbled. The annexationists hoped to shove victory down the throat of a threatening revolution, but the Left and Centre pressed hard for both democratisation and peace by negotiation. By July 1917 even Matthias Erzberger, a Catholic Centre Party leader who had flirted with annexationism, began to mock the ultra-patriots: 'One cannot pay any attention to the Pan-Germans, let them go berserk. It is cheaper to build sanatoria for them than to continue the war for another year'.[3]

Meanwhile, the leading Entente Powers, Britain, France, Russia, and Italy, could certainly be depicted as fighting *against* this aggressive German program. But what were they fighting *for*? As Fritz Fischer has written, 'all great powers had "annexationist" policies in the age of imperialism'.[4] This is often skated over. The

Entente's war aims – for which so many Australian lives were lost – are scarcely mentioned in speeches and popular books on Anzac. The military story blots out the diplomatic deals done to expand war aims and shore up the Entente coalition, deals that prolonged the war and the slaughter. At the beginning, under the Pact of London (September 1914), Britain, France and Russia became 'Allies' and promised not to conclude peace separately. Russia pressed for this and Britain and France gave in, to keep Russia fighting on the Eastern Front. Tsarist Russia – Europe's most reactionary power – was already eyeing annexations in Eastern Europe and beyond. Russia's 'Thirteen Points' set out annexations to buttress the old order. In agreeing to the Pact, Britain and France risked prolonging the war until Russia was satisfied.

The first major secret deal came in the Straits Agreements of March 1915, on the eve of the Gallipoli campaign. Russia urged Britain and France to agree to major Russian annexations at the expense of the Ottoman Empire. Russia wanted both shores of the Straits and Constantinople (Istanbul), Russia's great prize. As compensation, Britain secured Russia's nod to British acquisition of the oil-rich 'neutral zone' in Persia (Iran). France won Russian backing for her plans for expansion in Syria. To repeat, the agreements were secret. Unknowing Australians would die at Gallipoli so that Russia might rule in Constantinople.

At the same time, Lewis Harcourt, Britain's Colonial Secretary, drew up a Cabinet Paper entitled 'The spoils', which repartitioned the colonial world.[5] It assumed that the Entente Powers could 'dictate any terms they choose'. To balance Russian gains, Britain aimed for annexations in Mesopotamia 'from the Persian Gulf to Baghdad'. Harcourt outlined colonial seizures from the losers, and swaps among the victors, in the Middle East, the Mediterranean, Africa and the Pacific. Britain, her dominions and Japan would take all German Pacific colonies.

Also during March 1915, Italian negotiators in London bargained on the price of Italy joining the war. The Gallipoli landings on 25 April helped close the deal, for they seemed to foretell the collapse of the Ottoman Empire. So on 26 April the Italians signed the secret Treaty of London. The Italian elite agreed to bounce Italy into war. The bribe for them was the promise of great swags of Austro-Hungarian territory, a slice of the Ottoman Empire and a war indemnity. The Entente also contracted to shut down Vatican diplomacy aiming at peace. Meanwhile, there were Catholic Anzacs, perhaps 25 per cent of the AIF, digging in at Gallipoli. Then, in May 1916, British, French and Russian diplomatic negotiators struck another major deal, the secret Sykes–Picot Agreement, under which the victors planned to slice and dice the great bulk of the Ottoman Empire. This arrangement was quite inconsistent with British promises of independence made to the Arabs in 1915.

The Entente Powers bargained not only over territory but also over economic plans. At the Inter-Allied Economic Conference in Paris in June 1916, the Entente agreed to form a trade bloc against Germany. The 'Paris Resolutions' proclaimed a post-war economic boycott of the enemy to weaken German enterprise, while the victorious empires closed up economically. The plan marked the victory of protectionist lobbyists. Unfortunately, this strengthened Germany's militarists, for they argued their war was now self-evidently defensive.

The German and American Peace Notes of December 1916 forced the Entente Powers to issue their first declaration of common war aims – after 29 months of warfare. The 'Reply to

President Wilson' appeared on 10 January 1917. It promised the Entente was 'not fighting for selfish interests'. It proclaimed moderate aims: 'reparation, restitution' and 'guarantees' against aggression. The war was to liberate Belgium, France and Serbia, and obtain 'indemnities' for them. It gave prominence to high ideological goals such as 'the reorganisation of Europe' along lines of nationality, the liberation of the oppressed inside Austria-Hungary and the 'expulsion' of the Turks from Europe. The 'Reply' depicted the German, Austrian, and Ottoman empires as prison-houses of nations – as if the Entente Powers' empires were, by contrast, benign schools for future self-government – and kept silent on the Entente's secret treaties and on plans for economic boycotts against Germany. Soon after, in March 1917, France and Russia struck a deal in which France winked at Russian expansion in the east while Russia winked at French expansion in the west.

By 1916 the Entente Powers had already signed a string of secret agreements on disposing of the captured German colonies. More followed in March–April 1917. The Entente agreed to grant to Japan the German North Pacific Islands and Tsingtao. Various British War Cabinet committees recommended other deals that claimed Palestine and Mesopotamia for Britain, demanded African territory for Britain, recommended indemnities to pay for the war, and aimed to eliminate Germany as a colonial power.

## United States intervention

At this moment, in early April 1917, the United States inter-vened in the war, as an 'Associated Power', not an 'Ally'. President Wilson's War Message to Congress proclaimed ideological goals: 'The world must be made safe for democracy'. Wilson disavowed all 'selfish ends' and all plans for economic boycotts. Ostensibly, the trigger for US entry was the German decision to resume unrestricted submarine warfare. The pro-war pressures upon Wilson, however, included a demand that he protect the hugely lucrative war trade with the Entente. US intervention was scarcely driven by a desire to preserve all 'neutral rights' – the British Navy had routinely violated these for the past two years – yet Wilson was genuinely committed to liberal internationalist ideals. He did not pressure the Entente Powers to revise their war aims. 'England and France *have not the same views with regard to peace that we have* by any means', explained Wilson to his confidant Colonel House in mid-1917. 'When the war is over we can force them to our way of thinking, because by that time they will, among other things, be financially in our hands.'[6] For these reasons, Wilson did not make common cause with the liberal–socialist Provisional Government of Russia during 1917 in its efforts to revise war aims and prepare for a negotiated peace.

Entente ambitions were still off the leash. At the Saint-Jean-de-Maurienne Conference in April 1917, France, Britain and Italy agreed to parcel out more Ottoman territory so that Italy might gain defined shares. Russia was not told. Not until after the second Russian Revolution of November 1917 did Lloyd George and Wilson shift ground. In his Caxton Hall address in London on 5 January 1918, Lloyd George put up more liberal bunting over Britain's war. It was a war for Belgium and France. He promised there would be 'no demand for war indemnity'. Germany's captured colonies were 'held at the disposal of a conference'. Alsace-Lorraine needed merely 'a reconsideration'. Grand goals were back: the 'sanctity of treaties', 'self-determination' for all and, vaguely, 'some international organisation' to safeguard peace.[7]

Wilson immediately outshone Lloyd George. In his 'Fourteen Points' address of 8 January 1918, Wilson defined his goals in soaring terms: democracy, self-determination, free trade, open diplomacy, multilateral disarmament, and a League of Nations to replace the old balance of power. Germany was even promised an 'absolutely impartial adjustment of all colonial claims' and 'equality of trade'.[8] Later, in his 'Four Principles' address of February and his 'Five Particulars' speech of September 1918, Wilson promised Germany a peace of justice.[9] But he was already compromising on his ideals. In mid-1918 he approved a Japanese and British invasion of Siberia, setting aside Russian sovereignty. Soon there were 70 000 Japanese troops in Siberia. Such insincerities and inconsistencies in both Entente and US war aims undermined the chances of achieving a principled peace in 1919.

## Privation, conscription and atrocity

For ordinary people everywhere, the war meant conscription, inflation, impoverishment, shattered families and the mass movement of refugees. Australians quite rightly reeled at the hardships inflicted upon the AIF. But Australian tears may have distracted the nation from the scale of the tragedy endured by others. Soldiers and civilians across Europe suffered as the war machine swallowed up resources. In nations with a small industrial base, such as Russia, the result was extreme scarcity. Shortages of food and fuel hit families hard, inflation eroded living standards, and ordinary people experienced winters of terrible privation.

The world slid into a new kind of 'total war' that targeted civilians. The German military's appalling treatment of civilians in

Belgium from 1914 stood out as criminal. The Ottoman authorities' attempted genocide of the Armenian people from 1915 was even more ghastly, as Vicken Babkenian and Judith Crispin's chapter 3 in this book shows. Sadly, the repression of national minorities was widespread. Behind Russian lines, in East Prussia, in Poland, and especially in Russian-occupied Austrian Galicia, the Russian military – our allies – indulged in barbaric conduct against German and Jewish minorities. Russian mass expulsions, hostage-taking and pogroms created a flood of refugees beginning in 1914. During the Russian retreats of 1915, more than half a million Jews were expelled from Latvia and Poland and almost a million from Galicia. The number killed is unknown.

On the battlefronts, conscription fed the guns. Men – disproportionately young, voteless and without property – were pressed into uniform. The overwhelming majorities of the huge armies were conscripts. The warfare state insisted on its right to deprive men of their liberty and force them to kill. In Germany, conscription saw the total number of men drawn into the army exceed 13 million, almost one-fifth of the entire population, or 85 per cent of eligible males. There were 600 000 widows. During the last two years of the war, one in four German soldiers was aged just 20 or under. One Anzac veteran remembered the physical collapse of these soldiers between 1916 and 1918: 'Shocking damn thing. 1918 they were pasty-faced blokes, ill kempt, didn't look like soldiers even … The German nation was down to bedrock'.[10]

Britain adopted conscription in January 1916. Eventually, conscripts made up more than half the almost five million soldiers sent abroad. But abandoning the liberal tradition of 'free service' provoked resistance. The total of 'conscientious objectors' exceeded 16 000. Those who refused all service, often socialists and pacifists, were arrested and gaoled. More than 6000 endured prison and brutal treatment. Of these, 71 died in prison, 31 'lost their reason' and about 1500 were still in prison six months after the Armistice. When hundreds went on hunger strike, they faced force-feeding.[11] Vindictiveness followed victory. In a war of industrialised mass killing, atrocities were a daily event at the battlefront, but they also happened behind the lines. On the Italian front, the Italian commander, General Cadorna, ruthlessly applied against his own units his policy of 'decimation', the execution at random of conscripted men in order to punish 'cowardice'. Arthur Wheen, an AIF veteran and later translator of *All Quiet on the Western Front*, nailed it. The truth was, he wrote, 'the bestiality was wherever war was'.[12]

## Australia and a world tragedy

The war experienced by other people – the real war – was a much more complex and cynical phenomenon than most Australians realised. Australians could not truly comprehend this world tragedy; crucial facets were hidden from them. In their ignorance, Australian political leaders said the most naïve things. At a public meeting in Brisbane in January 1916 to launch the Anzac Day Commemoration Committee, the Queensland Labor Premier TJ Ryan told the crowd that 'at the conclusion of the war Great Britain will seek no territorial aggrandisement'.[13] Australians learned only scraps of information about the Empire's true war aims, which were mostly hidden in the diplomatic deals struck by Britain. When Australian politicians spoke of *our own* war aims, they spoke in generalities: to defend Australia, to help Britain and to defeat German aggression. One vital aim was often unspoken: to show such loyalty to Britain in this war that she would commit to defending Australia into the future – from Japan. Prime Minister Hughes did insist on Australia retaining captured German colonies, and he opposed Japan gaining any share. He also whipped up support for a post-war economic boycott of Germany, which he had urged at Paris in 1916. Beyond this, Australia contributed very little to the high diplomacy of war. Australia was seldom consulted or informed about British and Entente war aims.[14]

In late 1917 Russia's revolutionary government released the full texts of the key secret treaties concluded between Tsarist Russia and the Entente Powers. These were quickly republished in the *New York Times* and the *Manchester Guardian*. In faraway Australia, however, only a few Labor, feminist and Catholic newspapers gave summaries and extracts. For example, Catholic papers reported angrily from January 1918 that, under the Treaty of London of April 1915, Britain had agreed to block 'any diplomatic step' of the Vatican aiming at peace.[15] Months later, one paper, the *Woman Voter*, managed to get the texts of just two treaties past the censor.[16] The issue provoked debate in Labor circles, but the main newspapers buried the whole matter as they raged against Russia's 'betrayal'. Most Australians thus remained largely unaware of the escalation of war aims on their own side – the Entente – that had prolonged the war.

One hundred years later, Australians' lack of awareness is ingrained. The 'other people's war' is still almost entirely eclipsed by *our* war. Speakers at official Anzac events do little to disperse the fog shrouding war aims. Popular historians leave out the diplomatic underpinnings of the battles in which Australians fought. Purposes appear in rosy terms. 'Few of us can recall the detail', then Prime Minister Tony Abbott told the crowd at

Gallipoli in 2015, 'but we have imbibed what matters most: that a generation of young Australians rallied to serve our country, when our country called'. And fought for what? 'It was for country, Empire, King, and the ideal that people and countries should be free.' The Diggers fought 'for duty, loyalty, honour and mates: the virtues that outshine any cause'.[17] A century on, our soldiers in Afghanistan 'fought', said Abbott, 'for the universal decencies of mankind ... Australians don't fight to conquer; we fight to help, to build and to serve'.[18]

Should causes matter? Does the Abbott attitude respect the dead? From 1916 to 1918 on the Western Front, the Australian divisions lost 46 000 dead, of whom 10 892 have no known grave. They died mostly from shrapnel and high explosive shells designed to tear people to pieces or bury them alive. Surely the questions that haunt us should not begin and end with: Did our Anzacs fight well? Rather, we should be asking the only truly respectful questions: What happened here? For what precisely were Australian lives given up? Did our Australian government carefully weigh war aims, costs and alternatives? Or, in its servility to a powerful imperial friend, did it lose control over all these things? (Alison Broinowski's chapter 19 in this book has more to say on how Australia goes to war.)

We should reject the rationalisations of mass slaughter that find the complete cause of this disaster – the Great War – in the enemy. We should shrink from the sacrificial fantasies of the nation reborn through young blood. We should question the mindless fatalism that insists there was simply no alternative. We should shun the consolations of victory – because the end cannot vindicate all means. We should refuse to find comfort in the soldierly virtues, remembering poet and Great War soldier

Frederic Manning's remark that 'the extreme of heroism, alike in foe or friend, is indistinguishable from despair'.[19] The Tasmanian-born UK radical MP Leonard Outhwaite said it best when he scolded the ultra-patriots sitting safe in the British House of Commons in February 1916. Their demand for a military victory, he warned, would mean 'dragging in the last million men or the last hundred thousand men to hoist the flag of victory over an international graveyard'.[20] And so they did.

The Great War should rattle our souls, not rouse our national self-esteem.

# 3

# 24 April 1915: Australia's Armenian story over a century

## VICKEN BABKENIAN & JUDITH CRISPIN

On the afternoon of 24 April 1915 one of the most significant events in the military history of Australia and New Zealand began in Mudros Harbour on the Greek island of Lemnos. The island had become the base for a great Anglo-French assault on the Gallipoli peninsula. Other events were also underway: just hours before the Anzac landing, the Ottoman authorities arrested about 230 Armenian political, religious, educational and intellectual leaders in Constantinople. The arrests followed a directive sent by Ottoman Minister of the Interior, Talaat Bey, earlier that day. Even as the Anzacs were coming ashore, the Ottoman authorities deported the Armenian prisoners east by train from Haidar Pasha station on the Asiatic shore, inland to Angora (now Ankara). Only a handful of the 230 Armenians survived; the rest disappeared without trace. The 24 April arrests became a blueprint for the Ottoman government's systematic destruction of its civilian Armenian population throughout the Empire. The Ottoman commitment to eradicating Armenians extended well beyond ethnic cleansing to become a dedicated attempt to wipe out all traces of Armenian culture and history. Across the Near East, Armenian churches and cemeteries were reduced to rubble. A campaign of cultural genocide had begun, and it has continued across the region ever since.

For the Anzacs and their comrades, 25 April 1915 began an eight-month ordeal, a campaign that would see the deaths of 40 000 invaders and more than twice as many defenders. The failed campaign would later be celebrated as the making of the Anzac nations, while the Ottoman victory would contribute a figurehead (Mustafa Kemal, later Atatürk) and associated mythology to the idea of a Turkish nation. On that first Anzac Day, too, the train rattling eastwards from Constantinople marked the beginning of the extermination of at least one million of the Ottoman Empire's Armenian subjects. The fate of an already oppressed people, for centuries without a nation, who would wait decades to belong to a nation again, was bound up with the new Antipodean countries, whose soldiers were at that moment fighting on the hillsides of Gallipoli. How were these events connected?

The answer can be simply summarised, though the details are complex: Australians saw the attempted genocide of the Ottoman

Empire's Armenians and fought to liberate them; Australians were active in a massive humanitarian effort – the first in Australia's history – and later welcomed descendants of genocide survivors and victims. Today in Australia we know far more about what began on 25 April 1915 than what began the day before. Our lack of awareness of the Armenian tragedy epitomises Australian parochialism about our war history. This chapter attempts to redress the balance.

## The Armenian Genocide

The genocide of the Armenians in 1915 was implemented through what Turkish historian Taner Akçam called a 'dual track mechanism'. Deportation and resettlement orders came via official channels from the Interior Ministry to the provincial governors, who then circulated them to the security service units connected to the ministry. Concurrently, coded killing orders went to the provinces from the government in Constantinople.[1] Families then had a few days to collect their belongings. Their property was sold off or given to the local population. Men were rounded up and killed. Convoys of the elderly, women and children were sent on the road, and subjected to robbery, looting, rape, abduction and murder. From the Ottoman eastern provinces, the twin-track measures – deportations and accompanying mass killings – spread westward, spanning much of Anatolia, the major part of modern Turkey. Akçam estimates that between 600 000 and 1.5 million Armenians were killed. (Armenian volunteer battalions fighting alongside the Russian Army killed perhaps a few thousand Ottomans, although again exact numbers are unknown.) The number of women and children given to Turkish,

Kurdish or Arab families or just kidnapped is impossible to calculate, but some authorities suggest the number could have been as high as 200 000.[2]

## Anzac encounters with Armenians

During World War I, Australian Anzacs encountered Armenians wherever the Anzacs went in the Middle East. A community of several thousand Armenians lived in Egypt, mostly in Cairo. Anzacs, stationed at Mena Camp about ten miles from Cairo, patronised Armenian businesses. In December 1914, Lance Corporal Henry Miller Lanser of the 1st Battalion, a motor mechanic from Sydney, visited a recording studio owned by an Armenian, Setrak Mechian, and recorded a Christmas message to his family. He used a shellac disc instead of the card that was in normal use. Henry Lanser's disc is the only known recorded letter made by an Australian soldier during the Great War, perhaps the only one of its kind in the world.[3]

In late 1915, details of the escape and rescue by French cruisers of some 5000 Armenians from the Mediterranean coast began to be widely disseminated.[4] The heroism of these Armenians, and the suffering they endured, became a popular news item in Australia. When Ottoman orders to leave reached the inhabitants of six Armenian villages at the base of Musa Dagh (Mount Moses) near Antioch, Syria, in July 1915, the Armenians chose instead to defy the order and retreat up the mountain. With only a few hundred rifles and provisions from their village stores, the Armenians put up a fierce resistance against attempts by regular Ottoman troops to flush them out. Untrained, inexperienced, outnumbered and outgunned, the Armenians had little expectation of surviving the siege when their food stocks were depleted after a month. Then, gradually, despite the encumbrance of women and children, they retreated to the sea. They had resisted as best they could, but the situation seemed hopeless and, unless help came quickly, they would all be killed.

The only hope of rescue for these Armenians was if an Allied warship was patrolling the Mediterranean coast. When the Armenians hoisted two large banners – one a Red Cross flag and the other stating 'Christians in Distress: Rescue' – by an astonishing chance the banners were seen by a passing French warship. A squadron of Allied warships rescued the Armenians and disembarked them at Port Said, Egypt. A British staff officer used three Australian transport ships to meet the emergency. The Anglo-Egyptian government established a camp for the refugees where they were housed, fed and given medical treatment. Anzacs stationed close to the refugee camp would purchase the refugee women's handiwork to send to Australia as gifts.[5]

Australian encounters with Armenians proliferated after the Gallipoli landing in April 1915. Like the British and French forces, the Ottoman Army reflected the multi-ethnic composition of an empire. Despite being commonly referred to as 'Turks', the members of the Ottoman Army included Turks, Arabs, Kurds, Armenians, Greeks and more. On 25 April, Anzacs had captured at least one Ottoman Armenian. Interrogated by intelligence officers, this man reported that an Ottoman division of 18 000 men was advancing on the invaders. As the campaign continued, the number of Armenian prisoners increased. Since many of the prisoners had studied in American mission schools, they often had a good command of both English and Turkish. British intelligence officers examining Ottoman prisoners found many of the Armenians sympathetic to the Allied cause and saw them as trustworthy guides or interpreters. Still, the concept of an Ottoman prisoner being in sympathy with the Allies took time for some Anzacs to comprehend. Aubrey Herbert, a British intelligence officer and interpreter with the Anzacs, recalled his difficulty persuading Anzacs that the 'Greeks and Armenians ... were conscripts who hated their masters' and that just because a prisoner knew Turkish, this 'did not make him a Turk'.[6]

Anzac officers learned more about their enemy. In September 1915, Charles Bean reported from Gaba Tepe that the Turkish labour battalion – which largely comprised Greeks and Armenians – had been 'very active in digging and improving the trenches' for the upcoming winter campaign. Lieutenant Edward Gaynor wrote in November 1915 that the 'Turkish soldier does no work' but the Armenians and other Christians were herded together into battalions to do nothing else but dig trenches. Gaynor thought it would have been 'a boon and a blessing' if he had such working battalions: his fighting men spent 'half their time digging trenches'.[7]

## Anzac prisoners of war as witnesses

Among the many foreign eyewitnesses to the Armenian Genocide were the Anzac prisoners captured by the Turks. They included prisoners taken at Gallipoli, the Sinai and Mesopotamia (Iraq), as well as the submariners who penetrated the Dardanelles in 1915. Perhaps the best-known Australian prisoner in Turkey was Captain (later Sir) Thomas White, a pilot for the Australian Flying Corps and in later years a minister in the Menzies government. White was captured by the Ottoman Army while on a mission to cut telegraph wires near Baghdad in November 1915. He had his first encounter with the Armenian massacres when he reached a 'mainly Armenian town', Tel Armen, in northern Mesopotamia. White noticed that only a very few Armenian women and children had remained, 'the males being conspicuously absent'. He found 'thirty-six newly-made graves which spoke eloquently of what had become of the Armenian men'. He noticed a little girl looking pleadingly towards him. Powerless to help her, White was 'horrified at the Turk's handiwork, learning later that these massacres had been simultaneous and to order throughout the entire country'.[8]

As well as the demographic change caused by the forced deportation of Armenians and other Ottoman Christians, the Ottoman policy had served another useful purpose. The homes, churches and monasteries the Armenians had been forced to abandon became the prison camps where many Australian and other Allied prisoners were held captive. Lieutenant Leslie Luscombe of the 14th Battalion was taken prisoner at Gallipoli in August 1915. While he was being transported to the centuries-old Sourp Asdvadzadzin (Holy Mother of God) Armenian monastery in Ankara, he witnessed 'a sad and depressing sight' at the station in Eskişehir, a railway junction town in western Turkey. 'As our train pulled into the platform, Turkish soldiers armed with whips were driving the [Armenian] women and children into the sheep trucks. It was evidently intended to transport them to some distant concentration camp ...'[9]

Another prisoner was Able Seaman John Wheat, a crew member of the Australian submarine *AE2*, which had been captured shortly after penetrating the Dardanelles in April 1915. Wheat was taken to another Sourp Asdvadzadzin, an Armenian church at Afyonkarahissar, a town in western Turkey. Before the war, the Armenians comprised about one-third of the town's 30000 inhabitants. Wheat observed that '[a]ll the Armenians' had been 'driven from the town' before his arrival. Another Australian prisoner, Private Daniel Creedon of the 9th Battalion, wrote in his diary just two months later: 'The people say that the Turks killed 1¼ million Armenians'.[10] Creedon's figure was close to the accepted death toll for the massacres and suggests that the magnitude of the outrage was known and discussed by Anzac prisoners of war.

## The Syrian and Mesopotamian theatre of war

As the British forces advanced northwards into the Ottoman province of Palestine the Australian Light Horse encountered thousands of Armenian refugees. In Jerusalem, British Empire troops discovered around 500 deportees in the Armenian monastery of St James. During operations in February 1918, 900 deportees were recovered in Tafile on the Dead Sea, all of them in terrible health. They were the remains of a convoy of nearly 10000 people deported mainly from Cilicia on the south-eastern Mediterranean coast of Turkey. A month later, the British discovered a group of Armenian refugees and about 100 orphans near Es Salt, west of Amman. Lieutenant Colonel Arthur Mills of the 4th (Anzac) Battalion of the Imperial Camel Corps was among the Desert Column troops who helped rescue these Armenians. In a touching display of humanity amid the horrors of war, Mills carried a four-year-old Armenian girl asleep in his arms as he rode his camel to the safe haven of Jerusalem. In this way, individual Australian soldiers saw first-hand the victims of the war the Ottomans waged against Armenian civilians.[11]

Victorian Colonel Stanley Savige had a similar story. As a member of the elite Dunsterforce, Savige helped rescue tens of thousands of Armenians and Assyrians in the summer of 1918. Named after its commander, Major General Lionel Dunsterville, the Dunsterforce was an Allied military mission established in 1917 and comprising about 500 elite Australian, New Zealand, British and Canadian troops. In mid-1918 the force was deployed to northern Persia and the Caucasus to protect the Baku oilfields from the Ottomans. Savige was in charge of 22 men (including two other Australians, Captain Eric Scott-Olsen of the 55th Battalion and Sergeant Bennett Murphy of the 28th), helping the Armenian and Assyrian forces defend strategic areas of northern Iran. A successful Ottoman offensive against the Armenians and Assyrians resulted in a huge exodus of some 80000 refugees. Savige and his small party protected the refugee column against their pursuers, fighting off the Turkish cavalry and Kurdish horsemen, who outnumbered Savige's men ten to one. The demoralised crowds of men, women and children, with their carts, animals, flocks and herds, were ultimately shepherded to safety in Hamadan, through country almost entirely devoid of supplies. Savige received the Distinguished Service Order (DSO) for his role in the rescue effort. 'His cool determination and fine example inspired his men', the DSO citation said, 'and put heart into the frightened refugees'.[12] Many people today regard the Great War as a futile clash of empires, but those Australians who helped rescue and protect the war's Armenian victims may rightly have considered themselves to be fighting for humanity.

# Cultural destruction

The 1915 deportations triggered massacres of Armenian clergy, the destruction of churches and monasteries, and the burning of thousands of handwritten medieval manuscripts. As well as the seizure of personal property, by the end of the war Armenian communal properties (including some 2538 churches, 451 monasteries and 1996 schools) had been almost entirely transferred to the Ottoman state.[13] The Armenian atrocities were one of the foremost examples of 'asset transfer' – a euphemism for forcible economic dispossession – in modern history. Yet amid the cultural destruction there were stories of cultural rescue by Allied forces. On 16 November 1917, the New Zealand Mounted Rifles Brigade entered the port of Jaffa after its Ottoman defenders had been defeated by the Australian Imperial Force's 1st Light Horse Brigade. The Armenian cemetery of Jaffa was being destroyed by Ottoman soldiers; hardly a single tombstone had been untouched. The Anzacs arrived just in time to prevent the removal of the few remaining stones.[14]

The destruction of Armenian cultural heritage continued during the post-war Turkish republican era. Armenian monuments were used as targets for Turkish military training exercises or converted to mosques, shops and gaols. Across historic Armenia (today's eastern Turkey), 90 per cent of Armenian place-names and the names of geographical sites were replaced with Turkish names. This desecration of the most sacred symbols of Armenian culture, as well as their churches and monasteries, combined with a continuing attempt to erase Armenia from the history of the Near East, is a clear continuation of the Turkish policy of Armenian genocide. Still today, official travel guides published by the Turkish Ministry of Culture and Tourism often fail to mention Armenian cultural heritage in Turkey.[15]

## Australia's humanitarian response

Back home, the fate of the Armenians aroused the sympathy and interest of many Australians. In December 1915 Miss Edith Searle, the secretary of the Armenian Relief Fund (ARF), appealed by a letter to the editor of the Melbourne *Argus*. She said that the Young Turks – the government in Constantinople – were bent on 'exterminating the Armenians' and had made 'appalling progress' towards this goal. Searle urged her fellow Australians to 'spare something for these most pitiful of all'.[16] In late 1916 the Armenian relief movement gained momentum with the establishment of the Friends of Armenia organisation by prominent Victorians Alexander Leeper, Master of Trinity College at the University of Melbourne, and William Edgar MLC. The organisation took over the administration of Searle's ARF and began to expand the fund's support base. There were fundraising concerts as well as special church collections for the 'suffering Armenians'. By 1918, Armenian relief funds were also operating in Sydney and Adelaide, and more than £11 000 had been collected and sent to the London Armenian fund. The plight of the Armenians also featured in stirring speeches during recruitment drives: the outrages were a way of encouraging men to enlist.[17]

The Australian Armenian relief movement culminated in the establishment in Lebanon in November 1922 of an Australian-run orphanage for some 1700 Armenian orphans. A national executive committee called the Australasian Armenian Relief

Fund was formed a month later. Its secretary, the Reverend James Cresswell, a Congregational minister from Adelaide, made a fact-finding tour of the Armenian refugee camps and orphanages in 1923. At one camp near Aleppo, Syria, he saw 'women pale and emaciated, children with swollen abdomens, the result of starvation. Again, one saw little babies pinched and pallid – further on a little one just recently born, one tiny atom among thousands of the suffering children to be seen here'.[18] At this time too, the Prime Minister, WM Hughes, allowed free transport of relief supplies for Armenian refugees aboard the new Commonwealth Government Line of Steamers. Shipments of supplies went to the Armenian refugees from various Australian ports until 1929.

## Armenian migration

Before World War II, Australia had no more than a few scattered Armenian families, perhaps 100 individuals. After the war, though, the number of Armenian migrants to Australia began to increase, and by 1960 about 500 Armenians had migrated. At first, most came from British colonies in South and South-East Asia, where thriving Armenian trading communities had existed before the war, but Armenian migration significantly increased during the 1960s due to the political turmoil in the Middle East. The largest single group came from Egypt in 1962–63, when President Nasser began purging Egypt of Westerners and people like Armenians and Greeks, who were seen as pro-Western. The Australian government set up an office in Cairo to facilitate the entry of 'well-qualified Armenians, Italians and Greeks from Egypt'.[19] A one-year pilot scheme allowed entry without sponsorship.

After 1965 the presence of family and friends already settled in Australia became the major pull factor for Armenian migrants. Most of the new arrivals came on sponsorship or by qualifying for one of the immigration schemes operating during the period. Following the outbreak of the Lebanese Civil War in 1975 and the opening of Australia's doors to migrants from the war-torn country, a further small wave of Lebanese Armenians migrated to Australia. By 1976, an estimated 10 000 Armenians had settled in Australia, the majority of them in Sydney and Melbourne. They came from 43 countries, held 25 nationalities upon arrival and spoke 35 different languages, a reminder of the magnitude of the Armenian diaspora before 1915 and the exodus thereafter. The Iranian Revolution of 1979 led to yet another wave of Armenian migrants. Then, in the early 1990s, a small number of Armenians migrated to Australia to escape the hardships caused by the collapse of the Soviet Union (there had been a Soviet Armenian republic), the devastating Armenian earthquake of 1988 and the Armenian–Azerbaijani war over the enclave of Nagorno-Karabakh. Today, small numbers of Armenians come to Australia from many parts of the world, but mostly from the war-ravaged regions of Iraq and Syria.[20] (Gwenda Tavan writes about immigration and multiculturalism in chapter 11 of this book.)

## Australia and the Armenian Genocide today

Australia has had a long relationship with Armenia and its people. But since Australia also has a Turkish past – because Gallipoli in Turkey is such an important part of Australia's understanding of the place of the Great War in our history – Australia also needs to come to terms with what happened to the people of Armenia during and after that conflict. Since 1985, when the Turkish government agreed to rename a small stretch of Turkish land and water Anzac Cove (Anzak Koyu), Australians have been exposed to, and have largely swallowed uncritically, a version of the Gallipoli story that portrays the 'Johnnies' (that is, the invading Allies) and the 'Mehmets' (the Ottoman defenders) as common victims of a war engineered by Britain and Germany. A quotation attributed to Mustafa Kemal Atatürk and supposedly addressed 'to the Anzac mothers' in 1934 has been used repeatedly over the past 30 years, in Anzac Day ceremonies, in films and books, and on memorials erected all over Australia. The words reassure Australians that the Australian dead of 1915 are cared for by Turkey, whose people are said to regard the Anzacs as 'our sons as well'. As David Stephens and Burçin Çakır show in chapter 7 of this book, the celebrated words were almost certainly made up in 1953 by Atatürk's associate Şükrü Kaya, a man as guilty as any of crimes against the Ottoman Empire's Armenian and Kurdish minorities during and after the Great War. This is at best a terrible irony; at worst it is an insult to the memories of Australians who fought and died to defeat a power capable of perpetrating or permitting such a crime as the genocide of the Armenians.

The New South Wales and South Australian state parliaments have officially recognised the Armenian Genocide. A monument to the victims of the Armenian Genocide and all other genocides was erected in the grounds of the NSW Parliament House in 1998. A decision by the Parliament in May 2013 to reaffirm the genocide prompted the Turkish Foreign Ministry to ban the proponents of the motion from attending Anzac commemorations at Gallipoli.[21] The Turkish Consul in Sydney, Gülseren Çelik, made it clear that official Turkey saw suppression of the genocide story as the other side of the coin of Anzac commemoration.

'These people', she said, 'want to hijack this very special bond, the Turkish ANZAC spirit, this is their target … We expect Australians to show the same kind of respect that we have shown to their history and their ancestry'. Official Australia concurs. While the Australian government has historically maintained a policy of avoiding 'this sensitive debate', the Minister for Foreign Affairs, Julie Bishop, made her position clear in 2014. She wrote that the government does not recognise these events as genocide, adding that 'Australia attaches great importance to its relationship with Turkey, which is underpinned by our shared history at Gallipoli, and by the recent cooperation in the G20 and a range of other international fora'.[22]

Over the past century, in both official and popular works on Gallipoli, Turks have been variously portrayed as ruthless foes, noble enemies and, in recent years, national friends. What began as respect for the enemy at Gallipoli has 'now morphed into a nationally celebrated, government-constructed and media-supported friendship between Turkey and Australia'.[23] This unthinking acceptance of a Turkish (actually Kemalist)[24] approach to the history of the Great War suppresses Australian popular interest in narratives presenting a darker side of the Ottoman Empire's war. The Australian media has now fully committed to a view of the Great War, and especially of Gallipoli, that sees Turks as noble defenders – and, like Australians, the victims of an imperial power. The story of the Ottoman Empire turning on its Armenian minority and murdering a million innocent people sits awkwardly with this benign view. This view extends beyond the media, too. In Australian military history, the genocide and Australia's relationship to it are mostly ignored, so eager are Australian agencies to demonstrate a positive relationship with Turkey built around the shared Gallipoli story.

## Two defining moments

Many Australians recognise the Gallipoli campaign as a seminal event in the shaping of Australia's national identity. For Armenians, on the other hand, the genocidal eviction from their country was a defining moment in their quest for national survival. These two seemingly unrelated events had more in common than a mere coincidence of dates and geography – 25 and 24 April respectively – and a shared setting in Ottoman Turkey. They were also brought together by a humanitarian bond that helped save the Armenian people from complete annihilation. In the Ottoman war theatre, Anzacs witnessed the Armenian Genocide and helped rescue survivors of the death marches. At home, a combination of patriotism, Christian solidarity and public outrage at Ottoman atrocities sparked a relief movement in Victoria that eventually spread throughout the nation.

There is always more to war than heroism and fortitude under fire. Similar qualities can be displayed in a variety of settings, with or without proximate violence. Australians showed such qualities to the benefit of Armenians a century ago and since. Yet, despite the strong connection between Australia's Gallipoli experience and the Armenian Genocide, the latter does not form part of modern Australia's collective memory of World War I. The events that began on 25 April are burnished and sacralised; the events that began the day before are glossed over. The historical anthropologist Paul Shackel argues that 'public memory is more a reflection of present political and social relations [in this case, the relations between Australia and Turkey] than a true reconstruction of the past'.[25] After 101 years, it is time that Australia's connection to the Armenian tragedy formed part of our reconstruction of the past.

# 4

# Adaptable Anzac:
# Past, present and future

CAROLYN HOLBROOK

As I write this chapter, my 15-year-old is receiving the large dose of Anzac history the National Curriculum prescribes for all Year 9 students. She has designed a recruitment poster, delivered a presentation on Second Bullecourt, visited the Shrine of Remembrance and watched the movie *Gallipoli*. She seemed interested in the poster and the presentation, judged the Shrine 'dull' and thought *Gallipoli* was 'sad … too sad, I don't want to talk about it'. The contrast with my own education during the 1970s and 1980s is striking. Our lessons on

World War I had a much more international flavour: the Gallipoli campaign received less attention than the major battles in France and Belgium. In 1985 a historian from the University of Western Australia spoke to our class about the Battle of the Somme, using toy soldiers and a homemade diorama. I was entranced, but my teacher was not. After she thanked the speaker and showed him out, her expression changed from gratitude to disgust: 'He was glorifying war', she told us.

My teacher probably would have disapproved of the book I bought that same year. *Gallipoli: The Incredible Campaign* was published to mark the 70th anniversary of the landing. The author hoped the book might stir latent patriotism among his readers: 'Today, when "patriotism" appears to be passé and any form of national pride likely to raise a sneer, it might be as well to remember that most of those young men of Anzac had a deep love of Australia'.[1] It is hard to imagine an author feeling compelled to make the same observation in 2016, when Anzac is the cherished centrepiece of the flag-waving Australian nationalism that emerged in the mid-1990s.

How can we account for the massive change in public attitudes to Anzac commemoration between my generation and that of my teenage daughter? How did a legend whose 70th anniversary was barely acknowledged attract the commemorative frenzy of 2015?[2] This chapter traces the history of Anzac commemoration since 1915. It shows how enthusiasm for commemoration has waxed and waned, and how the Anzac legend has changed in response to shifting societal attitudes to such issues as race, gender and militarism.

I recorded my own experience as a schoolgirl to counter the assumption – implicit in the history lessons our children receive –

that the Anzac legend has always been as revered as it is today. In their landmark book *What's Wrong with Anzac?*, the historians Marilyn Lake, Henry Reynolds, Joy Damousi and Mark McKenna argued that our schoolchildren had been enlisted by the state as 'the inheritors of the Anzac spirit and its custodians'.[3] The authors documented the growth of a state-sponsored Anzac education industry and criticised 'the obsession with military history' at the expense of other significant aspects of Australian history, such as the Frontier Wars and the nation's early reputation as the 'social laboratory of the world'. But others have disputed the assertion that Australians are passive victims of Anzac brainwashing. They argue that state commemorative efforts merely respond to community demand: 'It's what the bogans want', a senior government official claimed a few years ago.

I believe that the most effective antidote to state-sponsored Anzackery is the very thing our national curriculum seeks to impart: historical knowledge. Indeed, the Year 9 history curriculum includes a strand of inquiry about 'the commemoration of World War I, including debates about the nature and significance of the Anzac legend'.[4] In my experience, young Australians are interested to hear that the Anzac legend has a controversial past. Otherwise inattentive teenagers take notice when they discover that Australia is vastly outspending other combatant nations on commemorating the Great War centenary.[5] If we give our children the perspectives of critics as well as of devotees of Anzac, and we encourage children to consider how the Great War should be remembered, not only do we counter the risk of raising a generation of jingoists, but we also impart invaluable skills of critical and independent thinking.

## The Dardanelles to Vietnam

Various explanations have been advanced for why the Anzac legend immediately established such a firm grip on the Australian psyche. Gallipoli's status as the first major Australian engagement of the Great War was significant, as was the setting, with its ancient echoes of Troy and Byzantium and its physical beauty. Much has been made of the British journalist Ellis Ashmead-Bartlett, whose purple prose brought Australians the earliest account of the Gallipoli landing. But none of these influences would have endured had the news of our 'race of athletes' not fallen on ears that were already cocked to tales of Australian exceptionalism.[6]

Why were ordinary Australians so willing to make a legend from the events of 25 April 1915? During the late 19th and early 20th centuries, the great nations and empires of Europe were engaged in a furious contest for territory and trade. The quasi-science of Social Darwinism underpinned the drive for colonial acquisition. This ideology proposed a hierarchy of races, whose fitness could be measured by their martial capacity and civilised qualities; the lowly status of the conquered justified the act of conquest. The contest between empires encouraged state-promoted patriotism and militarism, known as the New Imperialism. The glorification of war and soldiering seeped into popular culture; in adventure novels, school publications, magazines and toys, boys and young men were implored, in the words of Sir Henry Newbolt's famous poem, to 'Play up! Play up! and play the game!'

Though Australians belonged to the great British race, they felt deeply the shame of their convict heritage. It was gallant performance in battle, rather than the peaceful means by which nationhood had been achieved in 1901, that would redeem the original sin of convictism. The shedding of blood would demonstrate to 'the world that Australians were not degenerate sons of the gallant race from which they sprung' but 'worthy descendants of that noble stock'.[7] In early May 1915, Australian newspapers ran Ashmead-Bartlett's account, with one editor observing that our soldiers had 'shown that, though transplanted to these southern skies, the breed is still the same as that of the men of Mons and Waterloo, and a hundred other great battles'.[8] Australians' exhalation of relief breathed the first life into the Anzac legend. As tales of the Anzacs' fighting capacity spread through the years of the war, so did stories about passive and ineffective Tommies, ineptly led by pompous officers. Australian chests puffed with pride; our men were natural soldiers, we told ourselves, slack on the parade ground but highly disciplined and effective under fire. They were different from Britons but not inferior. The Anzac legend thrived under the umbrella of British imperialism, but it was a story about Australian distinctiveness and achievement.

When the fighting men returned home, politicians courted them, made speeches extolling their deeds, and assured families that the graves of the dead were being tended.[9] While the returned men demanded and received the patronage of the government, there were limits to the role of politicians. From early on, the veterans established themselves as the custodians of Anzac commemoration. Patterns of observance were settled during the 1920s; by 1927 all state governments had gazetted 25 April as a public holiday. Solemn remembrance was the order of Anzac mornings, while afternoons were given over to beer-fuelled sociability.

Veteran-led commemoration continued much the same until the 1960s, although Anzac was not free from controversy. During the 1930s, Labor governments in Western Australia and Victoria were criticised for trying to counter what they saw as the jingoistic and militaristic aspects of Anzac commemoration.[10] Catholics and Protestants squabbled over the religious content of Anzac services. From the mid-1930s there were calls for 'a brighter Anzac Day', for the solemn mornings to be followed by 'an afternoon and night of general rejoicing'. In 1946, a journalist lamented the 'unrelieved gloom' of Anzac observance: '31 years have passed away, and even the saddest memories have been softened by time. Nothing is more certain than that if the lads who fell on Anzac beaches could have their say, we should not be celebrating their heroism by a day of regimented gloom and sadness'. A Gallup poll in 1949 showed that a majority of Australians wanted organised sport with admission charges on Anzac afternoons.[11]

By the late 1950s, critics were attacking not merely the form of Anzac Day but its very substance. In 1958, Sydney University's student newspaper *Honi Soit* condemned Australians' attachment to the Anzac legend: 'Out of a rather speculative and routine beach landing has developed a festival of hero-adulation unequalled anywhere in the world'. The obsession with Gallipoli led Australians to believe 'that trained assassins are Australia's foremost export'. Condemnation from the RSL (at that time known in full as the Returned Sailors', Soldiers' and Airmen's Imperial League of Australia or RSSAILA) and the Sydney University Senate did not deter *Honi Soit*. In 1960, its editor denounced the Anzac spirit as 'one of the most pernicious which the human spirit possesses. The RSL calls it patriotism. Perhaps a better word would be jingoism – the same feeling that motivates Hitler's Germany and Tojo's Japan makes old soldiers march on April 25 of each year'.[12] Invective like this, considered sacrilegious by Anzac traditionalists, inspired the young playwright Alan Seymour to write *The One Day of the Year*. The play pitted the university student protagonist Hughie in generational conflict with his father, Alf. Hughie's condemnation of Anzac Day as a day of 'bloody wastefulness' perpetuated year after year by a 'screaming tribe of great, stupid, drunken, vicious, *bigoted* no-hopers' was incomprehensible to Alf, who had served in World War II.[13]

The Vietnam War was not, as popular memory would have it, the spark that ignited anti-Anzac sentiment. Rather, the unpopularity of the war following the introduction of conscription in late 1964 exacerbated the scepticism and hostility already in the community. To many Australians raised in the boom years after World War II, Anzac Day exemplified a society that no longer existed, one built on British race patriotism and a version of masculinity that prized martial prowess and assigned women an inferior role. A correspondent to the *Canberra Times* in 1967 articulated a sentiment common among young Australians about Anzac Day: it was 'the one day of the year for the glorification of war and the poisoning of children's minds with war pictures and heroes' stories'.[14]

## Popular culture and the (costly) transformation of Anzac

The decline of British race patriotism as the cornerstone of Australian identity led successive governments in the post-Menzies era to cultivate alternative sources of nationalist feeling.

Prime Minister Harold Holt established the Australia Council for the Arts in November 1967 to foster 'a greater awakening to the Australian people of Australia and its possibilities'.[15] Holt's successor John Gorton wanted to develop 'a feeling of real nationalism ... For a long time we stood not really as a nation in our own right, but as a nation the people of whom spoke of "home" and meant ... Great Britain'.[16] Comedian Barry Humphries both benefited from and satirised the state-sponsored search for a new Australian identity. In the movie *Barry McKenzie Holds His Own*, ocker Bazza tells his mate Col, who has moved to Paris: 'An arty-crafty bloke like you would be laughin' back in Australia right now. The government's shellin' out piles of bloody moulah for any bastard who reckons he can paint pictures, write pomes or make fillums'.[17]

Despite the splurge of subsidised creative expression and much rumination, the New Nationalism was unable to conjure a convincing substitute for British Australia. This failure to find an alternative wellspring of communal identity allowed for the emergence of a rejuvenated version of Anzac. During its period of popular exile, the Anzac legend had been undergoing a quiet transformation. *The Broken Years* (1974), Bill Gammage's history of Australian frontline soldiering during the Great War, pioneered the literary use of soldiers' letters and diaries, and offered what its author later described as 'an emotional history' of the war. While Gammage was effusive in his admiration of the Australian soldiers, he did not romanticise their experience. During the dreadful French winter of 1916–17, the Australians 'realised that they were assigning themselves to apparently endless agony, and were sacrificing their hopes and probably their lives to defend others. They had chained themselves to an odious necessity.

They had come to Armageddon'.[18] *The Broken Years* infused the experience of the 1st Australian Imperial Force with the gravitas of tragedy.

The rise of family history during the 1970s and 1980s was also important in the resurgence of Anzac; the children and grand-children of men who had fought in the Great War looked upon their forebears' experience with new eyes, particularly as these men began to die. Previously disregarded boxes filled with war letters and diaries became objects of intense historical curiosity. Family members painstakingly transcribed and self-published these documents, believing they comprised a significant part of the nation's history. Family histories offered an intimate and sympathetic perspective of the war, far removed from that of the curmudgeonly leaders of the RSL, whose outdated views regularly made the headlines. The soldiers depicted in family histories were pawns of government, like the young men conscripted for service in Vietnam. War was dreadful but the men who fought deserved our sympathy and admiration. From the 1990s, the efforts of descendants to discover the details of their soldier forebears were supported by the growing range of state-sponsored genealogical resources.

The effect of Peter Weir's film *Gallipoli* in changing popular attitudes towards the Anzac legend cannot be overestimated. The film, with Mark Lee as Archie and Mel Gibson as Frank, became a major commercial and critical success upon its release in 1981. Weir co-wrote the script with playwright David Williamson, and Bill Gammage was historical adviser. Born in 1942, Weir recalled childhood commemoration of Anzac as 'a very stuffy, almost religious sort of ceremony that would occur every year in school, and we really didn't know what it was all about'.[19] *Gallipoli* stripped the Anzac legend of its militarist and imperial connotations, and reduced it to a story of personal tragedy. In Weir's hands, Anzac was no longer a politically fractious medium for generational conflict but a means of indulging our growing taste for secular tales of suffering and tragedy. The film allowed audiences to put aside their reservations about the racism and militarism of Anzac and become immersed in the story of a group of naïve and beautiful young men sacrificed to the stupidity of British command. The altered representations of the Great War presented by family historians and filmmakers mirrored the growing emphasis in Western cultures on tales of trauma and suffering – 'victimhood'. The historian Christina Twomey has linked the revival of Anzac commemoration to its union with trauma culture, claiming that by the 1980s 'the suffering of soldiers in war and the potential for them to be traumatised by it became a central trope in the public discussion of Anzac'.[20]

Politicians have also played a significant role in the revival of the Anzac legend. (Frank Bongiorno's chapter 8 in this book says more about this.) Political leaders only began lending their rhetorical and financial clout to Anzac, however, once its restoration in the public conscience was apparent. They responded to demand. Robert Menzies was prime minister during the 50th anniversary of the Anzac landing in 1965. As well as commissioning a film and issuing a series of commemorative stamps, his government contributed the substantial sum of £20 000 towards a trip organised by the RSL that took a group of veterans back to Gallipoli.[21] Menzies' flagship Anzac jubilee project was the construction of Anzac Parade in Canberra, a new road that ran between Lake Burley Griffin and the Australian War Memorial. The road was opened by former Governor-General the Duke of Gloucester on

25 April 1965 in front of a large crowd that included 72 Gallipoli veterans.[22]

It was not until the prime ministership of Bob Hawke, however, that politicians really staked their claim as the new custodians of Anzac memory. Again, they took their cues from the public. The RSL's declining influence from its peak under Menzies had left a void at the heart of commemoration. Politicians were initially reluctant to fill the shoes of the RSL, given the controversy attached to Anzac since the late 1950s. But the Hawke government sensed that public sentiment was shifting. The mass goodwill towards Vietnam veterans at the official Welcome Home march in October 1987 provided an important clue; an estimated 110 000 people cheered as 25 000 veterans and families of the 500 Australians who died in the war marched from the Sydney Domain to the Town Hall. (Chapter 6 by Mark Dapin says more about Vietnam veterans.) When a veterans' representative suggested that the Commonwealth sponsor a trip to Gallipoli for the 75th anniversary in 1990, the government agreed and the Gallipoli 'pilgrimage' was a great success. Bob Hawke's knockabout patriotism and easy rapport with the remaining veterans smoothed the way for Anzac's re-entry into the Australian mainstream. Anzac was no longer about Australians' pride in the fighting prowess of their soldiers; it was a tale of mateship and tragedy. This recasting of the Anzac legend was embraced by a public that remained wary of militarism.

Hawke's successor, Paul Keating, felt great disdain for the sentimentality Australians attached to the Gallipoli campaign, though he kept such sacrilegious thoughts to himself while in office. While Hawke perceived Gallipoli as a defining moment in the assertion of Australian distinctiveness, Keating saw a subservient young nation doing the bidding of its imperial master in an ill-conceived campaign. As prime minister during the 50th anniversary of the battles against the Japanese during World War II, Keating tried to uproot the Anzac legend from its historical association with the Dardanelles and embed it in the Pacific. While Keating succeeded in piquing public interest in the Pacific War, Kokoda most notably, he was unable to loosen Australians' attachment to Gallipoli as the centrepiece of the Anzac legend.

John Howard had watched with mounting resentment as Paul Keating attempted to reorient Australian historical understanding away from the British legacy. As a shrewd student of history and well attuned to its ideological uses, Howard was determined to thwart Keating's revisionism. The Anzac legend became an essential element of Howard's drive to celebrate what he called the 'Australian achievement', a term he used to counter the dominant academic narrative of Australian history, which he believed was critical of the nation-building project and emphasised the suffering of Aboriginal people, women and minority groups. Howard wanted to give Australian children a more optimistic version of Australian history.

The Keating government had augmented the commemorative capacity within the Department of Veterans' Affairs (DVA) to run the 'Australia Remembers' campaign for the 50th anniversary of World War II.[23] But Howard took state patronage of war commemoration to a new level. His government gave prominence to the Anzac legend as a national myth that both promoted Australian distinctiveness in the form of such values as mateship and egalitarianism *and* celebrated the nation's historical and cultural links with Great Britain. *What's Wrong with Anzac?*, published in 2010, documented the early years of this educational mission, when programs like 'Their Service – Our Heritage' and 'Saluting Their Service' were launched. The Anzac educational industry has gathered much momentum in subsequent years. DVA's online Anzac Portal, launched in 2014, contains a mind-boggling array of resources for students and teachers. The resources are of varied provenance and quality, and cover World War II, Vietnam and Korea as well as the Great War. They encourage respectful and largely uncritical examination of Australian war experience. A 'Valuing Our Veterans' page urges students to record interviews with veterans, noting that 'it has been widely recognised since World War I ... that Australia's war experiences have played a key role in our evolving sense of national identity'. Whether a mistake of transcription or a sign of ignorance, the site's claim that Australia is approaching 'the celebration of 100 years of nationhood' illustrates the Anzac-centrism of the official version of Australian history.[24]

The Commonwealth and various state governments offer prizes to students for their Anzac-themed compositions. Winners of the Premiers' Spirit of Anzac prizes and the Commonwealth's Simpson Prize earn a study tour of old battlefields. Educational material of varying quality also continues to flow from the Australian War Memorial.[25] The memorial runs many heavily patronised onsite educational programs for school children on topics that include 'Anzac Legacy', 'We Will Remember Them' and 'Cobbers' Tales'. Visiting schools can book in for a special wreath-laying at the Tomb of the Unknown Australian Soldier or for the daily Last Post ceremony. The memorial's shop is well stocked with educational and recreational products for children. Among the soft toys on the memorial's website are Sarbi the Explosives Detection Dog, Murphy the Donkey and Florence the First World War Nurse. There is a Hall of Valour ruler and a trench whistle like those blown by officers in the Great War before men climbed over the top and ran towards enemy guns.[26]

John Howard watched with approval the increasingly bold displays of Australian nationalism during his prime minister-ship, frequently in the context of Anzac commemoration. None of his successors have proved as adept as Howard in weaving the Anzac legend into electoral gold, though all have tried. When former prime minister Paul Keating declared that 'Gallipoli was shocking for us', Prime Minister Kevin Rudd was strident in his condemnation, declaring it 'absolutely fundamental to the Australian national identity'.[27] Prime Minister Julia Gillard did not resist the political temptations of Anzac, announcing in 2012 an initial $83.5 million for commemorative activities. Failing to recall that the Hawke government thought the 1988 bicentennial commemorations were a flop, she hoped that 'Anzac Day in 2015 … will be like the bicentenary. It will be one of the commemo-rations that shape our nation and our understanding of who we are today'.[28] She was delighted that Australian children were such enthusiastic standard-bearers for the Anzac tradition.[29] But the former member of the Victorian Socialist Left stretched credulity in April 2012 when she announced that her forthcoming trip to Gallipoli for Anzac Day was a journey she had 'wanted to make all my life'.[30]

During his brief prime ministership, Tony Abbott spoke often of his desire that Australians understand more about the victorious battles of 1918. Abbott pushed through his pet project (first mooted by John Howard), allocating $100 million of mostly Defence Department money for the construction of the Sir John Monash Centre at the Australian memorial near the French village of Villers-Bretonneux. The interpretive centre is the most expensive single item in Australia's World War I commemoration. Despite speculation that Malcolm Turnbull might scuttle the project after he became Prime Minister in September 2015, his government announced the award of the construction contract. The timing of the announcement – two days before Christmas – suggested that the government had become sensitive to the growing criticism of its Anzac spending bonanza.[31]

## Suffer the children?

There is no doubt that our children are being reared in an era of unprecedented state patronage of Anzac commemoration. But does this mean they are being brainwashed? As the history of commemoration shows us, there is no pure and unbroken line of transmission between the rhetoric of our political leaders and teachers, and the minds of our children. How much of the material provided by DVA is actually used by schools? To what extent are these materials mediated by teachers, most of whom take very seriously their role of encouraging critical thinking?[32] My hunch is that teachers temper the celebratory excesses of government material wherever they find them. I am also heartened to remember that children absorb many more messages about war and violence than those suggested by the state. Peter Weir was turned off by the stuffy platitudes he heard about Anzac as a schoolboy in the 1940s and 1950s, when words like 'glorious' and 'gallant' were tossed around liberally. It is nonsense to suggest that Australians absorb the lessons of their politicians without demur; despite the best efforts of Paul Keating and his speechwriter Don Watson, Australians could not be persuaded to exchange their emotional attachment to Gallipoli for a Kokoda-centred Anzac legend.

When I asked my daughter if she thought she was being brain-washed about Anzac, she replied that we historians were all 'too sceptical, too critical. Why would I think that war was good when 60 000 people were killed [and wounded] on the first day of the Somme?' She gave me her impression of the Great War, based on her classes: 'The biscuits were so hard that the soldiers had to soak them in water so they wouldn't break their teeth. Rats grew as big as cats because they were eating dead bodies in no-man's-land. Men got such bad trench foot that their feet dropped off'. While I applaud the fact that war is not being glorified in our schools, we also need to inoculate our children against the slow accretion of Anzackery during their long years in the education system. We must remind them that there is much more to Australian history than the grim middens of Anzac. We must be sure they understand that the suffering of the Anzacs does not prevent us from questioning the cause for which they fought and the causes for which Australians fight in future wars.

# 5

# The Australian War Memorial: Beyond Bean

MICHAEL PIGGOTT

This is how the *International Encyclopedia of the First World War* introduces Charles Bean to those readers who do not know him:

> Charles Bean was Australia's official war correspondent who later wrote and edited the twelve-volume *Official History of Australia in the War of 1914–1918* and founded the Australian War Memorial. No other Australian has been more influential than Bean in shaping the way the

First World War is remembered and commemorated in Australia.[1]

When Dr Brendan Nelson arrived at the Australian War Memorial in December 2012 to take up the director's position, he clearly saw himself as Bean's disciple. He told the press, 'it will be a labour of love … it is a dream job'. He arrived with emotional baggage, including more than 70 visits to the Menin Gate Memorial at Ypres, and was clearly in thrall to Bean. The director's new business card and letterhead were embossed with Bean's description of the War Memorial: 'Here is their spirit, in the heart of the land they loved; and here we guard the record which they themselves made'. On his first day as director Nelson said, 'It is humbling to carry the legacy and vision of Charles Bean who envisaged the Memorial'.[2] He and Bean have been inseparable ever since. The war correspondent, war historian and founding father has served as muse and endless source of quotes, and as justification for both resisting and introducing change. Australia's attitude to the Anzac legend – and our national inclination towards Anzackery – have a lot to do with Bean as he has been filtered through the memorial.[3]

## Inevitably Bean

Up to a point, a War Memorial director quoting Bean is unexceptionable. Bean has always been held in high regard by people at the memorial and by many others, from eminent historians to prime ministers. Recent directors of the memorial have reflected a renewed public appreciation of Bean's writings and standing, linked with a resurgent interest in Australia's World

War I, battlefield tourism and family (military) history. In 1979 the memorial marked the centenary of Bean's birth with an exhibition, *C.E.W. Bean: Australian Historian*. Then, in 1981, Peter Weir's film *Gallipoli* was released. The following year the memorial inaugurated a CEW Bean Postgraduate Scholarship. In 1983 there was a biography, a guide to Bean papers, the first republication of Bean's single-volume World War I history, *Anzac to Amiens*, and an edition of his diaries.[4] Between 1981 and 1987, 11 of the 12 volumes of the *Official History of Australia in the War of 1914–1918*, edited and partly written by Bean, were republished by Queensland University Press and the memorial. The 1980s also saw new scholarship and new debates. David Kent analysed Bean's editorship of *The Anzac Book*; Robin Gerster produced *Big-noting: The Heroic Theme in Australian War Writing*, with Bean a major 'offender'; and Alistair Thomson examined Bean's idea of military manhood.[5] Then, as the Anzac legend began to be questioned in the new century, Bean's role came under renewed notice.[6]

Commemorations were also important. Republication of the *Official History* reinforced Turkish–Australian reciprocal remembrance in the early 1980s (as noted in chapter 7 of this book). Prime Minister Hawke led a pilgrimage of aged veterans to Turkey in 1990 to mark the 75th anniversary of the Gallipoli landing; in the same year Bean's *Gallipoli Mission* was republished and the ABC issued an audio version of his Gallipoli diaries. In 2001 a CEW Bean foundation and annual lecture were set up to commemorate war correspondents, photographers and cameramen.

> One only has to mention [says the foundation website]
> A.B. (Banjo) Paterson, C.E.W. Bean, George Morrison,

Keith Murdoch, George Johnston, Alan Moorehead, Chester Wilmot, Osmar White, Kenneth Slessor, Damien Parer, Lorraine Stumm, Denis Warner, Richard Hughes and Neil Davis to evoke a proud journalistic and literary tradition.[7]

From such an 'A list' of correspondents, why Bean? He was not Australia's first war correspondent and, by 2001, arguably not the best known. And yet the new foundation was named for Bean, perhaps because his post-war achievements had reinforced his war-correspondent associations but also, some have argued, because of the enduring hold of Gallipoli and the Great War on the Australian psyche.[8]

So it continued. In 2005 Jonathan King and Mike Bowers produced the book *Gallipoli: Untold Stories from War Correspondent Charles Bean and Front-line Anzacs* and the National Library and the Bean Foundation launched Despatches from Gallipoli: Scenes from a Remote War, a website of digitised reports from Gallipoli by Bean and others.[9] In 2005, too, the Australian Army History Unit established a CEW Bean Prize for the best honours or postgraduate thesis on the history of the Australian Army. In 2006, the memorial opened its CEW Bean Building. In 2007, Kevin Fewster produced a third edition of extracts from Bean's Gallipoli diaries, with a foreword by then memorial director Steve Gower. The book was reissued in paperback in 2009. In that year, memorial curator Janda Gooding wrote *Gallipoli Revisited: In the Footsteps of Charles Bean and the Australian Historical Mission* and the memorial launched a new website with digital copies of Bean's diaries and notebooks. In 2010, Wain Fimeri wrote and directed a dramatised documentary,

*Charles Bean's Great War,* and the memorial republished Bean's *Anzac Book.* In 2011, a valuable 'left field' study of Bean came from Judge Geoff Lindsay, *Be Substantially Great in Thy Self: Getting to Know C.E.W. Bean; Barrister, Judge's Associate, Moral Philosopher.*[10] Equally unexpected was Bruce Scates's 2012 time-shifting novel, including Bean at Gallipoli in 1915 and 1919, called *On Dangerous Ground: A Gallipoli Story.*

Inevitably, activities to mark the centenary of World War I included Bean. In 2014, Phillip Bradley's *Charles Bean's Gallipoli Illustrated* appeared, *Anzac to Amiens* was republished again and another biography of sorts appeared, Ross Coulthart's *Charles Bean.* (The book jointly won the 2015 Prime Minister's Prize for Australian History.) The following year there was a second and more rounded treatment, *Bearing Witness* by Peter Rees. In 2015, too, a War Correspondents Memorial was dedicated within the grounds of the main memorial, with the speeches full of eulogy to Bean. Finally, yet not finally, in July 2016, a two-day conference at UNSW Canberra (the Australian Defence Force Academy) focused on Bean and his legacy, one speaker foreshadowing an edition of Bean's diaries from the Western Front.

## Over the top

To reiterate, an Australian War Memorial director quoting Bean is unexceptionable – within limits. In recent years, however, the frequency and abandon with which Bean has been used has been exceptional. He features almost every time an address needs drafting – to give words gravitas, stories authenticity and opinion authority. He has been invoked, for example, in arguments about who should or should not be included on the memorial's Roll of

Honour and on whether the Frontier Wars should be featured in the memorial.[11] So often there has been unnecessary overreach, as the following three cases show.

The most recent fanciful use of Bean was when the memorial's director explained the location of the memorial below Mount Ainslie in Canberra.

> When Charles Bean first envisaged his plan to build
> a memorial to commemorate the commitment and
> sacrifice of Australia's servicemen and servicewomen, he
> wanted to ensure that the people making the decisions
> to send Australians to war – the politicians – had that
> commitment uppermost in their minds. That's why the
> Australian War Memorial is in direct line of sight of
> Australia's Parliament House.[12]

Now it hardly needs mentioning that Walter Burley Griffin's design for Canberra, prepared and accepted in principle by 1913, *did* include provision for a future Parliament House and monuments to civic deeds. But Griffin could not have predicted the need for a World War I memorial. In the 1920s, Bean among others sought a prominent location, nothing more, and when the site – originally earmarked for a 'casino', including a children's park, outdoor dining areas and a beer garden – was settled upon, Griffin's 'civic deeds' thinking had been reversed by placing the memorial opposite the proposed site for the Parliament and some distance north on the land axis. Yet nothing in the key literature on the location of what became the memorial – including the memorial's own official history, national heritage registration and the relevant official files – suggests the rationale might have been to form a visual reminder to parliamentarians when they were deciding to send people to war. If one had to nominate a single person behind the memorial's location at the base of Mount Ainslie, it would be the Federal Capital Advisory Committee Secretary, CS Daley. Historians of memorials Ken Inglis and Michael McKernan acknowledge Daley was a significant figure, and Daley himself explicitly stated that the 'casino' site for the memorial had been his idea in 1921.[13]

What then possessed director Nelson to express such a notion? Later in his article he reminded readers that it 'was on my watch as Defence Minister that Australian soldiers went to Afghanistan'. That Defence ministers, current or former, are aware their responsibilities can be associated with life-and-death issues is commendable, though both the 2001 decision to commit forces to Afghanistan and the 2006 decision to increase them when Nelson was minister were taken not by Parliament but by the government on the recommendation of its National Security Committee. It is doubtful whether the room where the committee met even had line of sight to the memorial.

The second case of Nelsonian overreach concerns the Tomb of the Unknown Australian Soldier. On 11 November 1993, a soldier's remains were interred in the Australian War Memorial's Hall of Memory. Speaking on that occasion, Prime Minister Paul Keating acknowledged that no one knew the soldier's identity, and added, 'We do not know his age or his circumstances – whether he was from the city or the bush; what occupation he left to become a soldier; what religion, if he had a religion; if he was married or single'.[14] This seemingly innocuous truth annoyed historian Geoffrey Blainey, who, as a member of the memorial's Council in 1998, ensured the words 'Known unto God' were inscribed on the tomb. Blainey knew the Kipling epitaph, 'A Soldier of the Great War, Known unto God', had been inscribed on the anonymous soldier's original headstone at Adelaide Cemetery and Villers-Bretonneux, and saw these words as a Judeo-Christian formulation and the cemetery as consecrated ground. He insisted the words be reused on the tomb in the Hall of Memory, and he protested when they were later obscured by floral wreaths.[15]

In September 2013, however, Director Nelson mentioned in a speech that 'Known unto God' on the tomb would be replaced by two quotes from Keating's 1993 speech, 'We do not know this Australian's name and we never will' and 'He is all of them. And he is one of us'.[16] The director explained that Bean's 'ambition was always that there would be no religious symbols or references in the memorial or indeed in the hall' and that, instead, he 'wanted a place of commemoration with a spiritual flavour but (which didn't) resemble a place of worship'.[17] Reaction soon followed. Murdoch press columnists saw political correctness at work. There were protests from Christians, historians and politicians. The Veterans' Affairs Minister directed that 'Known unto God' remain. While obeying, the memorial retained the 'He is all of them ...' words from Keating's eulogy on the tomb, displayed his entire 1993 speech in the Hall of Memory foyer and invited him to present a 20th anniversary address on Remembrance Day 2013.

While much could be said of this episode, our focus remains on the way Bean was used. This was full of inconsistencies, the unavoidable inference being that earlier War Memorial Council support for Blainey was ignorant of or repudiated Bean's thinking. It also suffered the same challenge as does anyone who cites scripture, with Nick Cater in *The Australian* attacking the removal of

'God' by quoting Nelson's most-repeated Bean lines concerning the memorial's very purpose: 'Here is their spirit, in the heart of the land they loved ...'[18] Nevertheless, anyone familiar with Bean's life and achievements would know that both Bean's religious beliefs and the history of the memorial's design were complicated, as was the relationship between the two. Bean did want to avoid both overt religious alignments and preferences in the memorial's architecture, and thus sectarian tensions at dedications and ceremonies. Yet personally, and in his memorialising ideas, Bean was spiritual, vaguely Christian yet strongly Arnoldian humanist. Because of his and others' influence, the memorial has never been totally secular.[19] The symbolism of the Hall of Memory's designs and installations is strongly spiritual, and in parts clearly Christian, as a careful reading of the 2016 version of the memorial's glossy Hall of Memory booklet shows.[20] The memorial has never completely shaken off Christianity. Representatives of the main Christian denominations have always been present at the big occasions in the memorial's history, with words and music to match. Would Bean have objected to 'Known unto God'? Given the words' use on unknown soldiers' headstones elsewhere, I doubt it, but there is enough evidence in both directions to counsel against certainty.

Now to our third case of 'over-the-top' action at today's War Memorial. Since Bean died in 1968, historians, biographers, commentators and memorial staff have struggled to find the right words for his relationship to the memorial. All have acknowledged his primacy in articulating and advancing the idea of a memorial museum, couched in the popular phrases 'conceived', 'the spirit behind' and 'central to the establishment of'. On the other hand, many people have attributed influence to administrative, military and political leaders other than Bean in ensuring the memorial became a reality, implying multiple agents were involved. These people have used such words as '[Bean] played an essential role in the creation of' and '[the memorial] owes its conception largely to [him]'.

Others, however, have not been so subtle. In the memorial's reception area and introductory gallery, Bean is described, without qualification, as 'Australian War Memorial Founder'. Brendan Nelson, in many speeches and statements since becoming director, has shown the same simple certainty.[21] The case for Bean, highly summarised, involves an idea (of a museum functioning as a memorial), a collection (basically 'sacred' records and relics), and an organisation (Bean's participation in the memorial's operations). The idea emerged in 1916, with Bean's diary musings imagining how Australia should remember the soldiers' sacrifice. It was refined in proposals to Defence Minister George Pearce over the following three years and to the public in Bean's 1919 booklet, *In Your Hands, Australians*. The collection grew from Bean's support for the Australian War Records Section (AWRS) in 1917, which formalised collecting during and immediately after the war. In the 1920s Bean began donating papers and eventually his prized personal diaries and notebooks.[22] As for the organisation, Bean's long formal association with the memorial began when he was acting director for two months in 1919, and included his membership of the first Board of Management, formed when the memorial's Act was proclaimed in 1926, and his chairmanship between 1951 and 1959.

The evidence for a qualified accolade attends every stage of this explanation. Even Bean's much-referenced 1916 diary musings, seen retrospectively to have had great significance, are pre-dated by a letter John Monash wrote from Gallipoli on 18 June 1915 to his wife Hannah, in which Monash anticipates 'a noble memorial erected by the people of Australia, to honour the memory of their fallen dead'.[23] Others who shared Bean's ideas, championed them politically and ensured they were implemented included HC Smart, John Treloar, Henry Gullett, Thomas Griffiths, Brudenell White, William Birdwood and George Pearce. Leaving aside these fellow toilers, the exclusively Bean argument also discounts Bean's own views. He took no credit for the AWRS, and late in life argued strongly for better acknowledgment of Brudenell White's role in the AWRS and the memorial's beginnings, for the Canadian precedent of each unit being allowed to control its own records, and indeed for the soldiers who had collected souvenirs. (Bean described one of these collectors, Corporal Ernest Bailey, as 'Founder of Australian War Museum'.)[24] Overselling Bean also ignores the pressure from elsewhere within Australia after the Great War for a national war museum, particularly from the Melbourne Exhibition Building Trustees, and the expressed need to assert a national approach to the distribution of trophies.[25]

## An honest approach

Writing in 2014, Gerard Windsor saw the resurgence of Anzac Day and interest in the Great War as partly due to 'the apotheosis of Charles Bean'.[26] The Australian War Memorial and its current leadership have played their parts. Their invocation of Bean is over the top, selective, factually flawed and, from what we now know from Peter Rees's fine 2015 biography, almost certainly would have appalled Bean himself: Rees concludes that few would disagree with RG Menzies' view of Bean as a 'man and scholar of self-effacing modesty'.[27]

Bean was a fascinating, complicated personality who cared deeply about his country and its soldiers, and went to great lengths to honour their sacrifice and preserve the relevant documentation. There are also his numerous lesser known publications, involvements and achievements. On the other hand, Bean could be irritating and interfering, historian and politician Paul Hasluck placing him, without malice, somewhere between prim and a prig.[28] Other observers have highlighted instances of Bean's poor judgment, his downplaying of the ugly edge to the larrikin Digger and his lobbying with Keith Murdoch against John Monash's promotion to lieutenant general in 1918, behaviour described by historian Geoffrey Serle as 'perhaps the outstanding case of sheer irresponsibility by pressmen in Australian history'.[29]

And yet. The answer Dudley McCarthy gave when asked in the early 1980s if he was writing a warts-and-all biography of Bean – that Bean 'had no warts' – echoes at the memorial 33 years later.[30] In 2017, relying so blindly on Bean's opinions is not necessary, and nor, as noted earlier, is it smart. If Bean can be cited to help explain, for example, why the memorial should not commemorate the Frontier Wars, then he can be readily turned against the memorial, too. Where is the special gallery Bean wanted, displaying drawings by the brilliant official war artist Will Dyson? (Dyson, of radical views, was also a political cartoonist and satirist.)[31] The memorial has evolved out of sight since Bean expressed this hope, but at least the first Australian war artist ever appointed should not be forgotten. When Senator John Faulkner noted in 2001 the formation of the CEW Bean Foundation, he also recalled Dyson's significance. More recently,

Dyson's absence from the memorial's galleries has been highlighted by historian Ross McMullin, who described the memorial's attitude as 'inexplicable. As the memorial confirmed earlier this month, the number of Dyson works on display there is zero. Charlie Bean would turn in his grave'.[32]

Finally, excessive concentration on Bean means numerous significant others tend to be overshadowed. A balanced and honest approach would recognise and better profile the dozens of people who encouraged, assisted and enabled Bean's many undeniable achievements. It would sharpen the focus on the other official war historians and official history general editors. Currently, for example, we have three Bean biographies but none of Gavin Long, the official historian of World War II. In 2017, despite the Great War centenary, we should take the 'Anzac auteur' off his pedestal.[33] Anzackery, the extreme version of the legend, has many progenitors, some of them unwitting. It is time to stop spouting single lines from Bean as if his words automatically settled an argument or definitively established a mood. It is time to move beyond Bean.

# 6

# 'We too were Anzacs':[1] Were Vietnam veterans ever truly excluded from the Anzac tradition?

MARK DAPIN

On 18 April 2016, I was interviewed by Richard Glover on ABC Radio 702. Glover was keen to have me argue that the popular view of the hostile reception Vietnam veterans received on their return home was 'overblown'. I would say only that there was another side to the story and that the largest of the wartime welcome-home parades were bigger than any of the Moratorium demonstrations.[2] Without warning, Glover opened up the phone lines. After a call from a veteran's son about the Returned and Services League (RSL) came a message from a woman named Jenny who suggested that Vietnam veterans were not allowed to march in Anzac Day parades during the war. I lost my temper and said, 'That's nonsense, Jenny'.

The truth is that Vietnam veterans were marching in Anzac Day parades even before an Australian battalion had come home from Vietnam. Alone among 'returned' soldiers, some men bound for the war marched in Anzac Day parades before they had been sent overseas. Vietnam veterans marched regularly, proudly and conspicuously, and their presence was generally highlighted in the press, along with the fact that they received a warm reception from onlookers. The myth that Vietnam veterans did not march on Anzac Day seems to have its roots in three interconnected ideas: first, that Vietnam veterans were not integrated into the Anzac tradition; secondly, that Vietnam veterans had no support from the wider public; and thirdly, that the RSL, which organised Anzac parades throughout the country, was institutionally hostile to Vietnam veterans. None of these ideas existed during the war itself.

The late Professor Jeffrey Grey, a giant among Australian military historians and the supervisor of my doctoral thesis on national service and popular memory, wrote that 'few wars in modern times have attracted such an accretion of myth, misbelief and arrant nonsense' as Vietnam.[3] Much of this misinformation gained credence not in the 1960s or 1970s but the 1980s. It tended to take the form of apocryphal stories, fables told to simplify complicated, sometimes barely expressible emotional truths. Many veterans felt the anti-war demonstrations were aimed at the soldiers personally, so – more than a decade after Australia's part in the war had ended – previously undocumented stories began to circulate about midnight protests at Sydney Airport, demonstrations apparently designed only to shame the returning troops. After the war, some veterans felt society rejected them as bloodthirsty war criminals, that civilians spat upon their service and scorned their masculine martial values in favour of feminist pacifism. Tales grew of screeching, spitting women and demonstrators who soaked the returned men in animal blood. With the exception of the young Nadine Jensen, however, who famously swooped on 1RAR's 1966 welcome-home parade and smeared the leaders of the march with a mixture of red paint and kerosene, these caricature protesters would seem to have been symbolic rather than real.[4]

'Honest' history is a dish best served cold, by uninterested wait staff, long after the banquet of lived experience is over. To the honest historian, the massacre at My Lai should arouse no more emotion than the rape of the Sabine women. I would not pretend to have no opinions or feelings about national service, the Vietnam War or the anti-war movement, but I can truly say that it is of no personal importance to me whether or not Vietnam veterans marched on Anzac Day. It is simply true that they did. In this chapter I lay out the evidence that, from the beginning of Australia's commitment of fighting troops for Vietnam, a conscious and sustained effort was made by the government and the RSL to integrate veterans into the Anzac tradition. I will then offer a theory as to why some veterans, journalists, popular historians and people who contact talkback radio shows do not believe this occurred.

## Returning from a faraway war

The first Australian troops sent to Vietnam comprised a small number of advisers whose unit came to be known as the Australian Army Training Team Vietnam (AATTV) and who arrived 'in country' in 1962. The first battalion of Australian infantry to serve in Vietnam, 1RAR, was despatched in May–June 1965, and was made up entirely of regular soldiers who operated under American command out of the American base in Bien Hoa. The first Anzac Day for Australian fighting troops in Vietnam fell on 25 April 1966, and the Australian Prime Minister, Harold Holt, flew to Vietnam for the occasion. Holt addressed Australian and New Zealand troops at a parade in Bien Hoa and told them, 'You may have written another chapter in the history of Anzac. Anzac Day has taken on a deeper significance here today. On another field of battle, remote from our countries, Anzacs are together again fighting for freedom'.

In Australia two days previously, federal Treasurer William McMahon had described the men of 5RAR, who had marched through Sydney before they became the second battalion to ship out to Vietnam, as 'the new Anzacs', and RSL national president Arthur Lee had delivered a special message saying the young Australians fighting in Vietnam were upholding the traditions of Anzac. The headline of *The Australian*'s front-page coverage of the 1966 Anzac Day parade in Sydney was 'Vietnam veterans join march'. While 1RAR was still in Vietnam, the newspaper noted 12 Vietnam veterans – including two army officers, an air force warrant officer and nine other ranks – at the head of the contingent of troops from the Korean, Malayan and Borneo campaigns. The *Sydney Morning Herald* reported that they received 'a special cheer from the crowd' and, 'when the march ended at the Domain, old soldiers broke their ranks to shake hands with the young Vietnam veterans'. One veteran asked a group of teenage spectators 'with long hair and duffel coats', 'Why aren't you demonstrating today?' A newsboy's cry of the day's newspaper headline – 'Conscripts fighting in Vietnam' – was said to have provoked the comment 'It'll do them good' from a veteran of World War I. (The story sounds apocryphal.) There were no conscripts in Vietnam on 25 April 1966 but three national servicemen were permitted to take part in the Perth parade, as they had completed their training and were scheduled to leave for Vietnam in the coming months.[5]

In 1967, members of 5RAR's advance party, who had returned by air before the majority of the battalion came home by sea, marched in Sydney, and veterans marched in Melbourne, too. The *Sydney Morning Herald* headlined its front-page Anzac Day report 'Vietnam gives new meaning to Anzac'. The report described how

> a wave of applause ran along the streets of Sydney in tribute to young veterans of Vietnam [who] looked tanned and tough, big youngsters in their prime. They were a small contingent … but they drew the loudest recognition. It came from youth [whose] strongest acknowledgement was for their own generation – the young Regulars and National Servicemen.

The Vietnam veterans marched near the end of the parade with the returned men from Korea and Malaysia, but NSW RSL state president Sir William Yeo said he would have preferred to see them marching separately. The state secretary, WG Osmond, said it was one of the biggest marches he had ever seen and attributed its size to 'public concern about Australians serving in Vietnam'. A lead photograph on the front page of the *Canberra Times* on 22 April was captioned, 'A veteran from Vietnam greets an original ANZAC at the RSL Club in Canberra, typical of scenes all over Australia as servicemen gather to attend pre-Anzac Day functions'. The picture showed Warrant Officer Don Stahl of the AATTV, who had also fought in World War II, having a drink with a decorated old soldier who had been wounded at Gallipoli. Vietnam was remembered in the Anzac Day requiem at the Australian War Memorial for the first time, and the marchers in Canberra included 'several' Vietnam veterans.[6]

In 1968, 100 000 people watched the Anzac Day parade in Sydney. Once again, the *Sydney Morning Herald* noted that the young cheered the most,

> particularly for those nearest their own age group – the
> recently returned Vietnam veterans … As the young
> Vietnam veterans came along, near the end of the
> parade, they [were joined] behind the barriers, by other
> excited young people – girlfriends, brothers, sisters, even
> a few of the younger Mums – in a way never before seen
> at an Anzac march.[7]

In 1970, *The Sun-Herald* reported that the biggest cheer of the parade was reserved for the first Vietnam veterans in the Sydney march. In an equal-and-opposite reaction to Nadine Jensen's 1966 action,

> [a] woman slipped under the barricades to throw
> confetti over the young, fresh-faced Vietnam troops,
> most of whom wore only two medals, indicating they
> had served 12 months in Vietnam. As police gently
> escorted her back, the woman said with tear-filled eyes:

'Oh, they are so young, as young as my son. It takes
me back to when I was a girl and my husband first
marched'.[8]

It is a puzzling truth that everybody remembers Nadine Jensen,
the woman with the red paint, but no one today recalls the
unnamed mother with the confetti.

The last Australian combat troops were withdrawn from
Vietnam in March 1972. The *Sydney Morning Herald* headlined
its front-page 1972 Anzac Day coverage 'A new generation leads
Anzac march' over a photograph of Vietnam veterans marching
at the front of the parade. The newspaper reported:

> The proud figures of 600 Vietnam war veterans at the
> head of yesterday's Anzac March through the city
> instilled a new enthusiasm into the crowds lining
> the streets. From the moment they swung past the
> Cenotaph in Martin Plaza, heads turned in salute to
> fallen comrades, the crowd was with them … Australia's
> newest veterans received generous applause amidst cries
> of 'welcome back, boys' and 'good on you, fellers'.

In Brisbane, 435 Vietnam veterans marched for the first time as a
unit, and 200 veterans marched in Perth.[9]

## The RSL and Vietnam veterans

There is no evidence-based argument that Vietnam veterans
were not permitted to march on Anzac Day, and their history
of appearing in the parade has to be seen in the context of the

overwhelming support given to them by the RSL during the war years. In 2007, author Paul Ham made the extravagant claim that, historically, 'most – although not all – RSL branches either refused or discouraged admission and membership to Vietnam veterans'.[10] Ham offered no statistics to support this proposition, only a handful of anecdotes, but it seems to have become the received wisdom. The story goes that the RSL did not consider Vietnam to be 'a real war'. While this might have been true of some individual RSL members in some clubs, the RSL nationally first sent Christmas parcels to Vietnam in 1963, when there were no more than 100 Australian servicemen in the country, all of them attached to the AATTV.

Although the Australians were in Vietnam as instructors, and ostensibly not taking part in the fighting, the RSL recognised they worked under 'conditions of great hardship with a considerable element of danger'.[11] The RSL had sent similar packages to Malaya during the Emergency but discontinued them when the Emergency was officially declared over, even though there were still Australian troops stationed in Malaya. In fact, the RSL judged Australians in Vietnam to be involved in a 'real war' more than a year before the Australian government officially committed fighting troops.

In January 1966, two RSL officials who embarked on a fact-finding visit to Vietnam and Malaysia came home determined to press the government to award a distinct decoration to Australian troops in South Vietnam. Brigadier WH Hall, president of the Victorian RSL and chairman of the RSL Defence Committee, said the troops were 'magnificent' but 'their biggest complaint is that they want a medal to be struck for the Vietnam War. They deserve one because this is a horrible war'. On

27 April 1966, a soldier reported to be the first Vietnam veteran admitted to the RSL joined the ACT branch. When Private Noel O'Halloran of 1RAR was presented with his badge by the ACT branch president, a photograph of the men together was printed in the *Canberra Times*.[12]

Far from habitually rejecting Vietnam veterans, the RSL officially feted them. In January 1968, *Reveille*, the magazine of the NSW state branch of the league, featured a poignant photograph of a man wearing striped hospital pyjamas with one leg bared to display an artificial limb. Standing with the aid of crutches between two smiling nurses was Private Denis Enright, a national serviceman who had lost his left foot, right leg and some of his fingers while serving with 2RAR in Vietnam. According to the story, the severely wounded man 'had one important thing to do shortly after he returned to Australia with multiple injuries. It was join the RSL'. So North Bondi sub-branch officials went to the hospital to present him with his badge.[13]

At a function in the Casino RSL Hall in January 1970, 40 'special certificates' were awarded to local men who had served overseas since World War II. Francis Maher, the NSW RSL state president, 'complimented Casino on their fine action in expressing thanks to those boys who had served in Vietnam'. The chairman of the 'Welcome Home' Committee, ER Mison, said the function had taken 18 months to organise because of 'the difficulty in obtaining information about the men who had served in Vietnam'. Maher added, 'On behalf of the R.S.L. I say we are tremendously proud of you and invite you to join our organisation'.[14]

*Reveille*'s 1970 Anzac Day editorial mentioned Vietnam in three places, each time explicitly including Vietnam veterans in the Anzac tradition. NSW state president Maher wrote of Australians who had 'sacrificed their lives fighting for their country in two major World Wars, in Korea, Malaysia and now Vietnam'. He said that enemies and allies 'from Gallipoli to Vietnam' had acknowledged the bravery of Australian troops who had 'fought in every major conflict including the treacherous, bitter and unusual jungle warfare now being fought in Vietnam'.[15]

In August 1971, *Reveille* wondered why, 'even though there are more members of the League than at any time since that period immediately after World War II', fewer seemed to be wearing their RSL badges. An anonymous – and therefore, perhaps, apocryphal – badge-scorning Vietnam national service veteran said, 'It's not that I'm ashamed of being a member, it's just that I work as an art director and the design offends my aesthetic taste'. Next to the story was a photograph of singer and actor Lorrae Desmond draped over a pile of boxes to illustrate a piece about the 7000 parcels the RSL's Australian Forces Overseas Fund (AFOF) planned to send to troops for Christmas 1971.[16] The gift packages the troops received throughout the war often came to them through the league, just as the entertainers who flew from Australia to perform for the troops – most famously Little Pattie and Col Joye on the day of the Battle of Long Tan in 1966 – were often organised by the AFOF.

In January 1972, Frank Buxton, formerly field representative of the AFOF in Vietnam, wrote in *Reveille* that

> every member of the League is obligated to do all
> within his power to assist the League in increasing its
> membership. At present a vast source of eligible League
> members are to be found in the National Servicemen's

> ranks, the majority of whom have now been discharged
> on completion of their service in Vietnam. The young
> veteran [sic] of Vietnam, now ex-servicemen, must be
> convinced by all means possible to join the League. They
> must be made aware that the League's future is theirs and
> that they now have obligations to care for the heritage
> handed down by past generations of ex-servicemen.[17]

The cover of the magazine shows an elderly woman embracing
Sergeant Ken Browning of 12 Field Regiment, who had returned
from Vietnam in November 1971 and had already joined the City
of Liverpool sub-branch of the RSL. (Many *Reveille* covers during
this period featured Vietnam men.) In April, NSW state president
Colin Hines's Anzac Day *Reveille* editorial noted 'growing feelings against war' and urged 'don't let us forget our troops – both
the National Servicemen and the Regular Army recruits who have
served in Vietnam. They have served their country with distinction in the same manner as their fathers and grandfathers'. The
NSW state branch appealed to all sub-branches to 'make special
mention of the Vietnam veterans in their Anzac Day services'
and requested every sub-branch to 'allow the Vietnam veterans to
lead their march and take pride of place at any ceremony'. These
Vietnam veterans, wrote Hines, 'must become the backbone of
the R.S.L. of tomorrow'.[18] This was how the 600 Vietnam veterans
came to be marching at the front of the Sydney parade in 1972.

## Protest: a minority occupation

Unfortunately, there is insufficient space in this chapter to
discuss the protests that occasionally occurred on Anzac Day

during the war, although these were few in number, generally silent and always sparsely supported. However, on the morning of Anzac Day 1972 in Sydney, at the moment the parade led by Vietnam veterans was scheduled to begin, a flare attached to a timing device was detonated among the wreaths laid around the Cenotaph. Several other wreaths caught fire.

Some men could have seen this as the final denigration of their service: a war bookended by Nadine Jensen and burning memorial flowers. I do not suggest the idea that veterans faced a hostile reception on their homecoming is 'overblown', only that there is another side to the story. Some veterans felt they were not permitted to stand beside the tall, tanned, larrikin youth of World Wars I and II, and join what General David Morrison referred to many years later as 'that long, loping column stretching back in memory's eye through the mist of time, of those who have worn the slouch hat and Rising Sun badge abroad in the service of their country'.[19] Instead, they felt they were regarded as murderers, rapists, baby-killers and mercenaries. A rash of feminist demonstrations at Anzac Day parades in the late 1970s and early 1980s seemed evidence of some veterans' conviction that the soldiers were being 'blamed for the war'. However, if some on the Left took this view in the post-war years, there is no evidence that it was a widespread sentiment among the electorate that returned conservative governments to power in federal elections in 1966 and 1969. But Menzies' 'forgotten people' were forgotten again once Gough Whitlam's Labor Party came to power, and the memory of the support given to the troops by the Right came to be eclipsed by recollection and reinforcement of the criticisms levelled at the war by the Left.[20]

In 1981, Peter Young, a Vietnam veteran, became national secretary of the RSL. By 1983 there were some 12 000 Vietnam veterans among the RSL's approximately 300000 members.[21] In 1988, Alf Garland, a Vietnam veteran, became national president of the RSL. It would be very difficult to construct an evidence-based argument for Ham's claim that 'most' RSL branches at any time refused or discouraged admission and membership to Vietnam veterans, so where do the roots of these stories lie? I suggest they originate in the well-documented dispute between the Vietnam Veterans' Association of Australia (VVAA) and the RSL over the Agent Orange issue. The VVAA was founded in 1979 to pursue claims by some Vietnam veterans that they had been affected by toxic chemicals during their war service.[22] Although the RSL provided assistance to the VVAA, some veterans felt the league did not advocate their case with sufficient vigour; certain RSL members and officials were openly sceptical of arguments that Vietnam veterans had suffered any unique hardship. In 1985 the Evatt Royal Commission into the use of chemical agents in Vietnam reported that the veterans' various medical problems were probably not caused by Agent Orange – although subsequent studies have pointed to the possibility of links between exposure to certain types of herbicides used in Vietnam and certain cancers. The VVAA spent several years publicly airing various complaints against the RSL – and the RSL fought back with the intemperate rhetoric for which generations of the organisation's leadership have become known – but until the mid-1980s the VVAA's accusations were based on the RSL's alleged neglect of veterans' post-war health issues rather than its rejection of individual membership applications. To date, I have been unable to find a single individual rejection story that was published before the Evatt Royal Commission reported its findings.

## The reckoning

There is a huge amount of contemporary documentary evidence that the government and the RSL did all they could to normalise the status of Vietnam veterans as returned Anzacs. There is only after-the-fact oral testimony that the reverse occurred. Why, therefore, do journalists, veterans and popular historians choose to ignore the former and accept the latter? I suspect that some of them simply conduct inadequate research and do not check their sources. Others, either by accident or by design, become advocates of the veterans rather than students of their experience. In most 'Western' societies, there has developed a post-feminist reluctance to challenge the testimony of 'victim groups' – and organised Vietnam veterans have, over time, established themselves in the Australian public consciousness as victims rather than prosecutors of their war. And the story works for everybody. Few on the Right question some veterans' version of history; they derive too much enjoyment from the idea that the Left in the 1960s was a spitting, blood-hurling, unthinking rabble. Few on the Left have much sympathy with the RSL, and an acceptance that even the league was somehow against the Vietnam War lends credence to their happy fantasy that the anti-war movement won some kind of cultural hegemony in Australia and forced the government to withdraw the troops.

Revisionist ideas about the veterans' experience gained strength with extraordinary speed. On 26 April 1987, 15 years after Vietnam veterans led the Sydney Anzac Day march for the first time, the Sydney *Sun-Herald* reported,

> Australia's Vietnam veterans came home yesterday,
> at long last. Steady applause, broken by spontaneous
> outbursts of cheering and whistling, accompanied the
> record number of about 2,000 veterans as they led the
> Army in the Anzac Day march for the first time.[23]

While it is axiomatically difficult to prove that something never happened – and in 2003 Victorian RSL state president Bruce Ruxton conceded that 'some secretaries of individual RSLs may have banned Vietnam vets' – it seems unlikely that many men were ever explicitly refused admittance to an RSL branch or sub-branch on the basis of their service *during the war*, although many felt alienated by the attitude of the RSL to their concerns *after the war*.[24] A feeling of quiet rejection – a cold shoulder, a limp handshake or a sarcastic sneer – is difficult to invest with narrative drama. It is clearer and simpler to say the Vietnam veterans were turned away at the RSL's doors – and thereby denied entrance to both the clubs and the Anzac pantheon – and banned from marching on Anzac Day. It may not be the truth of what happened, but it is the truth of the way some veterans felt. Like most of the stories of spit and blood and airport demonstrations, however, it is not 'honest history'.

# 7

# Myth and history: The persistent 'Atatürk words'

DAVID STEPHENS & BURÇIN ÇAKIR

Myth is not the same as history: the discipline of history is about the search for and presentation of evidence. Myth, on the other hand, is about providing comfort (Santa Claus, 72 virgins waiting in heaven for the martyrs) or causing fear (the Bogeyman, witches) or promoting an agenda. Mustafa Kemal, later known as Atatürk, was an Ottoman commander at Gallipoli who became the founder and first president of the Turkish republic. Some alleged words of his have become central to the received version of Anzac. This chapter questions those words and shows how they have been exploited; it undermines a central pillar of the Anzac legend.[1]

## The myth

On monuments around Australia, New Zealand, Turkey and elsewhere, these words appear, often with a Turkish version alongside them:

> Those heroes that shed their blood and lost their lives
> … You are now lying in the soil of a friendly country.
> Therefore rest in peace. There is no difference between
> the Johnnies and the Mehmets to us where they lie side
> by side in this country of ours. You, the mothers, who
> sent their sons from far away countries, wipe away your
> tears. Your sons are now lying in our bosom and are in
> peace. After having lost their lives on this land they have
> become our sons as well.[2]

There is another English version of the words, however, which says nothing about there being no difference between Johnnies and Mehmets. Instead, that sentence runs, 'You are side by side, bosom to bosom with Mehmets'.[3] This is a more accurate translation of the Turkish, '*Sizler, Mehmetçiklerle yanyana, koyun koyunasınız*'. The fact that there are competing English translations underlines the slipperiness of the 'Atatürk words', 82 (or perhaps 85) years after they are supposed to have been uttered (or perhaps written).

The extreme version of the myth is that Atatürk included the words in a speech he made at the Anzac Day Dawn Service at Gallipoli in 1934. There is no evidence that there was such a service, let alone that Atatürk was present. There are many other vague references to an Atatürk speech or message in 1930, 1931, 1933, 1934, 1935 and 1936. Another suggestion is that Atatürk wrote a letter to 'the Anzac mothers' of Australia and New Zealand; again, there is no contemporary evidence of such a letter.[4] The most common assertion, however, is that Atatürk dictated the words to his Interior Minister and close associate Şükrü Kaya, who then used them in a speech. The main problem there is that the evidence only dates back to 1953, 15 years after Atatürk died.

## Evidence: 1930s to 1953

The key document is the pamphlet *Atatürk and the Anzacs*, written by Uluğ İğdemir and published by the semi-official Turkish Historical Society in 1978. The pamphlet reprints (accurately) Şükrü Kaya's interview with the journalist Yekta Ragıp Önen, first published in the newspaper *Dünya* on 10 November 1953.[5] In the interview, Kaya recalls Atatürk giving him words to use in a speech Kaya was to deliver 'by the side of the Mehmetçik monument' on the Gallipoli peninsula. The words in Turkish commence '*Bu memleketin*' and, in English, 'Those heroes'. There is nothing in the *Dünya* article to date these words Kaya 'recalled' from around two decades earlier. İğdemir guessed 1934, perhaps because he knew there had been a ceremony on 18 March 1934 at Çanakkale to commemorate the Ottoman naval victory of 1915. This is the date the Turkish Embassy in Canberra gives for the Kaya speech, but there is no evidence that Kaya was even in Çanakkale that day, let alone making speeches partly written by

Atatürk. Even Utkan Kocatürk, a prolific author on Atatürk for a Turkish government publishing house, only 'cautiously' (*ihti-yatla*) accepts this date.[6] A published collection of Kaya's speeches includes no speech that looks like the one he 'recalled' in 1953, and no speech he delivered anywhere on 18 March 1934.[7] Some versions of the story have Kaya making a speech in *late April* 1934 to a group of Gallipoli pilgrims on the vessel *Duchess of Richmond*, but again there is no evidence for this. There were a couple of brief messages from Atatürk himself to the *Richmond* group but they were formal in tone and did not include the 'Those heroes ...' words.[8]

Kaya did give a speech *in 1931*, however, near the Mehmetçik monument and following a conversation with Atatürk, but his remarks distinguished clearly between defenders and invaders. There was nothing about soldiers lying bosom to bosom, dead but equal. Instead, there was this paragraph:

> Tomorrow, the history of civilization will judge those lying opposite each other and determine whose sacrifice was more just or humane and [which] to appreciate more: the monuments of the invaders or the untouched traces of the heroes left here in the form of sacred stones and soil, these traces of heroes.

The speech included some references to the fighting qualities of the invading troops, as did other Atatürk messages to Australia, but there is no sign of the 'Those heroes ...' words.[9]

Had Atatürk delivered such a significant and humane message sometime in the 1930s, whether personally or through a mouth-piece such as Kaya, it is reasonable to expect it would have been publicised as an example of Atatürk's greatness and magnanimity. Although İğdemir claimed in 1978 that the 'Atatürk words' spread around the world immediately after Kaya uttered them, the New Zealand researcher George Davis found no evidence of this, either contemporary or in standard Atatürk biographies. Atatürk's obituaries, too, are silent.[10] Perhaps Kaya remembered remarks that Atatürk had made at some point and he paraphrased them. Atatürk sent a message to Australia in 1931, for example, which said that the Anzacs 'will be in our thoughts as well as our own dead' as they, the Anzacs, 'sleep their last sleep on the windswept wastes of Gallipoli'.[11] Atatürk was a prolific speaker and writer, yet Atatürk scholar Cengiz Özakıncı says the style of the Turkish words is not Atatürk's. Instead, the tone is reminiscent of the legends of Ancient Greece, a field where Kaya was an expert and a published author.[12] Çakır checked Turkish language MA and PhD theses that refer to the 'Atatürk words' and found all of them gave Kaya (either in *Dünya* in 1953 or İğdemir in 1978) as the source.

What, then, were the circumstances of the Kaya interview with Önen in 1953? Önen sets the scene:

> I am in the house of Mr. Şükrü Kaya, a close friend of the Great Soldier, Great Reformer and Great Man, Atatürk. On the eve of the anniversary of Atatürk's death I am listening to Şükrü Kaya's reminiscences about Him … Carried away with the torrent of memories he was recounting in profound enthusiasm and great ecstasy. It is impossible to take them down in writing! … As he gets more emotional, new memories come to life and I ponder

in my incapacity for conceiving the greatness of the
Great Man.[13]

Why did Kaya speak out in 1953? Turkish politics then was
rife with competing personality cults and threats of instability.
Atatürk, the central pillar of 'Kemalism', had been dead for 15
years but there was mass hysteria in the streets of Ankara as his
remains were moved to a new mausoleum. In the background
was İsmet İnönü, Atatürk's successor as president but in opposition since 1950. By 1953 the Democrat Party (DP) government
feared İnönü might try to stage a coup to return to power. *Dünya*
supported the government against İnönü and Kaya himself had
reason to oppose İnönü, who had sidelined him after Atatürk's
death.[14] There was another element: Turkey at this time was reaching out to the West. It had troops in Korea, alongside Australians
and others. It had joined NATO in 1952 and its growing acceptance by the West was seen as a success for the DP government.
Kaya's 'Atatürk words' could have created an impression of
fellow-feeling between Turkey and its new allies.[15]

Of course, the absence of proof is not the proof of absence. Yet
there is a lack of evidence that the 'Atatürk words' were ever said
or written by anyone before Kaya spoke to Önen in 1953. (Önen,
the senior journalist – and devoted Kemalist – who wrote up the
interview did not take contemporaneous notes.)[16] It is not really
up to sceptics to prove the words were *never* said or written by
Atatürk. Rather, it is up to proponents to prove they *were* said or
written, and where and when. Producing evidence is what historians normally do; if they fudge the task, then wishful thinking
has overtaken the practice of history.

# Evidence: 1958–77

In the years after Kaya's 1953 *Dünya* interview, the 'Atatürk words' appeared occasionally in Turkish and in English trans-lation, without attracting much fanfare. The Çanakkale Martyrs' Memorial (*Çanakkale Şehitleri Anıtı*) was built between 1954 and 1958 and later extended. The original structure includes a stone carrying the 'Atatürk words' in Turkish identical to Kaya's in *Dünya*, and in English (but lacking any reference to equality between Johnnies and Mehmets – for reasons which will become clear shortly). The dissemination of the Kaya–*Dünya* version was probably responsible, too, for the words in Turkish Captain Akomer's speech in English to visitors from New South Wales in April 1960. While Akomer's words are close to İğdemir's of 18 years later, it is his vagueness about time and place that is signif-icant: 'I would quote what was said by Ataturk himself … *Upon an occasion*, he sent a deputation with a special message …' Bill Yeo (later Sir William), president of the New South Wales Branch of the then Returned Sailors', Soldiers' and Airmen's Imperial League of Australia, did not think Akomer's speech worthy of mention in the official trip report.[17]

Something similar happened five years later, when more Australians went to Gallipoli. According to Australian Associated Press reporter Norman Macswan, the Australians read copies in English of a statement from Atatürk; it was much the same as Akomer's in 1960. But Atatürk's pronouncements clearly lacked in 1965 the weight they later gained: his remarks made it into Macswan's story for *The News* in Adelaide but were missing in the *Canberra Times* version; historian Ken Inglis, who was there, did not mention them at all in his report.[18]

## Evidence: 1977–85

After 1977 the 'Those heroes …' words achieved an apotheosis that was due as much to the requirements of Turkish politics as to the sentiments the words expressed. Australians played a part, however, especially Alan Johnston Campbell of Brisbane. Becoming aware in 1977 of the Turkish version of the 'Atatürk words', Campbell, a Gallipoli veteran and head of the Gallipoli Fountains of Honour committee, determined that an English translation of the words would be ideal for the fountains. He embroidered the translation, however, to include the clause, 'There is no difference between the Johnnies and the Mehmets …' Campbell's Turkish contact, Uluğ İğdemir, went along with the change on behalf of the Turkish Historical Society, and the story of this exchange was recorded in İğdemir's 1978 booklet *Atatürk and the Anzacs*. In August 1983, the historical society became a government body under the Turkish Constitution of November 1982, following the coup by the Kemalist military in September 1980. One of the society's tasks, as part of the Atatürk High Institution of Culture, Language and History, was 'to disseminate information on the thought, principles and reforms of Atatürk, Turkish culture, Turkish history and the Turkish language'. The very first paragraph of the 1982 Constitution referred to 'the concept of nationalism introduced by the founder of the Republic of Turkey, Atatürk, the immortal leader and the unrivalled hero, and his reforms and principles'.[19]

Alan Campbell died in 1982, but his embroidered version emerged again – Atatürk had a profile at this time because of the 1981 centenary of his birth – pushed by the Turks onto Australians who were apparently unaware of the version's history (despite the story being set out in İğdemir's booklet, which the Turks were disseminating at the time). The revival was part of the bargain in 1984–85 where Turkey agreed to rename part of its Arıburnu area as 'Anzac Cove' (Anzak Koyu) in return for Australia renaming part of Lake Burley Griffin in Canberra 'Gallipoli Reach' and a stretch of water at Albany, Western Australia, 'Atatürk Channel', as well as constructing the Atatürk Memorial in Anzac Parade, Canberra, carrying the 'Those heroes ...' words over Atatürk's name. The Canberra memorial was dedicated on Anzac Day 1985, the same day as a memorial carrying the same words over the same name was dedicated at Anzac Cove. In both cases, Johnnies and Mehmets were equal, thanks to Campbell and İğdemir.[20]

As in 1953, Turkish political and diplomatic motives were crucial in 1984–85. The Turkish coup of 1980 had ended years of instability in the country, yet left Turkey seeking to shore up its Western networks. The Turkish Ambassador in Canberra, Faruk Şahinbaş, stressed to his superiors in Ankara that the renaming deal would enhance Turkey's standing in Australia, a small but significant Western nation. The visit to Australia of Turkish Foreign Minister Vahit Halefoğlu for the ceremonies in April 1985 – the first Turkish ministerial visit here – was significant in building relations with Australia – and, by extension, the West as a whole. The minister stressed Turkey's important role in the Western world and, in the Middle East, its geostrategic importance to the Iran–Iraq conflict, and the situation in Lebanon. He and his Australian counterpart, Bill Hayden, welcomed the further development of friendly relations between their countries.[21]

Even more than it was reaching out to the West, the 1980 junta was reaching back to Atatürk.[22] One of the regime's first acts was to revive the early Republican Kemalist doctrine. Only

Kemalism (*Atatürkçülük*), the regime believed, could foster national unity and modernity to reach the level of Western nations, bring the divided nation together after instability in the 1970s and restore the authority of the state. There was a massive campaign: Kemalist books were published; all educational materials followed Kemalist principles; streets, roads, buildings and airports were named or renamed after Atatürk; Atatürk's portrait proliferated on mountainsides and in classrooms, offices, homes and public places. The Atatürk High Institution had branches in almost every city in Turkey. These trends continued after the return to civilian rule – under close military oversight and with junta leader General Kenan Evren as President – late in 1983.

The Gallipoli story was central to this period, and rhetoric about it addressed both national and international audiences. New history textbooks from the Ministry of Education stressed the bravery of Turkish soldiers, the leadership of Atatürk and the ideals that Turks should adopt from this period of their history. War memorials had begun to appear on the Gallipoli peninsula from around 1960, but another nine were built between 1981 and 1984, most featuring words from Atatürk. The Gallipoli monuments and sites were brought under the protection of the Ministry of Culture, indicating their importance to the nation. Development of the Gallipoli area also fed into the Turkish government's desire to encourage international tourism. A 1982 law encouraging tourism marked Gallipoli sites for particular attention; the numbers of tourists, including from Australia, and facilities for them grew gradually from the early 1990s.

The 1984–85 deal – reciprocal renaming and memorial building – should be seen in this broader context. Ambassador Şahinbaş vigorously promoted the deal – including to Prime Minister Hawke

– and there is strong evidence that the inclusion in it of an Atatürk memorial carrying the Great Leader's likeness and words, rather than reciprocal renaming alone or renaming plus a simple plaque on a stone, followed the direct intervention of the Turkish Army chief, General Üruğ, and probably President Evren himself. The Turks even considered footing the bill for the Canberra memorial.[23] On the Australian side, official involvement in the deal was desultory and dilatory until Hawke acted to ensure the memorial was completed in time. Neither side questioned whether the words used on both the Anzac Parade and Arıburnu memorials were actually Atatürk's, although the Turkish side at least knew there were two different versions of the words and ensured that the 'no difference between the Johnnies and Mehmets' version prevailed. If any Turks knew of Alan Campbell's role they kept it quiet in the interests of Turkish–Australian relations. After all, as Şahinbaş told his superiors, the doctored version was the one that had become accepted in Australia.[24]

The Turks had more invested in the deal than Australia did: for Australia it was mostly about renaming Anzac Cove. Yet some Australians had a soft spot for Atatürk dating back to the 1920s. The Turkish historian Ayhan Aktar has described how Charles Bean, his British war historian counterpart, CF Aspinall-Oglander, and Winston Churchill cooperated to build up the then Mustafa Kemal's military reputation in the 1920s: it was easier to justify defeat at Gallipoli if it could be shown there had been a 'man of destiny' calling the shots on the Ottoman side. By the 1930s there were also diplomatic imperatives, as Britain cultivated President Atatürk.[25] Some old Diggers in the early 1930s were pleased to read Atatürk's testimonials about their fighting prowess. Australian visitors to the Dardanelles were touched by the reception they received. Alan Campbell referred to Atatürk as 'that Great Turk'.[26] While 1980s official Australia might not have placed a high priority on relations with Turkey, many Australians felt warmly towards the old enemy.[27] This facilitated the reception and consolidation of the poignant 'Atatürk words'.

## When myth prevails

Why does this case matter? First, because the 'Atatürk words' are famous. The British historian Jenny Macleod suggested in 2015 that they had become the most frequently quoted words about Gallipoli.[28] In Australia they are a central trope of Anzac commemoration. Any attempt to put Anzac in its proper, proportionate place thus needs to tackle the words head-on. To the extent that they are trotted out in other countries, robust evidence about provenance should matter there, too. Words matter; famous words matter more.

The words matter also as an example of how myth can drive out history. The 'Atatürk words' are almost certainly Kaya's – or possibly the journalist Önen's – embroidered by Campbell with the help of İğdemir and assiduously pushed by the Turks onto gullible or indifferent Australians. Historians are doing themselves and the profession a disservice if they forgo their normal evidentiary standards in the face of this attractive myth, if they fall back on the argument that such wonderful words must have been said by a great man, or if they pull their punches to avoid incurring Turkish disfavour. Insisting the words were written or said by Atatürk gives them extra weight because it takes advantage of his fame; something that Kaya or Önen made up, even if it was partly based on some recollection of a talk with Atatürk, is not the same, especially when the important 'Johnnies and Mehmets' gloss was added decades later. Hedging bets by using the formula 'attributed to Atatürk' changes little; the reflected glory remains. Think of the number of times the 'Atatürk words' are followed by another weighty phrase, 'the father of modern Turkey'.

The fact that Australian politicians – and some historians – still cling to the words says more about their attitudes to Australian–Turkish relations than it does about their respect for evidence or even for the dead. Myths comfort us. They are also a mainstay of diplomacy. Historian Peter Stanley said the 'Atatürk' paragraph was 'a useful vehicle to cement relations between Turkey and Australia and so has been endorsed and quoted by successive Australian prime ministers, even though it is not historically justifiable'.[29] When then prime ministers Tony Abbott and Ahmet Davutoğlu met in April 2015, Abbott referred to 'a great sense of mutual respect' he said existed between the two countries. The 'Atatürk words' serve that sentiment perfectly, reflecting two middle-sized powers, one firmly in the Western camp, the other wanting to be; one sending tens of thousands of immigrants to the other but earning lots of tourist dollars from it; one turning a soldier–statesman into a demigod, the other building a secular religion around ordinary men turned superheroes; and the soldiers on both sides equally honoured – and equally dead. Yet a trope based on myth is essentially a confidence trick, and the people most gulled by that trick are the bright-eyed children who are pushed forward, in Australia, Turkey and elsewhere, to recite what they have been told are the words of the great Atatürk.

Which brings us back to Şükrü Kaya, the man who claimed to recall Atatürk's words 15 years after the Great Leader died. It detracts from the dignity of commemoration to use bogus words. It detracts even more to rely on disreputable progenitors. Kaya was an unsavoury figure, for all his loyalty to Atatürk and his scholarly pursuits. He was arrested by the British in 1919 but escaped before he could be charged with war crimes relating to the Armenian Genocide, he supervised ethnic cleansing of Kurds in the 1930s and he may have plotted in 1938 to assassinate İnönü.[30] The words are cheapened by their association with this archetypal political fixer. (Chapter 3 of this book, by Vicken Babkenian and Judith Crispin, deals with Australia's links with the Armenians.)

Ultimately, though, it is how the 'Atatürk words' are used today that matters. Our yearning for comfort has been abused by the vision of dead combatants lying side by side, equal, with the Turks looking after all of them.[31] It is the right of adults touched by war to go on, if they wish, preferring myths to evidence-based history, but they should not encourage children to do the same. It is a cop-out to say – as Hume Council in Victoria said about its plans for a memorial or plaque carrying the 'Atatürk words' – 'these same words have been widely used by a number of military, State and Federal Government representatives'.[32] Writing about the Atatürk obsession, the translation expert Anthony Pym described 'a paroxysm of monuments and plaques, all reinforcing each other, with a certitude that creates its own history'.[33] That is dishonest history and dangerous myth.

# 8

# A century of bipartisan commemoration: Is Anzac politically inevitable?

FRANK BONGIORNO

I t has become common enough to hear complaints about the political exploitation of Anzac. Such criticisms often seem to assume that it might be possible to have an apolitical Anzac legend, one that was truly national in being above politics. In reality, Anzac has been a matter of politics from the jump; it has never simply been about remembering the glorious dead and honouring the noble service of the living. Even before Gallipoli, Labor leader Andrew Fisher's famous 'last man' and 'last shilling' pledge was as much about positioning his party in an election campaign as it was about pledging loyalty to the British Empire.[1]

This chapter will explore some political uses and abuses of Anzac since 1915, especially the ways the legend has figured in prime ministerial rhetoric. It is not that sinister calculation lies behind every mention of Anzac by a political leader: Anzac clearly has a public resonance that cannot be reduced to its political implications. Yet the Anzac legend's very resonance means it is a more or less permanent temptation for any national leader – regardless of party allegiance, for Anzac is bipartisan – to sanctify a particular cause, political or diplomatic, by linking it with the country's most respected civic language and symbolism. There can be little doubt, as Carolyn Holbrook has shown, that the habit has been more common since 1990 than it was in 1970 or even in 1950. As the hold of the Returned and Services League (RSL) over the legend (and Anzac Day itself) has weakened, the politicians and the bureaucracy have gradually tightened their grip.[2]

## Hughes to Menzies

WM Hughes began the political exploitation of Anzac. Hughes, in London as Australian prime minister at the time of the first Anzac Day in 1916, recognised in the anniversary a chance to draw attention to Australians' war contribution. The men of Anzac had not long evacuated Gallipoli and were just a few weeks away from the greater horrors of the Western Front; their march through London and then the Westminster Abbey service combined festivity and solemnity in a manner that would become familiar enough on many Anzac Days to come. Back in Australia, too, there was politics. State and federal leaders jostled to bathe in the reflected glory of Anzac warriors. Patriots such as Canon David Garland in Brisbane, who had promoted the observance of the day in a manner fitting a Christian nation fighting in a sacred cause, now used it to promote enlistment.[3]

After the war, Anzac continued to serve diplomatic and political purposes. Hughes again used the Anzac Day of 1919 – the first after the war – to display and celebrate the contribution of the Anzacs, this time to the Allies' victory. The Anzacs' London march was even more spectacular than in 1916. Hughes had been at the Paris Peace Conference, resisting Japanese pressure for the insertion of a racial equality clause in the League of Nations covenant and backing his demands by drawing attention to the scale of Australian sacrifice. The Australian contribution was dramatised by the sight of troops marching to the newly opened and extravagantly decorated Australia House, while borrowed Royal Air Force planes flew noisily overhead. Sir John Monash led the men on a grey horse.[4]

Hughes's Australian-born successor, SM Bruce, had served in the British Army as a captain at Gallipoli, where he was twice wounded; his war service bestowed on him a prestige that added lustre to polished manners, a Cambridge education and enviable wealth. Bruce was soon advocating Anzac Day 'as Australia's national day'. In 1925 he issued an Anzac Day message calling the day 'our most sacred and cherished memory', but he aligned the Anzac 'spirit' with a secular vision for Australia's 'development and prosperity' to be pursued by 'each and every section of the community'. While Bruce was criticising union militancy and the 'Bolshevik menace' as the enemy within, Anzac seemed to offer a consensual legend of national harmony and sacrifice. Despite walking with a limp that was a legacy of war service, Bruce did not much exploit Anzac for partisan political gain. His biographer David Lee reports that, while the war did not make Bruce 'a pacifist', it left him 'with an abiding detestation of war'. When there were hundreds of thousands of returned men in the country, most of them without Bruce's advantages, many of them more damaged than him, there was limited scope for making too much of the military connection, even if Bruce had been more inclined to do so. The dangers of Anzac partisanship were emphasised in 1925 when, at a public meeting in Perth, Bruce joined in criticism of the Western Australian Labor government for its decision to stop returned soldiers from giving speeches in schools on Anzac Day. The response from the Acting Premier, William Angwin, was fierce: 'The comments made were unnecessary, and, as one whose son made the supreme sacrifice, I personally resent them. I might add that others of my colleagues in the Ministry lost brothers in the late War, one losing two'.[5]

In contrast with Bruce, neither of Australia's two main World War II prime ministers, Robert Menzies and John Curtin, had served in a war. Curtin was a Great War anti-conscriptionist, then a World War II prime minister at the very moment when an invader most directly threatened Australia. The Labor Party has always been rather more invested in Anzac than historians have imagined, and Curtin's rhetoric was as fulsome as that of any other leader in Australia's history, as he called on Australians to 'work and fight, putting all else aside, so that Australia shall be for ever the home of the Anzac people'.[6]

Because of a family decision to keep one son at home, Menzies had not joined the Australian Imperial Force during World War I, although his two older brothers enlisted. The matter was almost certainly painful for the ambitious and patriotic young man at a time when the pressure to enlist was intense. It came back to haunt him when Country Party leader Earle Page launched a bitter parliamentary attack on him in 1939 over his lack of military service. Menzies' understandable sensitivity on this issue must have hampered any effort by him to connect his leadership conspicuously with the Anzac legend, which during much of his political career he identified as largely the property of returned men. In London in April 1941, Menzies expressed delight in his diary when *The Times* reported his 'Anzac speech verbatim on the cable page – an honour hitherto reserved for Winston'. But the speech was overshadowed by the disaster unfolding in Greece. 'This Anzac Day was a day of great anxiety', Menzies told the British Empire Service League. 'But if there was one great quality of our race it was that anxiety for us did not spell fear, or weakness, or hesitation, or vain repining.'[7]

Menzies might have found the Anzac theme easier to deal with when away from home. In Port Moresby for Anzac Day in 1957 he 'took the salute at an Anzac day march past', an event comprising 'green-clad native troops of the Pacific Islands Regiment, the regiment's pipe band and the black-uniformed native police'. Typical of Menzies' low-key Anzac Day activities was his unveiling in 1955 of a war memorial at Knox Grammar School in Sydney, but his government provided generous financial support to activities for the 50th anniversary a decade later.[8]

## The World War II men take over: Gorton and Whitlam

Knox's most famous student, Gough Whitlam, was standing on the steps of the Australian War Memorial for a ceremony when

Tasmanian Labor MP Lance Barnard suggested Whitlam should run for the Labor Party's deputy leadership. Both men had served in World War II, Whitlam with the Royal Australian Air Force (RAAF), Barnard in the 9th Division at El Alamein. (Whitlam became deputy in 1960. When he and Barnard formed a brief two-man government in December 1972, Whitlam boasted that it was the first entirely ex-service ministry in Australian history.) Indeed, in the era when Anzac Day is said to have been in decline – the late 1960s and early 1970s – Australia had two prime ministers who joined in Anzac Day ceremonies as old RAAF men. The Liberal Prime Minister John Gorton still bore the signs of an eventful war: his face had been badly battered in a plane crash. Later, the Japanese torpedoed his ship. HMAS *Ballarat* picked up the survivors, so Gorton, recently elevated to the prime ministership, was pleased to lead the Anzac Day march in Ballarat in 1968. 'The crowd clapped and cheered as he barked commands to the ex-Servicemen marching behind him', *The Age* reported.[9]

While Gorton sought to scale down Australia's involvement in the Vietnam War, the conflict was increasingly unpopular by the time he became Prime Minister. For anti-war protesters, Anzac Day itself became a target for its alleged role in fostering militarism. During a brawl following the wreath-laying ceremony at the Cenotaph in London on Anzac Day 1968, police arrested eight protesters from the group Australians and New Zealanders against the Vietnam War. The protesters carried a placard that declared 'Vietnam War explodes Anzac myth'; war veterans and their wives tore the sign to shreds. Anzac Day in 1969 saw protests in Perth, where students laid a wreath carrying the message, 'Remember the murdered Vietnamese', while posters proclaiming 'Anzac Day war worship' and 'Ban the RSL' also appeared. In Newcastle, protesters defaced two memorials with red paint.[10]

The Labor Party benefited electorally from the Vietnam War's growing unpopularity but, as Prime Minister, Whitlam himself was at the Cenotaph in London to lay a wreath in 1973. The following year he was among 22 000 returned service personnel who marched in Sydney: 'tall as a grenadier with his World War II medals sparkling', he chatted with the Liberal Premier of New South Wales, Sir Robert Askin, as they prepared to lay wreaths. It was no longer Vietnam that provoked Anzac Day contention, but whether 'God Save the Queen' or 'Advance Australia Fair' – the latter had recently been selected in a poll and then endorsed by Whitlam as the new national anthem – would be played. Both songs featured in the ceremonies in Sydney and Canberra but not elsewhere. In Perth, the 1902 anthem 'Land of Hope and Glory' stood in as the national song; those present expressed their attitude without ambiguity when they sang the chorus twice. Anzac Day's association with conservative imperialism was becoming looser but remained real enough: there was further controversy in 1984 after the Hawke government reversed a Fraser government decision to return to 'God Save the Queen' and again adopted 'Advance Australia Fair'.[11]

## Hawke to Rudd–Gillard–Rudd

Most accounts trace Anzac revival to the 1980s. The social movement and identity politics of this period saw Anzac Day develop as a day of protest by feminists against rape in war and as an opportunity for some ethnic communities to draw attention to their contribution to a multicultural Australia. Yet as the number of original Anzacs dwindled, it was broader trends in collective memory, popular culture and media coverage that had a larger impact than identity politics. As early as 1983 a journalist reported complaints from old Diggers that 'the real and personal Anzac Day was giving way to the mythological, nationalistic Anzac Day'.[12] Peter Weir's 1981 film *Gallipoli* registered the shift away from understanding World War I as necessary sacrifice on behalf of a loyal British dominion towards a sense of the ordinary Australian soldier – and the young nation itself – as victims of the English officer class.

Prime Minister Bob Hawke gestured gently towards the idea of Australian victimhood when he spoke at an Anzac Day ceremony in Greece in 1986, describing the original Anzacs as fighting 'in a war not of their making'. Hawke was a significant figure in this Anzac revival, and was the first modern prime minister to articulate a renovated post-imperial Anzac legend. This engagement occurred gradually, beginning with the announcement in 1984 that Australia would approach the Turkish Government with a proposal to rename as Anzac Cove the beach on which the Australians landed on 25 April 1915. (The change occurred in 1985: see chapter 7 of this book.) Hawke also addressed RSL national conferences, supported a Vietnam homecoming march in 1987 and led a well-funded 75th anniversary 'pilgrimage' to Gallipoli in 1990. He thereby became the first Australian prime minister to visit Gallipoli on Anzac Day. *The Australian*'s Paul Kelly, who reported on the event, declared that 'public interest in Gallipoli is growing, not receding. The Anzac Legend now has returned to its original role as a unifying force'. The process, however, was not spontaneous: the federal government's contribution to fostering collective war memory was increasingly conspicuous, even if still somewhat reactive; the flow of tax-payers' money was modest compared with the gargantuan amounts lavished on centenary commemorations 25 years later.[13]

Hawke largely invented the role of the prime minister as Anzac 'commemorator-in-chief' (to use Holbrook's phrase)[14] in April 1990, although most historians have insufficiently recognised that developments in the emotional register of Australian public life during the 1980s were a precondition for this change. Hawke's own occasional public tears had contributed something; one correspondent seemed impressed that Hawke 'didn't break down and cry' during the Gallipoli dawn service. Among the 10 000 who attended, however, '[m]any were moist-eyed at the end of the ceremony'.[15] No one seemed unduly concerned: it had become more acceptable for men – including public men – to display their emotions on occasion.

It is ironic that Hawke's successor, Paul Keating, who had so little time for the idea that Australian nationhood was born at Gallipoli that he tried to erect an alternative Kokoda legend, would speak the most eloquent words of any Australian prime minister about Anzac. Keating's 1993 Remembrance Day eulogy for the Unknown Australian Soldier, acclaiming him as 'all of them' and 'one of us' – the fruit of his powerful partnership with speechwriter and historian Don Watson – registered profound changes in historical consciousness. Keating celebrated the Digger as noble because he was 'one of those who by his deeds proved that real nobility and grandeur belong not to empires and nations but to the people on whom they, in the last resort, always depend'. Keating's speech drew on a sensibility about World War I shaped by social historians such as Ken Inglis, Patsy Adam-Smith and Bill Gammage, as well as films and television programs, of which Weir's *Gallipoli* was the most successful. 'It was a lesson about ordinary people', Keating explained of what the war had taught, 'and the lesson was that they were not ordinary'. Keating's was one of the finest ever expressions of Australian democratic egalitarianism: no prime ministerial speech about war would ever again rise to such heights.[16]

Keating's speech was also quietly republican. His description of the Unknown Soldier as 'one of us' evoked a sense of communal belonging that was centred on Australia itself; he would also use the phrase in arguing for an Australian head of state. His Liberal Party successor, John Howard, was, by contrast, a committed constitutional monarchist, but his speeches on Anzac were not a dramatic departure from the scripts of Hawke and Keating. (It is certainly incorrect to attribute the Anzac revival to Howard, as some have; the revived Anzac hare was well down the track before Howard became prime minister in 1996.) Commentators have nevertheless made much of Howard's emphasis on the foundational role of World War I in Australian nationhood – his father and grandfather both fought in that conflict – and his strong emotional commitment to the Anzac legend. Certainly, Howard aligned the legend with his favoured image of the patriotic, battling, matey Australian, but what mattered was less what Howard said than the context in which he said it. Howard's long prime ministership coincided with increasing stress on national security after 9/11, border security after *Tampa*, the Australian expeditionary force tradition, and military cooperation between English-speaking peoples, as well as some disturbing strains of militant white nativism and racism and a resurgence of flag-waving nationalism. Against the background of Australia's military commitments to East Timor, Afghanistan and, more controversially, Iraq, Anzac rhetoric became prominent during this period – including in Howard's own speech-making – with the Anzac soldier embodying a national 'spirit' that was as powerful and relevant now, when he (and now she) was serving overseas in the Age of Terror, as in the Age of Empire.

It is also significant that Howard's prime ministership coincided with the demise of the last Great War Anzacs, a passing that provoked massive media interest. In Hobart in 2002, in an impressive feat of rhetorical gymnastics, Howard managed to deliver a eulogy at the state funeral to the last of the Gallipoli Anzacs, Alec Campbell, full of references to the 'living values' for which Campbell stood, but without once mentioning the man's socialism. Howard seemed more comfortable paying eloquent tribute to Campbell's 'hard work', 'self-reliance' and 'self-improvement' – all very Victorian-sounding values and in line with Howard's own conservatism.[17] Through such performances, however, the Howard Anzac Day speech has come to be recalled as marking his persona and his era in a similar way to a Menzies visit to Lord's or the Palace. Howard was notably successful in claiming the legend in a manner that Menzies himself never dared (and probably never contemplated).

Subsequent Labor prime ministers Kevin Rudd and Julia Gillard added little to the contours of Anzac commemoration established by their predecessors, although Rudd's Anzac words were marked by a notable rhetorical extravagance.[18] There were plenty of references in Rudd's and Gillard's speeches to the 'national soul', courage, sacrifice, mateship, compassion and what Gillard called the Anzac 'tradition of arms'. Rudd even used Anzac at the national bushfire memorial service in 2009 when he defined 'courage' in terms of a 'new army of heroes in which the yellow helmet evokes the same reverence as the slouch hat of old'. He also tried to renew Keating's emphasis on the importance to Australia of the Pacific War – the latter consistent with his thwarted ambitions for the creation of an Asia–Pacific Community by 2020.[19] Gillard's 2011 speech in Korea recalled Keating's 1993 eulogy in her reference to Australia's 100 000 war dead – 'each of them one of us' – but she otherwise made no obvious attempt to impose a distinctive Labor Party – or Gillard – stamp on the Anzac legend.[20]

## Abbott and the sainted Anzacs

Until 2015, the dominant note had been secular. For this reason, Tony Abbott's centenary dawn service speech at Gallipoli in that year should be considered a bold turn in prime ministerial rhetoric, for all its occasionally bumpy phraseology. 'Yes, they are us; and when we strive enough for the right things, we can be more like them', Abbott declared in his peroration.

> They did their duty; now, let us do ours.
> They gave us an example; now, let us be worthy of it.
> They were as good as they could be in their time; now,
> let us be as good as we can be in ours.[21]

For Hawke, Keating, Howard, Rudd and Gillard, Anzac was the source and origin of a set of ideas about how to live well as an Australian. It meant looking after one's fellows (or 'mates'), displaying stoicism and endurance in the face of adversity, practising tolerance when confronted with difference and compassion when encountering suffering, providing hospitality to the stranger, and regarding everyone as of fundamentally equal worth. (That many of these 'national' values are actually cosmopolitan ones neatly expresses a key transformation of modern Australian life.) The Anzac legend made no claims for the afterlife; it did not promise an eternal reward to those who had lived up to the Anzac spirit, merely the fullest belonging to the national community. The men of Gallipoli who were seen to have provided the initial inspiration for this community's 'spirit' and 'values' were ultimately ordinary – they 'were exactly like ourselves', John Howard assured an audience at Lone Pine in 2000 – men who, in their very ordinariness, gave us 'a mirror in which we see ourselves'.[22] But a complete lapse into solipsism was avoided in the recognition that the extraordinary circumstances in which these men had found themselves, as well as what later Australians made of their origin story, gave the Anzac legend its spiritual meaning.

Abbott's assumptions appeared different. The Anzacs for him were no longer mere mortals. Like Christian saints, they had become exemplars of a personal holiness to which mortals could only aspire. Being an Australian politician, Abbott could not mention God directly in a speech of such national importance, nor could he attribute to the Anzacs the saintly power to intercede with God on behalf of the living. So the speech was not literally an expression of Catholic theology. Yet in it the Anzacs ceased to be merely virtuous democratic antipodean everymen, as they were for Keating and even Howard; Abbott had taken both 'them' and 'us' out of secular 'history'. And with a most peculiar turn of phrase – 'Yes, they are us' – Australians, dead and living, form into a single spiritual 'body', a nation reconsecrated as an Anzac Communion of Saints. This vision momentarily reconceived

Australia as a sacred fellowship, bonded by its descent from the original Anzacs and its continuing faith in what the Anzacs represent.

It remains to be seen whether Abbott's effort was anything more than a piece of cultural freelancing by a conservative Catholic and former seminarian. It might turn out to be as meaningless to the future of Anzac as his reintroduction of knighthoods is likely to be to the honours system. Certainly, his successor (and convert to Catholicism) Malcolm Turnbull has shown no inclination towards a similar rhetorical extravagance. (Meanwhile, the Catholic-educated alternative prime minister, Bill Shorten, heatedly cited Anzac relatives when he complained about the cancellation of a service at Lone Pine in 2016.)[23] But, if Abbott's canonisation of the Anzacs is not wildly out of kilter with the broader cultural patterns of our time, we might be entering a new phase in Anzac commemoration, a variety of state-sponsored ancestor worship, for the support of which we are paying more than half a billion dollars during the World War I centenary period alone. Less ambitiously, we could be witnessing the development of a spiritually charged, post-secular version of the old pioneer legend.[24] What seems assured is that Australian prime ministers, regardless of party, will continue to play a critical role in both registering and influencing patterns of remembrance, and Anzac will become ever more embedded in the nation's political life.

# 9

# Anzac and Anzackery: Useful future or sentimental dream?

DAVID STEPHENS

nzackery is hyperbole and empty rhetoric. Like this
from Dr Brendan Nelson of the Australian War
Memorial:

> In these First World War Galleries, our nation reveals
> itself in the men and women whose story it tells. It is
> who we were and who we are. Facing new and uncertain
> horizons, it is also a reminder of the truths by which we
> live, how we relate to one another as Australians and see

our place in the world … Every nation has its story. This
is ours.[1]

The second edition of the *Australian National Dictionary* defines
'Anzackery' as 'the promotion of the Anzac legend in ways that
are perceived to be excessive or misguided'.[2] The definition
allows for a legend but alerts us to perversions or distortions of
it. Beneath Anzackery, might Anzac still have something useful
to offer Australia and Australians more than a century on? Might
we wade through the emotional sludge to address some important questions about 'our place in the world'?

## Private and public

Anzac should be mostly private. It should be about the quiet,
within-family, remembrance of – and caring about – people who
have suffered in war, those who have been killed and not come
home, those who have come home injured in body or mind, and
those who live with the memory of the dead and the reality of the
living. Poet Laurence Binyon wrote, 'They shall grow not old, as
we that are left grow old'. Anzac is about both the forever young
and those who grow old. And their families. For most families
who are directly affected by war, commemoration is not speeches
by politicians, not parades and wreaths and children waving flags;
instead, it is something families live every day and every week,
forever and down through the generations.[3] It is the reparations
that families pay for the decisions that governments make to send
men and women to war.

Anzackery, on the other hand, is public, very public. It *is*
marches and flags and hymns and speeches. As far back as 2004

the writer Michael McGirr was saying, 'The remembrance of war is moving from the personal to the public sphere and, with that, from a description of something unspeakable to something about which you can never say enough'.[4] Nowadays, this means projections of pictures of soldiers onto the walls of the Australian War Memorial, promotions for 'the rarest tank in the world', battlefield tours and Gallipoli cruises and surf boat races, and boys and girls on their gap year wrapping themselves in Australian flags at Anzac Cove or getting drunk in the streets of Çanakkale and shouting 'Aussie, Aussie, Aussie, Oi, Oi, Oi'. And endless commemoration of 'the fallen'. Anzackery is also memorabilia and knick-knacks, the prime minister of the day describing the troops going off to Iraq as 'the proud sons of Anzacs', ministers and officials making emotional speeches to nostalgic audiences about the Anzac legend, Anzac football matches in various codes, and 11-year-old children recording the names of dead soldiers for playing on a continuous loop in the Roll of Honour cloisters at the War Memorial.

Anzackery is sentiment and nostalgia – and it is nationalism, which some people think is patriotism but is really jingoism. Anzackery tries to make simplistic sense out of war and its effects, to comprehend things that are not really comprehensible. It plays to our emotions because we prefer not to think too deeply about war. Historian Drew Gilpin Faust's remark about the American Civil War could apply to any war, certainly to Australia's World War I: 'The war's staggering human cost demanded a new sense of national destiny, one designed to ensure that lives had been sacrificed for appropriately lofty ends. So much suffering had to have transcendent purpose, a "sacred significance".'[5] King George V proposed such a purpose after the Great War. The words on the

'King's Penny' or 'Dead Man's Penny', the commemorative medal presented to bereaved subjects, were 'He Died for Freedom and Honour'. No need to question whether the death was worth it; the King had provided the answer and his answer would have been a comfort to many families.

Resisting or questioning this amalgam of comfort and patriotism is not easy, even a century later. The journalist Kate Aubusson, born in the late 1980s, grew up feeling it was somehow un-Australian not to empathise with the version of Anzac she encountered then. She describes it now as 'a learnt nationalistic sentimentality based on myth far removed from the reality of that visceral, horrendous experience and the repercussions for those who lived through it'.[6] Radio and television presenter James Valentine (born 1962), felt stifled by the outpouring of commemoration in April 2015. 'I'm being told repeatedly what I should feel', he wrote. 'Exactly how solemn I should be, which parts of the story I should mark and what lesson I should draw from them.'[7] The American musician and social commentator Michael Stipe could have had Anzackery in mind when he said, 'More and more, what we "feel" about collective history seems like something manufactured, and kind of pumped into us, rather than a real emotion'.[8]

## Individuals and the mass

An ideal Anzac would focus on individual soldiers, families and tragedies. Michael McGirr wrote that Anzac commemoration had drifted away from 'quiet remembrance' into something noisier, much more boastful, more self-indulgent, more narcis-sistic. 'People now seem to believe', he said, 'that in looking at the Anzacs they are looking at themselves. They aren't. The dead deserve more respect than to be used to make ourselves feel larger'.[9] More than a decade after McGirr wrote this, it is even more urgent for us, having survived 'Peak Anzac', the extreme commemoration of 2014–15, to get back to quiet remembrance of individuals, to think about what war did to them and their families. Historian Peter Stanley did this in his book *Lost Boys of Anzac*, about 101 Australians who came ashore on that first Anzac Day in 1915 and who died on the same day.[10] Half of Stanley's book is about what happened afterwards, as families tried to discover the fate of their son or brother at Gallipoli. Because Gallipoli was chaotic and men died and fell into ditches and their bodies were never found: someone's husband, someone's son, both Ottoman and invaders.

Stanley's central message about his Lost Boys was clear: they should not be abstractions in Anzac Day addresses. They were real people, with characters, flaws and strengths. They were not embodiments of an Anzac legend, not superheroes, but human beings. War produces many more victims than it does heroes:

> I was at the front for thirteen months, and by the end
> of that time … [t]he war had become an everyday
> affair; life in the line a matter of routine; instead of
> heroes there were only victims … Most people have no
> imagination. If they could imagine the sufferings of
> others, they would not make them suffer so.[11]

That voice was German, from World War I. An honest Anzac story would stress the victimhood of all soldiers on all sides, not the heroism of some of them on 'our' side.

Anzackery, on the other hand, is big on numbers, it looks at the mass far more than the individual. Prime ministerial Anzac speeches typically awe us with big numbers – 9000 killed at Gallipoli, 23 000 casualties at Pozières, 5000 casualties in one night at Fromelles, 61 000 killed in the Great War – but include only passing references to the individual men and women who made up the mass.[12] It is the big numbers that pull out the emotional stops. Anzackery is also strong on proportions: depending on whether the calculation is based on 18 to 60-year-olds or 18 to 40-year-olds, between one-third and 42 per cent of eligible Australian males enlisted. The more we obsess about big numbers, the more we obscure the individual and the family stories. One big number is stark, however: there were about three times as many families after 1918 living with returned, physically and mentally damaged soldiers as there were bereaved families.[13] Yet it is clear where the commemorative attention falls, even a century on. We relentlessly and repetitively commemorate the dead, but only in the last few years, against considerable resistance from the Commonwealth bureaucracy, are we starting to digitise the World War I repatriation files so that we can research the lives of those returned men through the 1920s, the 1930s and after.[14]

## Consequences and avoidance

Anzac should confront the consequences of our national decisions to go to war, the reparations that families pay. When the soldiers of the Empire came home after the Great War, they expected 'homes for heroes', land in soldier-settlement programs, decent jobs so they could support their families, and no more wars, since they had just fought the war to end all wars. Just recit-ing that list shows that the consequences of that war were not dealt with well. The soldier-settlement program is a good exam-ple: small, remote blocks with poor soil and little water; families living in tents or shacks until they could manage to build a house; struggles to make a block pay and to pay the block off; drought; debt. More than half the soldier settlers after the Great War had walked off their blocks by 1938.[15] Yet the clear-eyed and honest 'One Hundred Stories' project at Monash University had to fight Commonwealth officials to tell stories – about soldier settlement, post-war despair, death and family tragedy, and the bloody-mindedness of government agencies – that were not 'positive' and did not produce the 'warm and fuzzy feeling' demanded by the official commemoration industry.[16]

The fact that private organisations like Soldier On and Mates4Mates have had to be established to deal with the after-math of our more recent wars suggests we are not doing much better today. Yet, rather than fully addressing the challenges faced by those returning from modern conflicts, Australia is spend-ing around $600 million on commemorating the centenary of Anzac and 'a century of service' by our defence forces, and a large proportion of that money is going to projects such as modernis-ing the galleries at the Australian War Memorial, refurbishing the various looming monuments in our capital cities, and build-ing new monuments and memorial walks in suburbs and towns here and in New Zealand and – for $100 million – on the Western Front.[17] We are very good at dealing with the consequences when they are dead soldiers; with little provocation we will put on an exhibition of wistful (or even goofy) photographs of Diggers overseas, along with appropriate artefacts. On the other hand, we mumble and dissemble about the living consequences. The Australian War Memorial has many pictures of facial injuries suffered in the Great War but has been slow to digitise them. We should know just as much about Albert Ward, the World War I survivor who spent the remaining 43 years of his life 'living' in a bed with wheels (shown at the *Love and Sorrow* exhibition at the Melbourne Museum) and about the last mentally deranged men from that war (still around, living in secure wards, in the 1980s) as we do about Albert Jacka VC and the dead men of Fromelles. And we should know as much about 'enemy' victims as we know about 'ours'. This would help us to recognise the common human-ity beneath the 'team colours'.

## Honesty and euphemism

Anzac should be honest and avoid euphemism. When talking about past wars, we have well-honed rhetoric about 'the fallen', 'the supreme sacrifice', 'dying for freedom and honour', and 'nation-defining moments' amid blood and slaughter. We still use some of these terms today, along with neologisms like 'put in harm's way'. Anzac – the honest approach – would say 'dead' or 'killed' rather than 'fallen'. If it used the word 'sacrifice' at all it would say 'they were sacrificed'. It would not be afraid to use the truest description of the soldier's lot – not being put in harm's way but being set up 'to kill or be killed'. Euphemisms and dishonest terminology are the essence of Anzackery. An honest approach would not say 'they died for our freedom', as if there was some direct link between squalid death a century or 70 years ago and such liberty as we have today or had then. An honest approach would simply say 'they died serving a government policy' and then it would go on to question whether that policy made sense then or makes sense now. When we hear that mantra, 'They died for our freedom', it is usually a sign that someone is trying to stop us asking difficult questions about what they really died for.

Anzac should not turn soldiers into superheroes or saints, dying for grand causes. Anzackery does – or tries to. There are even euphemisms in quite sober books of military history. My uncle, Hector Charles Stephens, is listed in his battalion history as dying during 'guerrilla operations' in Malaya in 1943.[18] Now the war in Malaya effectively ended in February 1942 with the fall of Singapore. But my uncle and about a dozen others – we found this out 50 years later – were separated from their comrades after the Battle of Muar (where 300 Australians were killed in a single day) and they wandered around in the jungle for more than a year thereafter, most of the time without weapons, living on handouts from the local Malays (who were often on the verge of betraying them to the Japanese) and occasionally getting help from communist guerrillas. One by one, they killed themselves or, like my uncle, died of disease. One of them survived and was rescued by a British submarine in 1945.[19] So much for the euphemism 'guerrilla operations'. Anzac should not let soldiers be gods. It should allow for human frailties and failures and fear, for knaves and villains as well as for saints, and for people who stumble around in the jungle, dying of disease and not looking much like soldiers at all. Lots of mess and confusion and uncertainty. Just like real life.

Peter Stanley wrote a prize-winning book called *Bad Characters: Sex, Crime, Mutiny, Murder and the Australian Imperial Force.*[20] There were indeed mutinies among war-weary

Australian soldiers in France in 1918. Australian and New Zealand soldiers murdered a couple of hundred Palestinian Arab civilians at Surafend in 1918. They were retaliating for the killing of a fellow soldier; they had also had enough of war. These are awkward facts amid the bravery and the comradeship. Anzac should not try to suppress debate or discussion because of imagined sensitivities. Anzackery, on the other hand, does try to suppress and disguise. When ABC TV early in 2014 ran an item on the launch of the Honest History website – it was a scrupulously balanced piece but it included Peter Stanley talking about the unsoldierly exploits of some Australian soldiers in the brothels of Cairo – then federal Liberal backbencher Andrew Nikolic accused the ABC of lacking 'situational awareness' for broadcasting such material during the World War I centenary years. Later that year, the then federal Minister for the Centenary of Anzac, Senator Michael Ronaldson, attacked the ABC for being 'insensitive' towards the relatives of Australian soldiers in German New Guinea 100 years on when it broadcast an interview that suggested Australians might have massacred some of their opponents. Brendan Nelson of the Australian War Memorial said every Australian had 'a responsibility' to visit the refurbished World War I galleries at the memorial, and author Peter FitzSimons said Australians have 'a naturally bowed head' about Anzac Day.[21] (FitzSimons' refusal to call himself a 'historian' possibly exempts him from evidentiary standards for that claim. For more on how Australian attitudes have changed over time, see Carolyn Holbrook's chapter 4 and Frank Bongiorno's chapter 8 in this book.)

There is more involved here than concerns about sensitivities. Frank Bongiorno has written that '[t]here is a long history of contention over the significance and meaning of the Anzac legend'. The problem – particularly in the last quarter-century – is that anyone who decides they would rather not be part of that tradition can buy a lot of trouble:

> To question, to criticise – to doubt – can become un-Australian … Anzac's inclusiveness [trying to include everyone within the tradition] has been achieved at the price of a dangerous chauvinism that increasingly equates national history with military history, and national belonging with a willingness to accept the Anzac legend as Australian patriotism's very essence.[22]

So true Australian patriots have to accept the Anzac legend. Even if they have misgivings they should display 'situational awareness', which translates readily as 'pipe down, pull your head in and keep your awkward opinions to yourself while the rest of us have a good old patriotic celebration'.

## Context, parochialism and the future

Anzac, the ideal, should have context. It should allow us to empathise with the suffering of other nations in war. It should recognise our common humanity. We have extended the circle in recent decades to include Turks in the Great War but we need to bring in Germans, Austrians, Bulgarians, Japanese, Russians, Jews and Palestinians, and Indians and Newfoundlanders and New Zealanders and all the other soldiers of the Empire.[23] And our Indigenous warriors who fought to defend their country *on* their country, rather than overseas for an empire or for a large ally that had the safety of Australia some way down its list of war aims. And Anzac should encompass all of the civilians who were affected, which is a much, much larger number than those who wore a uniform. There were about 18 million deaths worldwide during the Great War, including those of around seven million civilians. American scientist Milton Leitenberg has calculated that about 231 million people were killed in wars and conflicts around the world during the 20th century and about 80 per cent of those were civilians.[24] Australian war deaths during the 20th century were only about 0.04 per cent of that total, and only a few hundred of them were not in uniform.

An Anzac ideal would also consider more explicitly the society that existed *before* wars and the very different society and community that existed *after* them; the changes that wars brought; how wars affected us as individuals, as families and as a nation; the changes that are all but ignored in, for example, the way the Australian War Memorial presents the story of World War I. Before this war Australia was in many respects a confident, socially progressive country, a social laboratory for the world, pioneering in labour and social policy and votes for women; afterwards, it was, in historian Joan Beaumont's phrase, a 'broken nation'.[25] People in those early post-war years intoned 'Lest We Forget'; people still do, but the words now mean something different. The obsession with remembrance has grown stronger as the reality has faded, as the number of living souls who actually remember total war has dwindled. What we are today urged not to forget is a false image – Kate Aubusson's 'learnt nationalistic sentimentality'. An honest Anzac would allow us to move on from this falsity. Yet the Anzackers – the purveyors of Anzackery – resist change. In so doing, they build in the possibility – even the probability – of war in the future. Former minister Ronaldson was fond of saying that today's children have a responsibility to carry forward the torch of remembrance; they 'must understand' that the freedom they enjoy today was 'paid for in blood'. The blogger James Rose detected in the Australian War Memorial 'a kind of imprinting ... While victory is not directly exalted, it seems the message is that war can be ok. If you win. Even if you die and win you can find honour. Dead losers stay silent in their unmarked graves'.[26]

Encouraging our children to take responsibility for the torch of remembrance only makes sense if we expect them at some time in the future to have to lay down that torch and take up weapons. The readiness to fight wars in future is affected by the way we look at past wars. Elizabeth Samet lectures to military cadets at West Point in the United States. She has written about the sentimentality of the way Americans – and, we can add, Australians brought up on Anzackery – talk about war, how 'emotion ... short-circuits reason', how people become 'exhibitionists of sentiment' in relation to war, and, most importantly, how sentiment stops them asking hard questions – Was that war worth it? Did those men die in vain? – about war, because they are afraid of being seen to disrespect the dead. Most importantly, Samet says, this attitude effectively supports jingoism – the inclination to wrap ourselves in the flag and go cheerfully off to war again.[27] Wallowing in sentiment – pickling ourselves in Anzackery – makes it more likely that we will do it all again next time.

## Another future

Anzackery takes a rear-vision mirror to Australian history, then distorts the image by overlaying it with jingoism and sentiment.

Could we instead imagine a peaceful Australian future – a future without war – and see if Anzac helps us get there? Australians commemorating war casualties routinely say, 'We are not glorifying war'. Yet such denials often come as an afterthought to regular, moving and colourful ceremonies that avoid asking hard questions. Only fools glorify war; Australians tend to normalise it.

The Anzac ideal described above emphasises instead the effects of war on those who fight it and on their families. It focuses also on the impacts on other countries besides our own. We should weigh these considerations more explicitly against the forces pushing us towards future military involvement. Being more honest about past wars would help us judge the costs and benefits of future ones. If those wars were not worth it, how can we be sure those in the future will be? Alison Broinowski's chapter 19 in this book supports such consideration.

Replacing a bloated Anzackery with a quieter, more honest Anzac means thinning the military strand in Australian history, putting Anzac in its proportionate place in our past, present and future. That, in turn, means devoting more attention to the non-military parts of our history. Part 2 of this book does that.

# PART 2
# AUSTRALIAN STORIES AND SILENCES

# 10

# Fires, droughts and flooding rains: Environmental influences on Australian history

REBECCA JONES

'The crops are done; ye'll have your work
To save one bag of grain;
From here way out to Back-o'-Bourke
They're singin' out for rain.

'If we don't get three inches, man,
Or four to break this drought,
We'll all be rooned', said Hanrahan,
'Before the year is out'.

In God's good time down came the rain;
And all the afternoon
On iron roof and window-pane
It drummed a homely tune.

And every creek a banker ran,
And dams filled overtop;
'We'll all be rooned', said Hanrahan,
'If this rain doesn't stop'.

And stop it did, in God's good time;
And spring came in to fold
A mantle o'er the hills sublime
Of green and pink and gold.

And each man squatted on his heel,
And chewed his piece of bark.
'There'll be bush-fires for sure, me man,
There will, without a doubt;
We'll all be rooned', said Hanrahan,
'Before the year is out'.[1]

Hanrahan laments the oscillation between drought, fire and flood that is part of the fabric of Australia. Dry and wet, scarcity and abundance are inevitable in a climate defined by variability and inconsistency, a natural flux of growth and decay, building and eroding. Droughts are periods of dormancy, fires stimulate growth, floods fill lakes, rivers and wetlands, and distribute soil, fertile sediments and seeds across floodplains, allowing plants and animals to grow and reproduce. The indigenous flora and fauna of Australia evolved to thrive with variability. The Kurrajong tree (*Brachychiton populneus*), a stalwart of the inland plains, goes dormant during drought, shedding leaves and limbs to conserve water. Rain following drought stimulates leaflets to form and the tree regrows. The river red gum (*Eucalyptus camaldulensis*), the giant of Australia's inland waterways, can survive many years of drought but still requires periodic inundation by flood to replenish and reproduce. Banksias, hakeas and acacias require fire to burst their seedpods for germination; fires encourage the native grass tree (*Xanthorrhoea*) to flower.

Just as fire, flood and drought have helped create the flora and topography of Australia, so they have helped define Australian human history. The Australian poet Dorothea Mackellar knew this: her poem 'My country' provides part of the title of this chapter. She wrote the poem in London just after the Federation Drought had ravaged her homeland and not long before young men and women who had grown to adulthood during drought joined what became known as the Great War. The natural events Mackellar wrote about and these men and women experienced are not simply backdrops to history but are players, shaping us, just as we shape them. And it has always been so.

The interrelationship that traditional Indigenous Australians had with the variable climate developed over millennia, allowing slow evolution and adaptation. By contrast, European settlers brought with them cultures, ways of life, technology and beliefs developed in very different places; settlers' acceptance of the frequency of climate extremes has been a turbulent journey, one that continues today. In the past 100 years Australia has experienced ten severe multi-year droughts, two of these lasting more than seven years, as well as 26 bushfires and 19 floods resulting in human fatalities. The most devastating of these occurrences, such as the 1939 Black Friday fires, the Clermont floods in 1916, the Brisbane floods of 1974 and 2011, as well as major droughts in 1914, the 1940s and the 2000s, were cataclysmic, forcing Australians to confront their relationship with the land. Climatic events have helped shape the way we live in Australia.

The interaction between settler Australians and the environment is often depicted as conflict, as adversaries pitted against one another. In these narratives, humans are broken and humiliated by the unwavering hardship of the environment, or the environment is plundered and destroyed by heavy-handed pioneers. Documentaries for 1950s schoolchildren and potential migrants proclaimed that nature was being 'tamed'.[2] Yet the relationship between settler Australians and climate extremes has always been more complex than one of conqueror and victim: it is bound up in ambivalence and contradictions. Droughts, fires and floods have become part of our national identity, celebrated in literature, art, theatre and film even though – or perhaps because – they threaten to destroy us. We fear and abhor them while also naming them: the Federation Drought, the Millennium Drought, Black Saturday, Black Friday, Ash Wednesday, Red Tuesday.[3] Naming mythologises these events while also making them familiar. Our relationship with drought, fire and flood during the last 100 years has been characterised by denial, opportunism, acceptance and control.

# Denial

By 1915 many populated areas of Australia had been occupied by Europeans and their descendants for more than a century, yet 20th century Australian history is strewn with examples of settler Australians behaving as if each fire, flood and drought was an unprecedented event. For example, following World War I, 37 000 returned soldiers were settled on agricultural blocks, often in marginal farming country. The size of the blocks and settlers' repayments were calculated in the boom years at the end of the war, when weather was favourable and the price of produce high. These calculations failed, however, to allow for the likelihood of poor seasons. The next decade saw intermittent drought combined with plummeting prices for produce, and it is estimated that by the end of the 1920s more than 25 per cent of soldier settlers had forfeited their blocks.[4]

Just as Australians denied the inevitable recurrence of drought, we also seemingly forgot our history of flood and fire. The intermittent saturation of floodplains is part of a river's make-up, and damaging floods are inevitable. This did not stop the development of riverside towns and cities. Queensland's capital grew around the meandering path of the Brisbane River. The area that is now the central business district was chosen as the site of a penal colony due to the physical barrier of the river and its provision of water, food, transport and fertile sediment for agriculture. Despite extensive flooding in 1841, 1890 and 1893, the growing city of Brisbane continued to embrace its river. Development continued, bridges spanned the river's width, large houses were built on the northern banks with views of the river, while industry and warehouses multiplied along the southern banks. Throughout the 20th century the river demonstrated its power and flooded – in 1916, 1924, 1927, 1928, 1931, 1933, 1934, 1935, 1937, 1938, 1939, 1951, 1955, 1970 and 1972. Then, in January 1974, after three months of heavy rain, a cyclone dumped more than 900 millimetres of rain on the metropolitan area. A vast 200-square-kilometre lake flooded the city, destroying bridges, roads, factories and warehouses, and more than 8000 homes were flooded. After the flood, the Wivenhoe Dam was constructed upstream of Brisbane to manage water flow and by the 1980s the city was again celebrating its river. Riverfront properties became desirable, and the waterway became a playground and transport highway. Inevitably, the river again overflowed its banks: in 2011 flooding swept away river infrastructure and inundated more than 28 000 buildings.

Similarly, Australians have repeatedly denied the dangers of bushfire and ignored the ecology of Victoria's forests, which are finely tuned for recurrent and catastrophic fires. After the Black Friday bushfires of 1939 devastated forest communities in the Yarra Ranges, Royal Commissioner Judge John Stretton concluded that the inhabitants 'had not lived long enough' – not lived long enough to accept that fierce fire, which cannot always be avoided or controlled, is part of these forests.[5] Following the annihilation by these fires, timber workers and their communities moved out of the forests to the relative safety of cleared areas. Yet in the following decades people slowly returned, building towns encircled by forest, carving roads through the bush and erecting houses on the ridgelines. Sixty years later, after the Black Saturday fires again incinerated the Yarra Ranges, environmental historian Tom Griffiths noted that we have forgotten all that we could have learned: '2009 was 1939 all over again, laced with 1983

… We have still not come to terms with what we have already experienced'.[6]

## Opportunism

Had Australians really forgotten that droughts, floods and fires are inherent parts of the climate that would come and come again like the Magic Pudding? What seems to be denial of the reality of extreme weather was often neither ignorance nor always wilful stubbornness, but opportunism. The continent's variable climate offered promise as well as failure, and people gambled with disaster to reap reward. The effects of floods, fires and droughts were devastating but, between disasters, there were great benefits. Settlers chose to live on floodplains and river banks because this provided the most fertile land, ready access to water, shade and shelter, and attractive living places. Similarly, other settlers braved the dangers of fire to live in the dry sclerophyll forests of southern Australia, harvesting hardwood and grazing cattle in forest blocks or clearing the bush for farming. Indeed, the flammability of these forests was harnessed for settlers' use. Just as Indigenous Australians fired grasslands and scrub as a tool for hunting and gathering, so settler Australians used fire as a tool for settlement. Pastoralists regularly burnt grasslands to encourage growth and rejuvenate pasture for their sheep and cattle, the impenetrable forests of South Gippsland in eastern Victoria were cleared with the aid of fire, and, on the other side of the continent, kangaroo hunters fired the jarrah forests to attract native animals to the new growth.[7]

Farmers also risked drought when cropping the wheat belt of south-eastern Australia. In the Mallee region of Victoria as much as one-third of the 30 years between 1915 and 1945 were in drought. Yet farmers persisted in growing wheat. Farmer Charles Coote's cropping records suggest why. Coote settled in the Mallee as a young man in the 1890s, and for most of the first half of the 20th century he kept meticulous records of wheat yields (using the imperial measures of acres and bushels). These records illustrate the huge variation in Coote's harvest yields, ranging from less than four bushels per acre during drought to more than 28 bushels per acre in good years. In the drought years of 1914, 1928 and 1945 he harvested nothing from more than 500 acres and yet, when rainfall was good in 1917, 1919, 1921, 1925, 1933, 1935 and 1937, he reaped bumper crops. In the good season of 1916–17, when Coote bagged 38 bushels per acre, he earned £3600. This was an exceptional income; his six-room house in the most salubrious area of town cost less than £200 and his new Ford car £265.[8] Farming in this extremely variable climate was a gamble on rainfall but, for many farmers like Charles Coote, one that was worth the risk.

## Acceptance

Denial is the story most often told about settler Australians' relationship with the land. Yet there is also a history of their acceptance of droughts, fires and floods. Reaping the rewards of the climate, while ameliorating its destruction, meant responding to the extremes, not with Hanrahan's fatalistic pessimism, but by accepting these events as catalysts for change. For example, over nearly 100 years, farmers and government authorities slowly learned to accept the frequency of drought in semi-arid regions. The story of cropping inland South Australia is a tale of learning, denying, then finally accepting the reality of recurrent drought. In the 1860s, the Surveyor-General, George Goyder, mapped a line through the south-east of the state to coincide with the southern boundary of saltbush, mulga and dwarf mallee. On the coastal side of the line, rainfall was generally reliable enough to grow cereals. Goyder recommended, however, that the land north of the line should not be settled for agriculture because, while some years had adequate rainfall, this could not be relied upon.

During a period of adequate rainfall in the 1870s, Goyder's findings were unpopular, as the population of South Australia was increasing rapidly and both farmers and the government were keen to settle new areas. Despite Goyder's recommendations, therefore, South Australians moved north during the 1870s, only to retreat in the 1880s as dry weather gripped the colony. During 1883 and 1884 nearly 600 000 acres of land were surrendered and, by 1911, almost 20 per cent of the people born in South Australia had moved to other states.[9] This was one of the greatest internal migrations in Australian history, and it was precipitated by recurring drought. Despite inclement weather, some farmers remained north of the Goyder line and struggled to grow cereal during dry years through the 1920s and 1930s. Where Charles Coote averaged 21 bushels an acre in the Victorian Mallee between 1926 and 1937, a farmer on the saltbush plains of South Australia, on the wrong side of the Goyder line, reaped only three and a half bushels an acre.[10] State and federal governments inquired into the viability of growing wheat in arid areas through the 1920s and 1930s and, by the early 1940s, the area being cropped in South Australia had been reduced by 1.75 million acres.[11] The long exodus from the drought-prone plains of South Australia had ended. Deserted stone houses in the Flinders and Gawler Ranges are evocative monuments to our final acceptance of the climate: that some areas are too marginal and the weather too unpredictable for agriculture.

Recurrent flood also forced many settlers to change. By the beginning of last century, the town of Clermont on the Wolfgang and Sandy creeks in central Queensland was accustomed to flooding. In December 1916, however, a cyclone brought a particularly severe deluge to the town. Rainfall over the town and in the upper catchment filled the creeks and destroyed the railway, telephone and telegraph lines and 50 buildings. From a population of 1500, 64 people drowned. Residents acknowledged that the location of the town on the river flats would bring further flooding and, once floodwaters had subsided, they relocated the town by shifting undamaged buildings one kilometre uphill on steam tractors and rolling logs. Nearly 100 years later, in January 2011, three-quarters of Queensland was again in flood. Heavy rainfall in December 2010 had saturated the Lockyer Valley west of Brisbane and torrential rain created what Premier Anna Bligh called 'an inland tsunami' through the townships of Grantham, Postmans Ridge, Murphy Creek, Helidon and Withcott. Nineteen people drowned, 14 in Grantham alone, and the southern part of Grantham was completely destroyed.[12] Just as Clermont residents had done decades earlier, most of Grantham's residents relocated to higher ground, acknowledging that flood would return to the valley again and again.

# Control

Other Australians have accepted the reality of drought, fire and flood by attempting to manage and control these events. By the mid-20th century, science, technology and engineering made many Australians, like people throughout the English-speaking world, feel it was possible to mitigate the unwelcome impact of climate. Beginning in the 1890s and accelerating in the next century, state and federal governments saw water as something that could be manipulated on a large scale. They began to reconstruct rivers to harness water and make its intermittent flow orderly. Dams and reservoirs were built to store water, weirs and locks to regulate it, and levee banks to control it. Water-engineering works became symbols of progress and mastery.[13] Rivers such as the Darling, Hunter, Snowy and Ord were dammed and channelled, while others like Melbourne's Yarra were straightened to reduce flooding. By the early 20th century the Wimmera–Mallee Stock and Domestic Water Scheme – 17 500 kilometres of channels carrying water from the River Murray and central Victoria – was a bold attempt to bring life to the waterless plains of the Mallee. This region has only 250–350 millimetres of rain annually (less than one-quarter of Sydney's annual rainfall) and has no permanent rivers or streams. Drought in the 1880s was the impetus for this ambitious scheme, reinforced by water shortage during droughts in 1895–1902, 1906–07 and 1914–15. Dams, weirs, locks and reservoirs were built along the Murray River and in the Grampian Ranges. By the mid-20th century the channel system supplied 36 towns and 28 500 square kilometres of farmland.[14] The Murray, so long characterised by irregular dry periods and flooding, became a managed asset.

One of the most enterprising – and least successful – attempts to ameliorate the effects of extreme weather was rainmaking. During the worst of the Federation Drought in 1902, Queensland meteorologist Clement Wragge experimented with cloud seeding to precipitate rainfall. He brought six specially manufactured rainmaking guns to Charleville in western Queensland and fired them into the clouds. Although there was huge public interest in the experiment, it failed to produce the desired rain and did not end the drought.[15] Encouraged by similar activities in the United States, the Commonwealth government again experimented with cloud seeding in the 1940s, and again, the effectiveness of the experiments was unclear. Hydro-electric companies in Tasmania and the Snowy Mountains still occasionally try cloud seeding.

## Increasing vulnerability

Australians' efforts to control and modify the extremes of drought, fire and flood have not abated. In fact, the way we lived and the ways we changed our environment during the 20th century increased rather than reduced the impact of extreme weather. The fringes of the Mallee region of Victoria and South Australia began to be settled for agriculture in the 1880s. Farmers felled the eucalypts, grubbed out large roots, fired the scrub and bared the soil. They introduced hard-hooved, heavy-grazing sheep, and ploughed and ploughed again. Water channels made the region more hospitable, and permanent farms, homes and townships appeared where previously there had been sparsely settled pastoral runs and transient Indigenous communities. Through the early 20th century, clearing and settlement of the Mallee continued haltingly. Ploughing increased the breakdown of humus in the soil and, within 15 to 20 years of cultivation, the soil's organic matter reduced by half, making it less fertile and more erodible.[16] When drought descended, as it does frequently in this region, wind whipped the bared soil into a frenzy. Choking sand filled the air, blinded inhabitants and filled their homes, beds and mouths with grit. Meteorological observers recorded 145 dust storms in the Mallee in the six years between 1936 and 1942.[17]

This escalation of vulnerability continued throughout Australia in the latter decades of the 20th century and into the next. Despite improved technology, better living standards, more efficient agricultural processes and global connections, we are even more vulnerable to extreme weather events such as drought than we were in 1915. Intensive agriculture, the high cost of agricultural inputs and machinery, the demand for ever-increasing production and larger properties, and consequent high debt and low margins, have meant that fluctuations in production are even more difficult to accommodate than they were for Charles Coote in the early decades of the last century. As well, the nature of our society has made us more susceptible to environmental challenges. In the last 100 years there has been a fivefold increase in the population of the nation. At five million, as many people now live in Sydney as lived in the entire country in 1915. When extreme weather occurs, therefore, many hundreds of people are affected, either directly or indirectly.

Over 14 million people cluster in the fire-prone capital cities of Melbourne, Sydney, Canberra, Perth, Adelaide and Hobart. As these cities have grown, suburbs have pushed into forested areas on the urban fringe: the Dandenong Ranges east of Melbourne, the Blue Mountains west of Sydney, the Adelaide Hills, the flanks of Mount Wellington close to Hobart, the Perth Hills and the peri-urban fringe of Canberra. The mix of bushland and high population density is an incendiary combination. The likelihood of fire ignited by accident or arson is great and, if this occurs, the impact on human lives and property is immense: in Hobart in 1967 when 62 people were killed and more than 1000 homes burnt; in the Ash Wednesday bushfires in 1983 when 75 people were killed and 2400 homes destroyed in Victoria and South Australia; during the Canberra bushfires in 2003 when four people were killed and 500 homes destroyed; in the Blue Mountains in 2013 when two people were killed and 250 homes burnt; and the Black Saturday fires in Victoria in 2009 in which 173 were killed and more than 2000 homes destroyed.

## Nature and culture

The profound effects of the events described in this chapter have helped to define Australian history and will continue to do so. Our relationship with environmental extremes has been a heady and contradictory mixture of denial, acceptance, opportunism and control. What Tom Griffiths said of fire could be said also of drought and flood, 'that nature can overwhelm culture'.[18] While we have, at times, adapted to the extremes of Australia's climate during the last 250 years, anthropogenic climate change is introducing a new degree of uncertainty. What we have slowly and laboriously accepted as normal is, again, changing. Scenarios suggest that Australia's variable climate will become even more unpredictable. There is likely to be a decline in rainfall in southern Australia, with increased intensity and frequency of drought and fire. By contrast, rainfall may increase in north-western Australia, and the severity of cyclones and storms may intensify along the east coast of Australia, which, combined with rising sea levels, may increase the likelihood of damaging floods. The Millennium Drought of the 2000s, the Black Saturday fires of

2009 and the Queensland and Victorian floods of 2011 show us that climate extremes continue to have the power to change our lives – and in ways as fundamental as our wars have. It is possible, indeed likely, that climate extremes will become an even more potent force in the future.[19] We may hear from new Hanrahans but they are likely to have reason to complain.

# 11

# From those who've come across the seas: Immigration and multiculturalism

GWENDA TAVAN

ontemporary Australia is an immigrant nation yet that fact is not central to our self-definition. Indeed, if recent polls are correct, many Australians remain anxious or ambivalent about immigration, especially non-British and non-European. These concerns show up in the high value placed on settler (white, Australian or British-born) experience, our vulnerability to panics about immigration (currently Muslims and asylum seekers), and the resurgence of right-wing, anti-immigration movements. Australia's anxieties are not unique, echoing those of many countries struggling with globalisation, mass migration, refugee movements and international terrorism. They also lack a single cause or focus. There is, still, a broader historical, symbolic and cultural context for our current anxieties, including a long record of elite-induced neglect of our immigration history. This neglect by historians, politicians, opinion leaders – our 'migration amnesia' – has undermined popular understanding of the importance of immigration in our national story, reinforced the dominance of a narrow, Anglo-nativist view of Australia in which the so-called 'Anzac legend' is central, and perpetuated a tension between Australian nationalist ideals and our multicultural, settler-state reality. Indigenous Australians excepted, all of us came here from somewhere else.[1]

Overcoming this amnesia requires Australians to reject views that have privileged white, Anglo-nativist and settler achievement. It demands that we engage with how a small population defining itself in rigid racial–cultural terms developed remarkably quickly into a successful multicultural society. In doing this, we need not substitute one foundation myth (the evolution of multicultural immigrant Australia) for another (white, British settlement and achievement). Rather, we should accept the complex historical logic of the colonial settler-state experience, in which successive waves of migration since 1788 (forced and free, British and non-British, white and non-white) have helped develop modern Australia, albeit at terrible cost to our Indigenous population. As I will show, engaging with our immigration story is not just more 'honest', more 'interesting' history – it is the basis for a powerful reimagining of the Australian community. This reimagining acknowledges the inherent worth and interdependence of all our inhabitants, celebrates all our achievements and fully realises the potential of our multicultural society.

## Australia's migration amnesia

In 2014 more than 28 per cent of Australia's resident population were overseas-born; migrants and their children make up more than 40 per cent of the Australian people today.[2] Australia has achieved this diversity without enormous social and political upheaval and rapidly, mostly in the last 70 years or so, even if some parts of the country remain steadfastly monocultural or bicultural. Yet immigration has never been central to our nation's self-definition. Successive generations of politicians and community and business leaders have paid lip-service to the important contribution of immigration to the development of the Australian nation-state while simultaneously reminding us that the best marker of immigrants' success is their capacity to become *invisible*, through absorption into the national community.

Historians have contributed to this neglect, repeatedly asserting the centrality of immigration to the modern story but engaging only superficially with immigration's complex dynamics. Immigration history is a relatively small academic field in Australia, and those who take an interest tend to be immigrants or the children of immigrants.[3] Immigration historiography is fragmented, focusing predominantly on specific groups or schemes or events rather than broad historical forces and trajectories. Only a handful of works have ever attempted a comprehensive narrative of Australia's immigration history.[4] George Megalogenis's *Australia's Second Chance* is a recent valuable attempt to put

Australian immigration at the centre of the national narrative.[5] But more work needs to be done.

This neglect also permeates our educational and civic institutions. In Victorian secondary schools, migration history is a minor subset of VCE (Year 12) history. It attracts very few students – far fewer than the hundreds who study World War I. Another example is the booklet *Australian Citizenship: Our Common Bond*, distributed by the Commonwealth Department of Immigration and Border Protection – the second part of the departmental title says a lot about our attitudes to newcomers – to prepare immigrants for membership of the Australian community.[6] The booklet proudly proclaims the contribution of immigrants to the country's prosperity but emphasises they are socially on the margin. The booklet is peppered with pronouns ('we', 'us', 'you') that reinforce assumptions of an Australian 'in-group' and a migrant 'out-group'. The 'we' at the heart of the imagined Australian nation is so self-evident as to need no explanation. Whether the migrants it identifies can ever reach a point where they will be considered part of the Australian 'we' is not made clear.

The booklet also contains a summary of 'important national days for Australia'. It is a very short and unashamedly Anglo-centric list. Australia Day is described as

> the anniversary of the arrival of the First Fleet from Great Britain in 1788 to set up a convict settlement for the British Government … the day that we honour our history and all the people who have made this nation great. It is a day to rejoice in the present and commit to a happy and prosperous future together.[7]

There is no explanation of why more than 200 years of British and European endeavour and experience has been distilled into one event whose relationship to Australian nationhood is tenuous at best. There is no admission either that this anniversary is an occasion for deep sorrow and mourning for Indigenous Australians who regard it as Invasion Day. (Larissa Behrendt's chapter 16 in this book has more on this subject.)

The other nominated national day in the citizenship booklet is Anzac Day. It is described as 'a solemn day when we remember the sacrifice of all Australians who served and died in wars, conflicts and peacekeeping operations. We also honour the courage and commitment of all servicemen and women'.[8] This phrasing suggests some attempts at social and cultural inclusion (*all* Australians who served and died) yet the effort is undermined by the depiction of the event that anchors this solemn ritual of national commemoration: 'Anzac Day is named after the Australian and New Zealand Army Corps, which landed at Gallipoli in Turkey during World War I on 25 April 1915'. What is memorialised on this de facto 'national day' are the sacrifices and loyalties of 'old' white Anglo-Australia. Anzac Day's relevance to contemporary multicultural Australia is completely ignored. So is the question of why such a tragic military event should have more symbolic potency than 'positive' nation-building milestones, including Federation in 1901 and the start of the postwar immigration program in 1945. The knowledge (unstated) that many contemporary migrants come from countries against which Australia fought in previous wars only reinforces the illogicality of claims that Anzac Day can speak to all 'Australians'. The official commemoration industry has in recent years recognised the need to reach out to non-Anglo-Celtic Australians, some of whose children might have had difficulty in grasping the relevance of Anzac Day.[9]

The neglect of our immigration history is not benign. It feeds popular assumptions that only white, British settlers and the white native-born have contributed to the nation-building project; that *only* they have the cultural, social and political authority to define the nation's values and identity. It leaves Australians vulnerable to scare campaigns about foreigners and the mistaken belief that immigration and ethnic diversity can be wished or legislated away (by abandoning multiculturalism, or banning Muslim immigration, or keeping refugees in our care in indefinite detention on remote islands). It also undermines our capacity for Aboriginal reconciliation, since the denial of our immigration history is also a denial of the Indigenous dispossession on which this settler state was founded. It ensures that the migrants and minority groups in our midst continue to face inequality, injustice and neglect. It means policymakers pay inadequate attention to the lessons of our immigration history. Not only does this undermine Australia's vaunted egalitarianism, it also challenges our capacity to fully realise the human potential of our rich and diverse society. (Carmen Lawrence's chapter 13 in this book has more on the contrast between egalitarian myths and Australian reality.)

## Australia's immigration paradox

Our compulsion to bury our immigration history is a legacy of our colonial past. This compulsion began as a powerful psychological defence against the reality of our British settler-state origins – convict transportation and the acts of Indigenous dispossession and destruction upon which white settlement was founded. White settlers sought to appease deep anxieties about the legitimacy of their claims to sovereignty and to overcome the terrible psychological and physical dislocation they felt as a small, transplanted population in a harsh and isolated continent far from the British metropolis. As historian Keith Hancock put it in 1930: 'That is the aim of so many, to forget that they are exiles in Australia ...'[10]

Australian nativism was intimately connected with this historical amnesia; it manifested as an exaggerated pride in the racial and cultural superiority of the white Australian-born population over their convict forebears and over more recent arrivals from Britain and Europe. Nativism emerged out of the growing self-confidence and prosperity of mid-19th-century colonial society, as thousands of people from around the world flocked to the Australian goldfields, and as colonial cities like Melbourne grew dramatically in size and wealth. It was reinforced by the major demographic shifts of the period that saw the proportion of white native-born population finally overtake that of the overseas born. Australian nativists generally did not reject their British cultural and political heritage. Rather they argued that the superior values and environment of the colonies were creating a new and better type of Briton, a new and better type of society.

Exclusivism, isolationism and racism – the prejudicial treatment of 'out-groups' based on racial and cultural characteristics deemed inferior and hostile to white, British-Australian ones – were the other side of 19th-century white Anglo-nativist pride. These attitudes reflected the vulnerability of a people on the edge of Asia who feared they might be physically overwhelmed. The attitudes simultaneously reinforced the interests of the national 'in-group' and provided powerful rationalisation for discrimination, violence against and dispossession of non-British and non-European out-groups. The Chinese, in particular, were seen as threats to sovereignty and living standards, against which only the homogeneity and unity of Australians would ensure national survival. These assumptions merged with the flourishing nationalism of the late 19th century to produce a rigid racial–nationalist doctrine – 'White Australia' – and a complex legislative regime with its centrepiece, the Immigration Restriction Act of 1901, aimed at severely restricting non-European entry and assuring white, British–Australian dominance.

The pro-British, anti-Asian biases of early Federation immigration policies proved remarkably successful. The national census of 1911 showed great cultural and national homogeneity, with almost 83 per cent of the population Australian-born, more than 13 per cent natives of the United Kingdom, and just under one per cent natives of New Zealand.[11] Australians revelled in this 'sameness', frequently boasting they were '98 per cent British'. There were social and political costs, nevertheless: cultural insularity had a self-perpetuating logic, feeding Australian xenophobia and creating a political buffer around White Australia that would take decades to overcome. Immigration restrictions set Australia at odds with neighbouring countries, which recognised the racial slight beneath the diplomatic veneer of the dictation test, the tool of the policy.[12] It deprived Australia of badly needed population and labour at a critical time in its economic development. Nativism and the familial embrace of Empire could not contain the significant social cleavages – class, religion, ethnicity – of the fledgling nation. The vicious sectarian and anti-Irish conflicts during the Great War, spurred by Prime Minister Hughes's conscription crusades, split and scarred Australian society for decades. Then, class conflict was rife in the inter-war period, fuelled by economic decline and the divergent interests of the labour movement and the capitalist class. If anything, social conflict reinforced popular and political faith in racial–national loyalty. The economic and political crises of the 1920s and 1930s entrenched anti-foreigner sentiment and led to the effective ending of immigration, despite growing concerns about Australia's declining population growth. Australia's entry into World War II saw a repeat of the xenophobic anxieties of the previous war, with German, Japanese and Italian enemy aliens summarily detained, regardless of how long they had been in the country or where their political loyalties lay.

Australia's need for population for defence, labour and nation-building eventually grew so great that the momentous decision was made in 1945 to introduce a mass immigration program. The program became one of Australia's most extraordinary achievements. In the short term it contributed to population and economic growth. In the longer term it dramatically changed the nation's ethnic character. That the program was introduced during significant social instability – military demobilisation, international upheaval, social and economic uncertainty – makes the achievement even more remarkable.

This profound change required delicate management by the Chifley and, later, Menzies governments, balancing population realities with the desire to hang onto old racial and cultural ideals. Ultimately, the political success of immigration lay in the bargain between governments and the Australian people, the bargain that perpetuated the myth that, while immigration might be an economic necessity, it would remain tangential to Australian national identity. Immigrants ('New Australians') could come, but on the condition that they would give up their foreignness and assimilate into the 'Australian Way of Life'. Europeans, not just Britons, would be allowed to enter, but 'White Australia' would remain intact.

As it turned out, though, Australian immigration took a different track to that promised by governments in the 1940s. There were insufficient numbers of British and northern European immigrants, which meant that the hierarchy of preferred nationalities quickly broke down. By the 1950s, European migrants, including previously despised southern Europeans, made up the majority of settlers. Then declining European immigration, the shift to universalist, anti-racist principles and increasing diplomatic pressure led to the gradual abandonment of the White Australia policy by the early 1970s. Even assimilation was rapidly undermined, replaced by the more enlightened multicultural policies of the 1970s. These policies emphasised the rights of migrant groups to maintain their cultural heritage and the responsibility of the host society to provide adequate integration services. Again, that these changes were achieved with limited disruption is one of the most remarkable stories of Australian 20th-century history. It also shows the important role that government leadership has played in managing the politics of immigration. Finally, it suggests Australians' capacity to transcend isolationism and xenophobia in pursuit of the national interest.

Australia today is a vastly different society from that of 100 years ago. The most dramatic changes have occurred in the last 70 years, successive waves of immigrants presenting specific new challenges and opportunities. Australia's immigration history lends itself to easy periodisation, in line with shifting policies: 'British colonial Australia', 'White Australia', 'post-war immigration', 'multicultural Australia', 'John Howard's Fortress Australia'. Periodisation, however, can obscure more nuanced historical dynamics. In 2016–17 Australian immigration is undergoing one of the most radical policy shifts in its history, a change that is undermining the old nation-building, citizenship model of migration and recasting it in more instrumental, neo-liberal and globalised terms.[13] This is shown by dramatic immigration increases since the mid-1990s which are continuing unabated. Current immigration rates are close to 200000 per year.[14] There are other important changes: growing transnationalism, an increasingly strong bias away from family reunion towards economic migration, and increasing barriers to citizenship. One of the most profound shifts is the dramatic increase in temporary migration.[15] Yet we are also seeing intensified immigration control and compliance, containing unauthorised maritime arrivals, deporting undesirable migrants (even those with permanent residency) and using prohibitive powers to exclude people (particularly Muslims) deemed a threat to national security or national values.

These forces present real challenges for governments and citizens. Trade liberalisation, movements of people, and transnationalism are creating new opportunities for international economic and cross-cultural exchange. On the other hand, many people clearly feel alienated from the promised pay-offs of a globalised world. Dramatic cultural and social change has merged with economic insecurity and concerns about international terrorism to produce deeply felt anxieties among sections of the population. Some Australians have reverted to old cultural–racial certainties, including the view that white Anglo-nativism and cultural homogeneity are the natural state of affairs, and the mistaken belief that Australia's immigration reality can somehow be overturned.

Pauline Hanson's One Nation, the Cronulla rioters who attempted to rid their suburb of people of 'Middle Eastern' appearance in 2005, and, more recently, the virulently anti-Muslim Reclaim Australia group are the most extreme and visible manifestations of this outlook. They have the potential to directly harm members of minority groups and the body politic as a whole. More moderate in tone, but no less politically potent, has been the mainstream conservative backlash against the progressive politics and histories of the 1970s onwards, which took into account the experiences and contributions of Indigenous and immigrant populations.

This conservative backlash has taken the form of a strident rearticulation of Anglo-nativist values, ideals and institutions. Prime Minister John Howard played a key role in the 'culture wars' of the mid-1990s onwards, with his aversion to 'black armband history' and his interventions in cultural, civic and educational life (for example, citizenship testing, demands for changes to secondary-school history curriculums, his refusal to apologise to Australia's stolen generation, and his overt rejection of multiculturalism). There is nothing innocent or arbitrary about the reconstruction of Australia Day and Anzac Day as Australia's national days. This has been part of a self-conscious governmental strategy to undermine post-colonial, multicultural understandings of nationhood and reinvigorate a narrative of white, Anglo-Australian (masculine) achievement.[16]

The irony of this backlash is that its most fervent political supporters have also been the architects of the dramatic shifts in Australian immigration policy referred to earlier. Annual immigration intakes more than doubled during the Howard years, despite his 'tough on immigration' policies.[17] Intakes also continued to diversify, with Asians making up an ever-increasing proportion. Yet the *Tampa* crisis of 2001 and the 'Pacific solution' were a radical retreat from post-war Australia's generally admirable approach towards refugees and international norms. A question Australians must ask themselves is whether Howard's hardline anti-asylum-seeker, anti-multiculturalism discourses were a cynical attempt to distract Australians from the fact of increased migrant intakes, or whether he genuinely believed that the reinvigoration of Anglo-nativism and nationalism could curb the forces for social and cultural change that were implicit in his immigration policies.

There are still grounds for optimism. Australia's immigration statistics disprove the hope held by some of us that our national identity can remain resolutely Anglo-nativist, or that our immigration reality can remain hidden. Australia will continue to be an immigrant nation. Recent Australian history decrees it, as do broader international forces. The signs are visible. Howard's loss of his Bennelong seat at the 2007 federal election was partly attributable to the changing demographics of that seat, including its large Asian-born population.[18] His conservative successor Tony Abbott's attempts to reinvigorate British imperial sentiment (by bringing back knighthoods and publicly declaring that the arrival of the First Fleet was *the* defining moment in the history of Australia) were generally met with derision and reinforced the view that Abbott was out of touch with modern Australia. These examples remind us that, whether our political leaders admit it or not, Australia has been fundamentally changed by its immigration experiences. Many immigrants and their children vote, a fact that politicians ignore at their peril.

## Reclaiming Australia's immigration history

In his recent book *Australia's Second Chance*, George Megalogenis urges us to acknowledge the centrality of immigration to Australia's national history:

> The thread that connects the past to the present and future is the ongoing conversation between those who came to these shores, and those who received them. This dialogue has always been central to the national story ... but it is too often reduced to its social dimensions only. The economic side of the equation is rarely considered, even though Australians would acknowledge they obsess about economics more than most.[19]

Drawing on history, economics and public policy, Megalogenis argues that since 1788 Australians' *collective* economic fortunes, not just those of immigrants, have risen and fallen on the back of specific immigration decisions. His evidence is convincing: the dynamism of free immigration and technological innovation in the Victorian colony compared with the exploitation, racism and violence of Queensland's pastoral, forced-labour economy; the negative consequences of the White Australia policy; the destructive economic and demographic impact of immigration restrictions in the 1920s and 1930s; the dramatic effects of the post-war immigration program; the positive outcomes of Australia's refugee policies in the 1970s and 1980s; and, more negatively in recent times, the moral, political, economic and reputational costs of Australia's harsh response to unauthorised asylum seekers.

Megalogenis's account also reinforces how interesting and dynamic this history is, filled with human drama (a cast of millions!), providing public-policy lessons, and reminding us that Australia's development is firmly tied to regional and international affairs. Unlike the foundation myths upon which we have relied in recent years, this history is positive, inclusive and highly relevant to our post-colonial, multicultural reality. It tells us how we got to be who we are today.

There are some tensions and traps, however, in Megalogenis's work. His claim that immigration has been *the* central driver of national development underestimates, I think, the multicausal nature of historical processes – not singular forces but a conflation of ideas, events, policies, structures and systems of government. Surely, for example, social liberalism and Australia's historically interventionist state must qualify as a central driver of national development. Megalogenis's overt commitment to open immigration also discourages him from pursuing some tough questions. Even if migration has generally been good for this country, does it mean it always is or will be? What limits, if any, might there be to immigration's benefits in the future, especially in social and environmental terms? How do we reconcile the tragedy of Aboriginal dispossession with immigration's positive narrative?

Megalogenis's book has still made an important contribution to Australian immigration history. There are many more immigrant stories to tell, many more analyses of the social and economic consequences of specific schemes, policy lessons from the past that can steer the country through difficult times, engagement with the bureaucratic framework in which our immigration history has unfolded. Through such histories, we may finally start to close the gap between our multicultural reality and the narratives we have so far used to define ourselves. We may finally make our peace with our immigration story.

# 12

# Bust and boom: What economic lessons has Australia learned?

## STUART MACINTYRE

During the early 1930s most Australians lived in a state of chronic economic insecurity. In the depths of the Great Depression one-third of all trade unionists were unemployed; others worked only intermittently and many who described themselves in the 1933 Census as self-employed were earning less than the basic wage. Recovery from the Depression was slow and incomplete; when war broke out in 1939 the unemployment rate was still ten per cent.[1] Yet by 1943, with so many people called up for military service and others directed into war industries, there was an acute labour shortage. At a conference called to discuss the question of post-war reconstruction, Sir David Rivett, the head of the Council for Scientific and Industrial Research, said that 'the only completely satisfactory method of dealing with unemployment seems to be war'.[2]

Rivett brought together in a sentence two of the great influences on Australian lives in the first half of the 20th century – war and the economy, specifically the Depression. But today's Australians seem to know and care a lot more about what we did in our two major wars than the economic crisis that came after the first of them. Not so HC (Nugget) Coombs, Director-General of the Ministry of Post-War Reconstruction. In a radio broadcast at the end of 1942, Coombs said the aim of reconstruction after the war was to ensure full employment, economic growth and improved living standards. Full employment was an ambitious goal. As Coombs explained how the country's resources could be used to produce a larger volume of goods and services for the common benefit, he reminded listeners that one in three people in the Australian workforce had been idle in the depths of the Depression. Apart from this human tragedy of deprivation and despair, he said, there was an irretrievable economic loss: 'We have our fields, our mines and our factories, but these are barren and lifeless without the work of our hands'. And, while it was possible to delay the use of physical resources, labour does not keep: 'the power and ability to work must be used or it is lost forever'.[3]

In the midst of the first Great Depression in the 1890s, Joseph Furphy wrote *Such Is Life*, his sprawling novel of the Riverina, its narrator a bullocky who exchanges stories around the campfire with various other itinerants. The mordant irony that runs through the book leaps from the opening sentence: 'Unemployed at last!'[4] But there was no such irony in the historian David Potts's 2006 book *The Myth of the Great Depression*, a revisionist account of the Depression of the 1930s – revisionist because it downplayed the Depression's effects. The unemployed might have been hungry, Potts conceded, but they did not suffer malnutrition. Besides, underfeeding enhances 'mental functioning and the vigour of the disease-fighting immune system'. Potts claimed that people unable to find work, many evicted from their homes, did not despair; on the contrary, they maintained a fortitude that added purpose to their lives.[5]

Until World War II, economists regarded business cycles of expansion and contraction as inescapable. Writing in 1942, the economist Joseph Schumpeter said that a 'perennial gale of creative destruction' was an 'essential fact about capitalism'.[6] The drive to invent new products, find new methods and establish new markets was always destroying old industries as they lost out to new ones. Schumpeter gave the example of the railway that, by carrying mass-produced goods, displaced small-scale local producers as it spread over the American West. Today we may think of the contraction of newspapers as their readers desert to digital providers. World War II was a striking illustration of creative destruction: both Germany and Japan afterwards rebuilt their shattered industries, using the most advanced technologies to achieve prosperity, whereas Britain was left with obsolete factories. Maynard Keynes regretted that the German Luftwaffe had not concentrated the Blitz on the Lancashire cotton mills, to allow industrial and community rejuvenation.[7]

## Salad days and dog days

If success sows the seeds of subsequent failure, the most serious mistakes are made during periods of prosperity. In 2005, when Australia was enjoying what the economist Ross Garnaut described as its longest period of expansion and the most rapid rise in incomes that a developed country had ever known, Garnaut warned that the salad days would not last. The economic bonanza came from a resources boom and all such booms come to an end. Too much of the windfall was being spent on personal consumption, not enough on investment that would lift productivity for Australia to remain competitive when the resources boom was over. Too much of the public revenue was dissipated in tax cuts and middle-class welfare. In 2013, when the salad days gave way to the dog days, Garnaut worried about the 'veil of ignorance' that had descended on public life, delaying remedial action. He thought the nation's good fortune had closed off any capacity for foresight, reinforcing 'the great Australian complacency'.[8]

The predicament that exercised Ross Garnaut is not new. Ever since European settlers first took possession of Australia, they have sought prosperity by exploiting its resources, including agricultural production. At first whale oil and sealskins were shipped to foreign ports, then wool and timber, followed by gold and a variety of agricultural products and minerals. There was an abundance of natural resources after they were seized from the Indigenous owners. Using these resources to create successful and profitable industries, however, required capital, labour and appropriate technology. Australia grew rich because it was able to attract these factors of production. We continue to rely on foreign investment, immigration and technology transfer.

Australian export industries supported a high standard of living. By the second half of the 19th century Australians enjoyed the world's highest per capita gross domestic product (GDP). The demand for labour kept Australian wages higher than in Europe. Food was cheaper, home ownership more accessible and a wide range of consumption goods was available. Governments had favourable access to capital markets, and used it to build ports and railway systems, and provide urban facilities and free education for all. Yet an economy built on resource abundance was vulnerable to external shocks. When foreign demand fell, there was not just a loss of income but a withdrawal of foreign capital, an interruption of population flows and the stagnation of local enterprise. These misfortunes were particularly pronounced during the country's two major depressions, the first in the 1890s and the second in the 1930s, though in both cases economic historians have looked beyond the initial fall in export prices to deeper causes.

The Depression of the 1890s came after Australia used heavy borrowings to finance speculation in real estate. With the flight of foreign capital, many companies failed, and by 1893 eleven of the country's banks had suspended operations. Wage cuts and industrial disputes compounded the ruin: between 1889 and 1895 GDP fell by 30 per cent. The Depression of the 1930s, similarly, followed a period of high levels of foreign borrowing applied to unrealistic schemes of rural settlement. With the abrupt fall in overseas earnings, a contraction of similar magnitude occurred.[9]

# The role of government

In neither depression was government able to stave off a painful adjustment. Economic orthodoxy dictated that a country with a deficit in its external account must reduce its cost structure to restore competitiveness, including labour costs. In any case, the reduction of economic activity meant a fall in public revenue that ruled out remedial measures. During the 1890s colonial governments provided emergency relief work to indigent breadwinners, and charities distributed rations to women and children. The results were apparent in the enlistment records for the 1st Australian Imperial Force: recruits born during the 1890s were shorter than their older counterparts.[10] In the 1930s both the Commonwealth and states were pledged to a reduction in outlays: the Commonwealth cut old-age pensions, the states again provided relief work that paid a fraction of the basic wage. Many victims had to fall back on assistance from family and friends.

In both cases a creative response came only when the emergency had passed. With Federation and economic recovery in the early years of the 20th century, the new Commonwealth built a policy framework to safeguard living standards. Local industries were to be protected behind tariff walls and, in return for this protection, employers would be required to provide a living wage. The determination of that wage fell to the Arbitration Court, a new tribunal established to resolve industrial disputes, and it decided on a minimum or 'basic' wage for men that was calculated to support a husband, wife and three children. This system of wage determination has been described as creating a 'wage-earner's welfare state' and it was accompanied by an old-age pension, a maternity benefit and other measures of social protection, as well as renewed public investment in education and health.[11]

Both at the time and later there were critics of these experiments in state regulation. An economic historian has argued that the changes stifled greater economic growth, and it is true that Australia failed to achieve any increase in per capita incomes between 1890 and 1940.[12] But this is to ignore the substantial improvements that were made. There was an increase in leisure as the working week was shortened. Infant deaths fell, along with maternal mortality, and life expectancy increased. The quality of housing improved, as did domestic conditions: candles and lamps gave way to electric lighting, wood stoves to gas ovens, fresh water was on tap and human waste could be flushed. By 1939, one Australian in ten had a phone, one in eight a motor car and one in six a radio – all consumer durables that were not available in 1890.[13]

Another criticism came from the political commentator Paul Kelly. His account of the opening up of Australia to market forces in the 1980s begins with the protective measures created at the beginning of the century, measures which he said left 'a young nation with geriatric arteries'.[14] A more recent assessment from the economic historian Ian McLean sees the new arrangements having very little effect on an economic upswing that continued until the Great War. McLean points out that World War I hit Australia hard. It closed the London capital market, brought an acute shortage of shipping to disrupt international trade, and burdened the country with a large war debt. The import-replacement industries established during the war faced stiff competition during the 1920s, requiring further protection and pushing up the cost structure while a world oversupply of agricultural commodities reduced export prices.[15] More than this, the peace settlement, with its heavy reparations, left an imbalance between the major industrial countries that crippled international trade and brought a financial crisis at the end of the 1920s. Australians' ability to deal with bust was about to be tested again while they were still dealing with the aftermath of war.

The Great Depression of the 1930s was global. The economic collapse and the inability of government to protect living standards brought a crisis of capitalism and democracy. Fascist regimes came to power by overriding the market, directing resources into armaments industries and fanning national animosities. When the Western Allies were finally drawn into World War II, it was little wonder that they embarked on extensive reconstruction. The successful prosecution of the war required an unprecedented effort by entire populations. If only to secure acceptance of the sacrifices demanded of the people, it was necessary to provide assurance that there would be no return to pre-war conditions. A lasting peace also required a secure prosperity, hence the creation of the International Monetary Fund and the General Agreement on Tariffs and Trade. That framework for the international economy would bring sustained economic growth for the next quarter-century. War followed bust and boom followed war.

## World War II and after

Australia's post-war reconstruction went further than making good the wartime loss. It involved major programs of public investment in housing, migration, retraining, health and welfare; the munitions factories were turned over for civilian production, the airstrips used for domestic aviation, a car industry was created, farms re-equipped. The full employment pledge was formalised in 1945 and was supported by a central bank. Post-war reconstruction came to an end in 1950 with the return of Menzies to office, but the Coalition government retained its Labor predecessor's methods of economic management, using fiscal and monetary levers to maintain full employment and economic growth.[16] Australians adjusted readily to this new prosperity. For the first time in living memory there was steady work for all. Those in previously casual employment now had security; the 40-hour week was achieved shortly after the war, and paid annual leave would follow. Home ownership rose from the pre-war norm of around 50 per cent to 70 per cent by 1966, when the overwhelming majority of households owned a car – and a refrigerator, a washing machine and a television. The car was reconfiguring patterns of work and leisure. Most men drove to work, and the family car allowed trips to the new shopping centres as well as weekend drives and interstate holidays. The birth rate rose markedly, from no more than replacement rate in the 1930s to 3.5 children per woman by the early 1960s, and the children born after the war enjoyed greater educational opportunities. As more children stayed on to complete secondary education, the number in higher education rose from 31 000 in 1950 to 175 000 by 1970.[17]

An overriding concern for those who managed the economy after World War II was how to ensure full employment did not spill over into excessive demand and inflation. There was indeed a spike of inflation when the Korean War sent the wool price soaring, but it was soon brought under control. One reason for this was that the system of wage determination prevented a wage-price spiral. Another, perhaps, was that most Australians could still remember the Depression and were prepared to moderate their demands. Of greater importance, surely, was that this was a period when the gap between rich and poor was narrowing. At the beginning of the 20th century the top one per cent of income earners took 12 per cent of all personal income. In the 1950s that share slipped below eight per cent and by 1970 it was just six per cent. All incomes were rising, but they were rising faster at the bottom than at the top, and equal-pay decisions by the wage tribunal in 1969 and 1972 would narrow the gender pay gap.[18]

When the long economic boom ended in the early 1970s, there was no lack of culprits. Unions were blamed for escalating their wage demands. Business was accused of lacking enterprise; this was particularly so with manufacturers, who were content to exploit their advantages in the domestic market and failed to innovate. Government was criticised for a lack of planning and leadership. Yet the difficulties Australia encountered in this decade arose from world conditions. By this time the United States had lost its economic advantage and no longer underwrote the financial system. The sudden lift in oil prices in 1973 by a producers' cartel sent shockwaves through the international economy, reducing demand for Australian exports at a time when globalisation was shifting low-skilled jobs to low-wage countries. For the next decade the country searched for a solution to the twin problems of unemployment and inflation. As after previous booms, the adjustment was protracted and painful. It came in the 1980s as a new Labor government floated the dollar, eased restrictions on capital movements and reduced tariffs, opening the economy to greater international competition. A series of changes in domestic arrangements followed, corporatising or privatising public enterprises in telecommunications, banking, transport and utilities. Soon there was substantial deregulation of the labour market and to these economic measures can be added a determined engagement with the Asian region to finally lay the ghost of White Australia to rest.

## The longest boom

From the early 1990s, as Asian markets opened up to the country's exports of minerals and energy, sustained growth finally resumed. Australia would withstand subsequent international recessions and even weather the global financial crisis of 2007–08. To be sure, the government embarked on a major spending program to ensure Australia came through that crisis, leaving a budget deficit that remains unclosed nearly a decade later. But other countries that suffered severe austerity, blighting the lives of a generation of school leavers, could only envy the good fortune of this country. This quarter-century boom was the third and most bountiful of our long booms. It was accompanied by a new wave of immigration, so that around 30 per cent of today's population was born overseas. The population increased from 17 million to 24 million, GDP doubled and real wages now are 20 per cent higher than they were at the beginning of the 1990s.

The years on either side of the new millennium have reinforced the importance of economic influences on the Australian national story. But we need to use a wider lens. The United Nations devised a Human Development Index to create a broader measure than average income; to GDP per head, the Index adds life expectancy as a guide to a long and healthy life, and years of schooling as a guide to educational provision. Australia has consistently been near the top of this index; in 2014 it ranked second, behind only Norway. The improvements are thrown into bold relief by comparing the three components of the index over a longer time span. In 1901 Australian GDP per head was $10951; by 2010 it was $61 813.[19] Life expectancy in 1901 was 56.5 years; by 2010 it was 80 years.[20] In 1901 the overwhelming majority of Australians left school at the age of 13 or 14; by 2010 two-thirds of adults aged between 21 and 65 had a post-secondary qualification.[21]

In other respects Australia fares less well in international comparisons. As more women joined the workforce, the labour-force participation rate rose. The hours worked by full-time employees have increased since the 40-hour week was introduced after World War II, so that by 2007 the working week was longer in Australia than in other advanced economies. Australia was also close to the top of the table for part-time workers, even though a substantial proportion of them would have preferred full-time employment.[22] Australia has one of the highest rates of car ownership but one of the lowest rates of travel by public transport.[23] Australians have always liked to claim that we punch above our weight, but more of us now fight in the heavyweight division. A quarter of recruits to the armed forces in 1914–18 and 1939–41 – in both cases following an economic depression – were at risk due to an extremely low body mass index; decades later, when the army's dress uniform was redesigned in 2016, the trousers came with a stretch waist.[24]

There have been improvements in military habits. The troops in World War II were given a special allocation of beer and cigarettes; indeed, tobacco was sent from the United States under the Lend-Lease scheme as an essential war material. Alcohol consumption has declined since 1980 and now only 12 per cent of all Australians smoke. But two-thirds of our adults are obese or overweight. One factor cited for increasing obesity is a lack of exercise. Fewer families live on a quarter-acre block with a back-yard for play; fewer children walk to school, and it is younger, inner-city adults who fill the bicycle lanes. The rising cost of housing has pushed many families to the outskirts of the major cities – in 1990 it took 312 weeks of average weekly earnings to buy a house with the median price; by 2010 it took 544 weeks.[25] Home ownership peaked in the 1980s and new housing construction is now split between grandiose McMansions and luxury apartments on the one hand, and shrunken and poky rental properties on the other.

The last quarter-century has also seen a marked rise in inequality. For a number of reasons, one of them the decline of trade union membership and a consequent loss of bargaining power, the lower-paid have failed to keep up with the increases enjoyed by the wealthy. The top one per cent of income earners increased their share of all incomes from five per cent in the 1980s to over eight per cent by 2010.[26] The share of wealth held by 'the one per cent' was even greater: they held 15 per cent of total wealth by 2014; the top ten per cent held over half.[27] Various studies have linked a country's level of inequality to its incidence of ill health, violence and incarceration; the OECD has recently warned that inequality reduces economic growth, in part because it restricts consumer demand.[28] The growing inequality is particularly disturbing in a country that prides itself on its egalitarianism. (Carmen Lawrence says more about inequality in the next chapter of this book.)

It is still hazardous, though, to extrapolate from these patterns to politics and public attitudes. There would appear to be a disenchantment with the major parties – evident in the growing support for fringe candidates – and a lack of faith in the capacity of government to provide leadership. When problems emerged with the provision of insulation batts in homes, part of the stimulus program of the Rudd government in response to the global financial crisis and global warming, it was suggested that the public sector lacked the capacity to administer such projects. Such a suggestion would have astonished an earlier generation that witnessed the Curtin government organise the country to fight and win a total war. It is a similar story with the repeated efforts to 'close the gap' between Indigenous and other Australians: each new strategy over-promises and under-delivers. Perhaps it is this lack of government capacity that leads politicians to take refuge in border security and punishment of asylum seekers and refugees as diversions from less tractable policy areas.

Surveys show that Australians feel uncomfortable with increased inequality, but few of the beneficiaries of our generous treatment of capital gains and large superannuation benefits show willingness to give up their advantages.[29] There is criticism of the bonuses paid to chief executive officers, who now expect more than a hundred times the average salary of their employees, but the decline in benefits for the unemployed goes largely unremarked. If Ross Garnaut laments that there is no longer an Australian appetite for economic reform, there seems to be scepticism on the part of the Australian majority that they will share in reform's benefits.

# 13

# 'Fair go' nation? Egalitarian myth and reality in Australia

## CARMEN LAWRENCE

Perhaps there is no more widely claimed Australian value than the right to a 'fair go'. Indeed, egalitarianism is frequently invoked as a quintessentially Australian virtue, as a defining national characteristic, on display in our commitment to 'mateship', our comradeship under adversity in war – egalitarianism in step with the Anzac spirit – and our expressed 'Jack's as good as his master' attitude to wealth and status. It is not just the way things should be, but the way they are. Egalitarianism is a central strand of our national Australian story.

It is routinely invoked as a founding principle of our democracy – the wage-earners' welfare state – and solemnly endorsed by politicians of all stripes. Conservative Prime Minister John Howard said in a speech in 2000, for example, that Australia's 'social cohesion, flowing directly from a quite unique form of egalitarianism, is arguably the crowning achievement of the Australian experience over the past century'.[1] (This was despite Howard's advocacy over many decades for dismantling many of the institutional arrangements that had enabled the egalitarianism to be realised.)

Egalitarianism is on display, too, at our borders. People applying for visas to Australia have to sign an 'Australian Values Statement', which says that applicants should understand that shared Australian values include 'a spirit of egalitarianism that embraces mutual respect, tolerance, fair play and compassion for those in need and pursuit of the public good' as well as 'equality of opportunity for individuals, regardless of their race, religion or ethnic background'.[2]

So ubiquitous and forthright are Australian public statements about equality that it is tempting to conclude that egalitarian values must be deeply embedded in our institutions and public policies, and evident in the status of our citizens. Given, however, the data indicating continuing group inequalities and the discrimination faced by significant numbers of Australians, our egalitarianism may be better characterised as a myth, functioning to provide comfort and to inspire us and offer moral guidance, rather than being founded in fact.[3] The myth may have been a factor in our history, honed by bush mateship and battlefield experience, but the evidence suggests the reality is far removed from the myth.

After decades of monitoring Australian attitudes, social researcher Hugh Mackay warned that myths may often seem benign: they 'can be a great source of comfort' but 'they can weaken us by blinding us to the way things really are. We can take refuge in myth; anaesthetise ourselves; insulate ourselves from reality'.[4] Evidence of inequality may be discounted or re-interpreted to diminish our discomfort at the discrepancy between myth and reality. Indeed, it is not easy to determine precisely what Australians mean when they commit to 'a fair go' or what form of egalitarianism they are signing up to. On the face of it, a 'fair go' denotes equality of opportunity, but that too can be highly variable in meaning and scope. In endorsing equality, some of us clearly intend little more than equality before the law, ensuring that 'the legal, regulatory and institutional framework does not impede Australians from competing on equal terms'.[5] This means endorsing '*formal* equality of opportunity', the 'equal treatment of all people regardless of circumstance'.[6] It typically includes ensuring that discrimination based on age, religion, gender, ethnicity, race and sexual preference are not officially condoned and that there is a basic 'safety net' of social security, decent wages and conditions, and affordable health care and education. For people who have this view, as long as the classroom door is open, the handicaps some students bring with them are not seen as worthy of policy attention. This perception is often accompanied by the attitude that success or failure is entirely due to individual effort and merit: 'You get what you deserve and deserve what you get', the so-called 'Just World Hypothesis'. Significant inequity is tolerable because it is seen as an inevitable consequence of the unequal distribution of capacity.

Conversely, those who embrace 'substantive equality of opportunity' – the need to achieve equitable outcomes as well as equal opportunity, and to take account of past discrimination – judge that all people should have the chance to develop to their full potential, regardless of the circumstances of their birth.[7] This view of a 'fair go' clearly requires a more muscular intervention by governments to remedy the disadvantages people face because of their early lives or the lack of wealth, status and power of their parents or their social group. As President Lyndon Johnson explained in a 1965 speech about equal opportunity, 'You do not take a person who, for years, has been hobbled by chains and liberate him, bring him up to the starting line of a race and then say you are free to compete with all the others, and still believe that you have been completely fair'.[8]

It is true that, whenever Australians are asked about what we value and what values we think should define us, we place ensuring a 'fair go' near the top of the list. A 2006 survey for the Australian Council of Social Service (ACOSS) found that 91 per cent of the people in a national sample believed that 'a fair go for all' is an important Australian value. Asked what was necessary to make Australia a fairer place, most of those surveyed pointed to policies that underpin formal equality: human rights, education, decent wages and conditions, health and a safety net for struggling people.[9] In surveys and opinion polls over many decades, significant numbers of Australians have also endorsed the idea that people should not only get the same opportunities, regardless of parental income or privilege, but also that policies should aim to compensate for disadvantage in order to ensure greater equality of outcomes. That is probably one of the reasons for the strong endorsement of the needs-based funding for education recommended by the Gonski Review, whose explicit brief from government was to find ways of funding education so that differences in children's *achievements* are not the result of differences in wealth, income, power or possessions.[10]

Studies of Australian attitudes to economic inequality indicate that most people judge the gap between rich and poor as too large, and that this concern has been growing in recent years.[11] The proportion of respondents in the regular Scanlon surveys agreeing that the gap is too large has hovered between 71 and 78 per cent, with the highest level of agreement – 77–78 per cent – being recorded in 2015–16.[12] Australians show somewhat less willingness to contemplate redistributive measures that might reduce these gaps, although this too may be changing. Survey data collected by the Australia Institute in 2014 indicated strong backing for income support measures and universal services, and showed that people are willing to pay the taxes needed to fund them.[13] Similar sentiments are revealed in the latest Per Capita survey of taxation policy, which shows that people are worried that the quality and availability of public services are declining and, while people are willing to pay higher taxes themselves to fund this spending, they also think the tax system should be improved by governments, cracking down on tax avoidance and insisting that high income earners and big businesses pay their fair share.[14]

There is, however, an uncomfortable tension between this apparent commitment to a 'fair go' and attitudes toward the groups who are conspicuously not faring well in contemporary Australia – the unemployed, single parents, recent migrants and Indigenous Australians. Significant minorities of Australians appear to believe that this disadvantage is self-inflicted, that some people, when offered opportunities, perversely refuse to take them. When directed at Indigenous Australians such perceptions, paradoxically, are often couched in terms of 'equity'.[15] While most settler Australians believe that Indigenous Australians have the right to equality, some settlers resent what they perceive as 'special treatment'. They actually believe that Indigenous people are getting *more* than others – generous 'handouts' – that being Indigenous, for example, entitles people to receive more welfare payments than non-Indigenous people, that the Government helps Indigenous people make loan repayments on cars and so on. Such prejudices are fuelled by the very few instances where additional resources *are* made available to try to redress Indigenous disadvantages. They are also reinforced when public policy and political positioning are marked by a persistent refusal to acknowledge the effects of Indigenous dispossession and childhood separation and disadvantage. (These issues are addressed by Larissa Behrendt in chapter 16 of this book.) Such 'split consciousness' about inequality, reporting support for egalitarian principles (such as distribution according to need) while simultaneously endorsing inegalitarian attitudes (such as the moral depravity of the poor), appears in many political debates.[16]

## Universal values?

While many Australians believe we are exceptional, the claim that we are more passionately wedded to 'a fair go' than others is challenged by international data on attitudes toward various forms of (in)equality. The Canadian sociologist Lars Osberg points to the 'near ubiquity' worldwide of a preference for greater equality.[17] This indicates that such values are actually the touchstones of modern, liberal democracies. While there are clear national differences in both the type of values endorsed and the importance ascribed to them, there is also surprising consensus on the importance assigned to particular values. A survey of 54 nations found similar high rankings of core egalitarian values; that study suggested the similarities arose from the way values sustain societies and from our shared nature as human beings.[18] Values promote group survival and prosperity, which is why egalitarianism is at the core of many societies: its cultivation helps people recognise that they share basic interests and need to look out for everyone's welfare. The Norwegian government, for example, tells intending international students that 'Norwegian values are rooted in egalitarian ideals' and that 'egalitarian values ... are at the root of the welfare state' and 'manifest themselves throughout Norwegian society in many ways – for instance in the field of gender equality'.[19] (Readers will note similarities in these sentiments to those in the Australian Values Statement quoted above.) Similar statements are commonplace around the world, and opinion polls continue to reveal strong egalitarian preferences in most contemporary societies.

Global surveys also show a near universal antipathy toward conspicuous inequality of wealth and income. While the people surveyed may not estimate the degree of inequality with any accuracy, everywhere they do appear to care about it. According to various surveys, a large majority of people – between two-thirds and 90 per cent in a survey by the International Social Survey Programme – judge income differences in the countries where they live as 'too large'. In these surveys, clear majorities in all countries either agree or strongly agree with the question, 'In [your country] are income differences too large?', although, contrary to our self-image, Australians appear less emphatic in this view than the citizens of some other countries (for example, 60.3 per cent of respondents in France 'strongly' agreed compared with Australia's 17.8 per cent).[20]

## International and Australian evidence

How accurate are these perceptions of inequality and do they generate pressure for policy action – in Australia or elsewhere? If Australian unequal reality does not match Australian egalitarian rhetoric, does the rest of the world offer us any guidance for dealing with this gap? Answering these questions requires evidence about various forms of inequality within and between societies and about changes over time. Both types of assessment are extremely difficult, but since there is now considerable evidence that places with the greatest differences in wealth and income are also the most unequal in other respects, including power and influence, economic inequality can be used as a proxy for other forms of inequality: societies with the greatest income inequality are the most likely to discriminate against minorities and to limit universal access to public goods, such as education and health services.

Globally, while there has been material progress on many fronts, economic inequality has been increasing. A 2014 report by the United Nations Development Programme (UNDP) showed that one per cent of the world's population owned about 40 per cent of the world's assets, while the bottom half of the globe's people owned around one per cent.[21] Humanity, the report concluded, remains deeply divided, and recent trends are not very encouraging: over the last two decades, income inequality has grown both within and between countries. A majority of the world's population lives in societies more unequal today than they were 20 years ago. Evidence from the developed world confirms a significant and widespread increase in income inequality over the same period.[22] Whatever its precise causes – the prevailing neo-liberal economic model is certainly implicated – income inequality is almost universally on the rise.

Within this world picture, researchers generally agree that inequality among Australians is also increasing. While we are collectively wealthier than we have ever been, that wealth is spread less evenly than in the 1960s and 1970s, and we are now a good deal less equal than such countries as Japan, Sweden and Norway. In fact, Australia has now slipped into the bottom half of the OECD league table on equality, and the gender pay gap, for example, is growing, not decreasing. Today, the wealthiest 20 per cent of Australians own 61 per cent of the nation's wealth, the poorest 20 per cent just one per cent. Although the income disparities are less marked, they too have been increasing. OECD data show that the richest ten per cent of Australians captured almost 50 per cent of the growth in gross domestic product (GDP) over the last three decades. A significant minority of citizens live in outright poverty, this figure being estimated by ACOSS in 2015 at approximately 12.8 per cent.[23] Most at risk are Indigenous people, the unemployed, children (especially in lone-parent families), and people whose main source of income is social security payments. Overall, the evidence strongly suggests that the egalitarian strand of the historic Australian tapestry is fraying or, put another way, the gap between myth and reality is widening along with the gap between rich and poor.

## The effects of inequality

Even the World Bank now acknowledges that inequality jeopardises economic growth and the reduction of poverty.[24] As the UNDP documents, inequality has also stalled progress in education, health and nutrition for large sections of the globe's population, undermining the potential to develop the human capabilities needed for a decent life. Furthermore, it is likely that inequality is driving conflict and destabilising societies; when incomes and opportunities rise for just a few, when inequalities persist over time and across generations, then those at the margins, excluded from the gains of development, will at some point contest the 'progress' that has passed them by.

Clearly, the case for equality is not simply a moral one; there is now a well-established association between income inequality and health and social problems, including life expectancy. Many of these linkages mirror the 'social gradients' in health and social indicators within societies. Data from many countries show that 'the societal scale of income inequality is related to morbidity and mortality, obesity, [high] teenage birth rates, mental illness, homicide, low trust, low social capital, hostility, and racism'.[25] Poor educational performance among schoolchildren, imprisonment rates and deaths from drug overdoses can be added to this list.

One of the more troubling adjuncts of inequality is the collapse in intergenerational mobility: children born into disadvantage in the most unequal societies have reduced prospects of improving their circumstances compared with their parents and grandparents. Although which factor comes first is necessarily uncertain, it seems fair to conclude that greater income inequality is associated with a greater prevalence of ill health and social problems, and that the whole society is affected.

To date, the relationship between these outcomes and income inequality within Australia has been little studied. Australia does, however, rank among the more unequal nations, with a larger catalogue of social ills than more equal societies – higher levels of illegal drug use and mental illness, lower levels of trust, less child wellbeing, more obesity among both adults and children, higher levels of imprisonment, less social mobility, and lower scores on a composite index of health and social problems.[26] The drag of inequality is particularly obvious in the deepening impact of social disadvantage on children's educational chances. Research has also documented the association between inequality and the symptoms of civic discord, such as distrust, poor social capital, hostility and racism. Analysis of data across countries and among American states reveals substantially lower levels of trust where income differences are large, as well as a reduced willingness of people to volunteer, to contribute to the common good.[27]

While the research is extensive, the processes underlying these linkages are not clear. One possibility is that inequality flows from the basic social, political and economic characteristics of a society. These characteristics also influence the quality of the social and physical environment. Economic ideologies, cultural values (individualism, materialism), and attitudes toward consumption, work and environmental protection, all influence policies that, in turn, affect both income distribution and people's wellbeing. The German-based sociologist Nate Breznau showed that people with strong egalitarian values, including in Australia, are the most likely to support government services designed to reduce inequality. Conversely, those who support 'economic individualism' and neo-liberal economic policies are the least likely to favour such a role for government.[28]

Such attitudes are reflected in government expenditure on health, education and environmental services: countries with higher scores on 'economic individualism' have lower levels of government spending per capita.[29] Within the OECD, Australians are more tolerant of inequality than the average of other countries, and Australia's family policies are among the least generous. This less generous provision is, in turn, related to greater child poverty and higher child mortality in Australia than in countries that are more generous to their children. Reinforcing this view is the demonstration that the American states with the greatest income inequality have lower spending on education and literacy programs, and poorer educational outcomes.[30] It also appears that high levels of inequality are linked to more corruption in government and greater exploitation of workers (where workers are underpaid relative to the market value of their productivity).[31]

Such effects may be detrimental to democracy itself. As economist Paul Krugman has argued, 'extreme concentration of income is incompatible with real democracy'.[32] The evidence backs him up. A study of citizens' political engagement in 24 wealthy democracies showed that greater income inequality reduced 'interest in politics, views of government responsiveness and participation in elections'.[33] On average, people are less supportive of democracy if they live in a country that has a high level of income inequality.

## What can be done?

All this evidence needs to be set against the Australian myth – that there is something in our customs, our history (including the history of our wars), our literature, that makes us instinctively egalitarian, both towards each other and compared with the rest of the world. We have seen that the rest of the world does not seem to be particularly equal in 2016–17, but then neither does Australia, regardless of our national myths. Given the apparently near-universal commitment to equality as an ideal, a general perception that inequality is too great, evidence that inequality is growing and that it has detrimental effects on any society, we might expect that governments would be motivated to develop policies to reduce the divide. Until recently, however, awareness of the need to reduce economic inequality had largely disappeared from the policy agenda in Australia and many other countries. Inequality was routinely overlooked in public discussions about solving our social problems. Indeed, some people clearly regard inequality as an inevitable consequence of the operation of free markets – in the words of economist James Galbraith, a kind of 'black rain, a curse of obscure origin with no known remedy, a matter of mystery covered by words like downsizing, deregulation or globalization'.[34] Some economists particularly appear to believe that capitalism has just become more savage, that the new brutality of markets is inevitable and unavoidable, and that inequality is a price we must pay for the efficiencies of worldwide production and trade.

More likely, as economist Joseph Stiglitz argues, the widening gaps, at least in the developed world, are the result of government policies (or the lack of them) on taxes and income transfers, non-cash benefits in housing, health and education, and labour market and corporate regulation. As Stiglitz says of the United States, 'even though market forces help shape the degree of inequality, government policies shape those market forces'.[35] While deliberate government policies in the post-war period produced steady increases in economic equality, in the United States and elsewhere the momentum stalled and then reversed under the neo-liberal experiment. In Australia, we have progressively neutered many of the instruments designed to spread our wealth more evenly. Despite much recent commentary on the need to reduce inequality, there are no clear signs yet that the mounting evidence of the destructive effects of growing inequality is being translated into public policy to close the gaps.

Much can be done to reduce inequality, however; many countries have managed this through a combination of progressive economic and social policies. The lessons of these policies are as relevant to Australia as to other countries, despite the 25 years of growth in our GDP that have made some of us better off. (Stuart Macintyre considers economic influences in chapter 12 of this book.) Much can be learned from those experiences: approaches that shape growth so that market outcomes do not further divide societies but deliver shared prosperity; fiscal and monetary policies that allow governments to intervene to realign market outcomes through redistribution; policies that ensure universal access to critical services, especially education, health and social protection, that strengthen labour markets and democratic institutions, and seek to redress disadvantage and ensure people are not marginalised because of who they are.

The key test is whether the public policy choices we make reflect a genuine commitment to equality of opportunity: do we give it more than token weight or do we subordinate it to other economic and social goals? Are we really the nation of a 'fair go' or are we kidding ourselves? In reality, it seems that our comforting and comfortable egalitarian myth, passed down to us in stories of brothers in the bush and mates in the trenches, is blinding us to the growing divide in our society and the need to do something about it.

# 14

# Australian heroes: Some military mates are more equal than others

PETER STANLEY

Every human group – family, community, state or nation – has its heroes: celebrated individuals who illuminate the group's values, and how it sees and represents its identity. Medieval Europe venerated saints and princes. Victorian England celebrated imperial heroes exemplifying the virtues of character or religious zeal. Americans celebrate entrepreneurial individuals. The Soviet Union valued contributors to the collective good. What heroes do Australians now hold up as exemplars of their society as it developed and changed, and what does our choice of heroes say about us?

## The one and the many

Australian history has always seen a tension between the collective and the individual. This was perhaps the natural consequence of a settler society that began with voiceless convicts, visionary governors and bold explorers, but by 1901 showed both a robust individualism and a strong tendency towards the collective. Colonial society had both the acquiescent and the anti-authoritarian. It had notable individual contributors, such as Lachlan Macquarie, Henry Parkes or 'Banjo' Paterson, but also celebrated bushrangers like 'Bold Jack' Donohoe, Captain Moonlight and, pre-eminently, Ned Kelly. Above all, colonial Australia created and acclaimed anonymous archetypes – the free settler, the pioneer, the goldminer, the bushman, the selector. World War I added to that pantheon 'the Digger' – the citizen soldier representative of those who fought and died in that conflict. At the beginning of the 21st century that easy connection between the individual and the mass has been broken. We are arguably more aware of exceptional individuals in Australian history now than at any time in the past; the current centenary of Anzac exemplifies who and what Australians seem to value in that conflict. Our Great War hero is no longer the anonymous archetypal Digger: now Australia's heroes have names, ranks and decorations.

A list compiled for Australia Day 2013 by *The Australian* newspaper identified 50 'great Australians'.[1] The first ten were (in order):

- Andrew 'Banjo' Paterson, poet and author of 'Waltzing Matilda'
- Don Bradman, champion cricketer
- Howard Florey, scientist, joint discoverer of penicillin
- John Curtin, Prime Minister 1941–45
- Mary McKillop, Catholic nun, canonised 2010
- Eddie Mabo, Indigenous activist
- John Monash, commander, Australian Corps, 1918
- Douglas Mawson, Antarctic explorer
- Edith Cowan, first woman parliamentarian
- Albert Jacka, timber worker; first Victoria Cross winner in World War I.

This list is illuminating in that it is carefully balanced between civil, military, cultural, political and sporting figures. It includes two women and an Indigenous representative and – pointedly – the explorer pioneered Antarctica, not outback Australia. The list offers a reminder that heroes are made by the survival of their reputation, not by the inherent qualities of their achievements. They include a Great War general – John Monash – and the war's first Australian VC, Albert Jacka. These two seem to embody our Australia's view of that war.

The 'Hall of Fame' of Australian 'heroes' is constantly refreshed but constantly eroded. As Bradman's taking second spot confirms, sporting champions are so prominent and newly minted with every season and Olympic cycle that they especially rise and fall. In, say, swimming, once famous figures such as Annette Kellerman (1887–1975), Fanny Durack (1889–1956) or Andrew 'Boy' Charlton (1907–75) are supplanted by Ian Thorpe, Leisel Jones and Grant Hackett. Explorers once familiar from school texts are now probably largely obscure, with the exception of, say, James Cook. Some labels become interchangeable, even if only on social media, where a meme has appeared occasionally with Bradman and cricket bat photoshopped into a famous (but staged) propaganda photograph of a soldier carrying a 'wounded' mate. The sportsman hero is seen as a warrior, just as in the Great War 'eligibles' were encouraged to volunteer for 'The Sportsmen's Thousand'.[2]

*The Australian*'s list suggests 'heroes' in popular Australian usage (with the media taking the lead) includes many more than those who have performed heroic deeds in war. Australian heroes encompass not only 'classic' heroes who contribute mightily in war or in conditions of hardship – such as military figures or philanthropists or surgeons Fred Hollows and Victor Chang – but also sporting figures and eccentrics – Daisy Bates, Bea Miles, 'Prince Leonard' of Hutt River – and, more recently, entertainment or media 'personalities' such as Paul Hogan or rock musician Michael Hutchence. A peculiarity of Australia's conception of heroic worth is that it extends to failure, including characters like Burke and Wills (died returning from an incompetently managed cross-continental journey), the boxer Les Darcy (died of septicaemia at the height of his fame, possibly evading war service), the airman Charles Kingsford Smith (lost during an air record attempt in 1935) and Phar Lap (the celebrated race horse supposedly poisoned in the United States in 1932). Perversely, Australian heroes include criminals, such as brothel madam, sly-grogger and drug-peddler Tilly Devine; career criminal Joseph 'Squizzy' Taylor; and even multiple murderer and war criminal Harry 'Breaker' Morant. Australia's heroes at any time reflect the values the nation shares in aggregate.

## Egalitarianism as an Australian value

Paradoxically, one of the values most cherished by Australians for much of our history has been egalitarianism (as Carmen Lawrence shows in chapter 13). Historian Nick Dyrenfurth argues that mateship is 'part of our cultural DNA', 'a de facto religion. Symbolically speaking, mateship is said to embody our secular egalitarian predilections'. By 1914, Dyrenfurth writes, 'a brash egalitarianism stood at the heart of Australian identity' – white male identity, at least. Egalitarianism meant fairness and equality, at least for white men. Dyrenfurth traces the lineage of mateship and equality from the itinerant pastoral workers of the 19th century, through the gold rush period, down to World War I, where egalitarianism seemed to reach its zenith. Bill Gammage, the chronicler of the Diggers in that war, believed they saw mateship as 'a particular Australian virtue, a creed, almost a religion'. Decades later, prime ministers Hawke and Howard, political custodians of a revived Anzac, struck the same note. Returned from Gallipoli in 1990, Hawke argued that the original Anzacs were defined by their 'sense of mateship – in a word ... sheer Australianness'. Howard dedicated his new government to 'the maintenance of traditional Australian values. And they include those great values of mateship and egalitarianism'. 'Equality of sacrifice' had been the watchword, too, for Hawke and Howard's prime ministerial predecessors WM Hughes and John Curtin. Hughes used it as an argument for conscription in World War I, Curtin to justify the all-in war effort two decades later.[3]

Charles Bean, Australia's Great War official historian and the progenitor of the 'Anzac legend', saw and presented the men of the Australian Imperial Force (AIF) as an expression of the egalitarianism of the progressive Australia with which he had fallen in love after his return from Britain and his visits to the pastoral west of New South Wales, where bushmen mates still roamed. The footnotes in Bean's *Official History* and the Roll of Honour in the Australian War Memorial he helped conceive (arranged in alphabetical order, not by rank) testify to the value he placed on egalitarianism. 'As Bean saw it', writes his biographer Peter Rees, 'egalitarianism was fundamental to Australia's national tradition'. He was 'captivated by the mateship and egalitarianism that he saw in outback Australians, and then in Australian soldiers in the Great War'.[4]

## Egalitarian values and the Victoria Cross

Recent developments in the presentation of the Great War in Australian society suggest that this historic Australian commitment to egalitarianism is weakening. (Carmen Lawrence's chapter 13 in this book explores other angles of this phenomenon.) The creation of the Digger archetype, so fundamental to the birth and dissemination of the Anzac legend, seemed to resolve the persistent tension in Australia between the individual and the mass, between individual notoriety and mass anonymity. Individuals might be celebrated (by telling the stories of heroic individuals at Anzac Day services, for example) but the egalitarianism inherent in the legend acted against the valorisation of just a few notables. Perhaps the only individuals to truly transcend this representative tendency were John Simpson Kirkpatrick, 'the man with the donkey', for World War I and Edward 'Weary' Dunlop, the prisoner-of-war surgeon, for World War II.

By contrast, during the centenary of the Great War, we have seen notable men – almost all of them are men – portrayed as exceptional rather than representative. This tendency to highlight individuals is perhaps a consequence of other processes at work in the cultural industries. It is now common in both print and electronic journalism for reporters to use individuals to illustrate the effects on society of broader movements and developments. A story about globalisation or rapacious cheque-cashers will invariably be framed by the experiences of individuals. It is also now much easier to find individuals' stories ('stories', the word, and the concept, is now endemic) than before, thanks to the widespread digitisation of sources. And much easier to turn ordinary people into celebrities.

These changes have profound implications for the way Australians have told – and been told – stories about notable individuals. Midway through the centenary of World War I, we can now see how Australians understand the war through their focus on the most highly decorated members of the AIF and its most senior commander. Ironically, one reason Australians tended to pay attention to their wartime heroes is that formal awards for gallantry historically have been relatively rare here. Like other British Empire and Commonwealth armies, Australia's was niggardly in awarding medals. In the Great War the 300 000-odd other ranks – that is, non-officers – of the AIF between them garnered only 12 935 British decorations and that total mostly comprised the 9891 men awarded the Military Medal, the lowest award recognised by a medal. By comparison, though, the AIF's officers – numbering probably not more than 20 000 – gained 3879 awards of all kinds.[5] In other words, it was four or five times 'easier' for officers than men to get an award.

The 16814 British decorations awarded to the AIF during World War I included 60 Victoria Crosses (VCs), the British Empire's highest gallantry award. The men who received these awards were understandably regarded as the 'bravest of the brave'. They have rightly always been described and feted, but it seems incontrovertible that VCs have become in the past decade or so much more prominent in the telling of the Australian story of war in general and of the Great War in particular. Australian military history has enjoyed an unending boom for more than 30 years. Books about VCs are notably more popular in that field. More books on individual VCs have appeared in the past decade than at any period: ten between 1930 and 2000, but 17 since then.

Arguably, Australia now venerates the VC more than ever before. The Australian War Memorial has shown a strong interest in promoting the VC since the 1980s, and this has done much to enhance the award's stature. The memorial's VC collection went from being negligible 50 years ago to occupying a gallery at the memorial's heart. A 'Hall of Valour' opened in 1981 and has been enlarged twice. This room now displays 68 Australian VCs (and several British VCs with Australian associations) and comparable decorations, such as the George Cross for bravery by civilians.

Though the greater prominence VCs are accorded is inspired by genuine regard for heroism, it also helps neutralise critical attention. It will undoubtedly be regarded as in poor taste for me to criticise what is perhaps Australian military history's last remaining sacred cow. Yet scrutiny of the awards made in World War I to Australians suggests the process was not free from pragmatism and political opportunism. The timing of awards, the recommendations rejected, the language of the citations, the circumstances of the awards, subjectivity and serendipity, all suggest that the process was very human and indeed political. As the research of Victoria D'Alton shows, VCs were not simply awarded because a few soldiers performed brave deeds.[6] Rather, they were very much the product of an imperial system under stress. It is surely significant, for example, that half the VCs awarded to men of the AIF on the Western Front came in 1918, when the Australian Corps was under the most severe strain and the supply of volunteers from Australia had almost dried up. Awards were intended to bolster Australia's faltering commitment to the war. Arguments within the chain of command over the nature of 'deeds' to be rewarded – with aggressive actions preferred over rescuing wounded comrades – show the process to have been all too political.

As the VC became more valorised it aroused extremes of passion, with individuals advocating the claims of those allegedly 'denied' recognition, who may themselves have lobbied for years for redress. In 2013 an inquiry into such claims reported after two years, receiving dozens of written submissions and holding public hearings into the claims of 13 individuals.[7] They included John Simpson Kirkpatrick, already perhaps the most famous Australian soldier of the Great War. In a detailed and well-justified report the tribunal recommended that no retrospective VCs should be awarded. Interestingly, while professional historians generally argued against retrospective awards, popular writers mostly urged that the awards were justified.

The growing number of books on VCs means that these men – they are all men – are overwhelmingly the best-documented and celebrated members of Australia's military forces. While some of the books are works of quality, they invariably celebrate heroic 'deeds'; they are rarely portraits of what war does to men as well as what men do in war. Still, there is no doubt that these men did perform acts of individual bravery meriting recognition. Even if other men performed brave deeds that were not recognised, or there were anomalies of recognition, surely there is no harm done? Actually, there is. It could be argued that the recent concentration on 'Victoria Cross heroes' as major bearers of the Anzac legend has meant skewing the presentation and perception of Australian military history. Veneration of VCs challenges Australia's tradition of democratic commemoration. Robert Macklin, in his book, *Bravest* (which deals with a selected few VCs), paradoxically claims that the VC 'has a particular appeal to the egalitarian streak in the Australian character'. But even Macklin concedes that the VC 'has become ever more prized, its story ever more gloriously arrayed with myth and legend'.[8]

Surely the undue focus on the VC story actually *denies* the egalitarian streak in Australian military history? It emphasises the few rather than empathising with the many, the 300 000 who did not receive the VC. Writing in 1916, Charles Bean reflected on the AIF's part in the great offensive. He praised its men but insisted that 'they are not heroes. They are just ordinary Australians doing their particular work as their country would wish them to do'.[9] While Bean's official history duly noted each Australian VC, he knew that those who were decorated were not the only heroes. A century on, Bean's admiration for the egalitarian, volunteer citizen force he documented, celebrated and mourned seems less accepted than once it was. The emphasis on 'Anzac VC heroes' ensures that Australia sees glory in its war history rather than the horrific reality. Focusing on VCs helps us rise above the ruck of suffering and victimhood that characterised military work; at the same time, however, it denies the egalitarianism that was central to what the mass of soldiers would, if asked, have said they were fighting to defend. Our reputed aversion to tall poppies notwith-standing, our growing preoccupation with VCs gilds the lily of war.

## Sir John Monash as celebrity general

Perhaps the most striking manifestation of the change in the way Australia now represents the Great War can be seen in another recent concentration in Australian military historical publishing: the extraordinary slew of books about General Sir John Monash that have appeared in the past three decades. Monash's story is now familiar, even among those uninterested in Australian military history. The son of German-speaking Jewish immigrants, Monash became both a successful businessman and an officer in the part-time militia. In 1914 he took command of the 4th Brigade, which he led on Gallipoli, then in 1916 the newly raised 3rd Division and in 1918 the Australian Corps, which he commanded at Hamel, Amiens, Mont Saint-Quentin and the breaking of the Hindenburg Line. He gained further renown, at least in Victoria, by running the State Electricity Commission, and he died in 1931. He is familiar now because his portrait adorns one side of the hundred-dollar note.

By the time Geoffrey Serle published his 600-page *John Monash* in 1982, Monash had already been the subject of no fewer than 18 books or substantial articles, including a couple of books by the man himself. Serle's biography, though magisterial, did not analyse its subject as a general, but a book complemen-tary to Serle's soon appeared, *Monash as Military Commander*, by Peter Pedersen, a military officer who became a respected mili-tary historian. By the mid-1980s, Monash had not only not been forgotten but had been accorded more biographies than any other Australian soldier. Twenty years later a second Monash boom began with Roland Perry's *Monash: The Outsider Who Won a War*. Perry's title had two important flaws – Monash was not an 'outsider' and he did not 'win the war' – yet his book set the tone for those that followed, notably *Monash: The Soldier Who Shaped Australia* by Grantlee Kieza, which added little but bulk.[10]

Then there was a film. *Monash: The Forgotten Anzac*, produced in 2008, was inspired by the idea that Monash had been forgotten and that he had triumphed over adversity, 'winning the first world war on the western front'.[11] In this Monash represented an Australian victory: over anti-Semitic prejudice, over imperial 'English' condescension – oh, and over the Germans. The film perpetuated the idea that Monash looked after his men, in contrast to British generals, who were supposedly prodigal of men's lives. In fact, the death toll for the AIF in 1918, with Monash in command, was the same as in 1916, when the ANZAC corps were commanded by British generals. In his polemic 2014 book *Maestro John Monash: Australia's Greatest Citizen General*, former soldier and politician Tim Fischer argued that Monash deserved a posthumous promotion to field marshal; this for a man so modest that he instructed that his headstone should bear only the words 'John Monash'.[12]

Monash is now central to the retelling of the Anzac legend on the Western Front. In 2015 the Abbott government committed $100 million to the creation of a Sir John Monash Centre, to be built beside the Australian National Memorial at Villers-Bretonneux, France.[13] The interpretive centre, which will use 'immersive' multimedia to communicate with visitors (some of whom will be Australians), is expected to tell essentially the story of the 'Australian victories in France' as Monash described them and as his admiring biographers have retold them in the ensuing century. Then, in 2016, when the ABC called for filmmakers to tender for a documentary marking the centenary of the end of World War I, the national broadcaster did not seek to explore the trauma of the conscription referenda, sectarian antagonism or even the grief of mass deaths. Instead, it seized on Monash. The ABC decided, in advance of filmmakers pitching their own ideas, that the film should help Australians 'understand why Sir John Monash is widely regarded as a Great War hero who changed the face of traditional warfare and became a great Australian and a pivotal figure in the nation's history'.[14] In this production the VCs of 1918 may also get a mention, though it is less certain there will be room for the anonymous dead of 1918, among whom is probably numbered the Unknown Australian Soldier who was disinterred from Adelaide Cemetery in France in 1993. Monash's place as the new representative figure of the Great War seems to be confirmed by the recent announcement that there is to be placed in the grounds of the Australian War Memorial a statue of Monash, in post-war civilian clothes, wearing medals and RSL badge. In every sense this will be some distance from the Unknown Australian Soldier.[15]

## Egalitarianism and celebrity culture

What does all this military hero-worship mean for the way Australians relate to the egalitarianism once central to our popular culture? The question is particularly important because the Anzac story has been seen as the apotheosis of mateship, of egalitarianism. It would seem that history has come to be understood not just through the lens of the personal stories beloved of publishers and documentary filmmakers, but also through the obsession with celebrities that permeates popular culture. The experience of the mass of people who lived through or died as a result of an event such as World War I remains as distant as ever. On the other hand, the lives and actions of a few notable individuals, generals or VCs from this time will massively and disproportionately dominate popular historical understanding. The egalitarian basis of Australian culture, in which privates are mentioned alongside generals, regardless of decorations, is massively diminished.

The representation of war itself is skewed. War is presented not as a matter of mass slaughter but as a celebration of individual heroism. 'They are not heroes', Bean wrote in 1916 of Diggers on the Somme. Yet today the formula 'Anzac heroes' or 'our heroes' crops up regularly in children's books, family history sites, local history collections, military history buff sites, school projects, and op eds by the director of the Australian War Memorial.[16] Victoria Cross winners have been used in promotions at the memorial for private organisations and for football codes, where loose comparisons between war and sport are occasionally attempted.[17] (Ironically, today's popular focus on heroes resembles the way the Great War was reported at the time, when the need to convey useful propaganda impelled journalists to celebrate heroes and leaders, regardless of egalitarian traditions.)

The novel emphasis on Australian generalship in 1918 implies both that an Australian took a leading role in gaining 'victory' and that *command* made the difference, rather than the endurance, resilience, initiative, skill – and yes, heroism – of the mass of men who fought. The concentration – in the press, on television, in books and in memorials – on VC heroes transforms the traditional and long-accepted view of World War I as a great challenge faced by the Australian people, and a test they faced collectively and equally. Australians met the ordeals of the battlefield and of waiting and worrying in Australia, and sharing the burden, the cost and eventual victory. In all of this, the highest virtue was mateship at war and solidarity at home. The more recent celebration of both Monash and the VCs elevates individual rather than collective achievement; it is the antithesis of the mateship at the heart of the Anzac legend, an egalitarianism seen as defining Australian society. This concentration on heroes and generals, like the celebration of pop stars and sportspeople as our modern Australian heroes, says a great deal about the values of a very different Australia a century on from the Great War.

# 15

# Hidden by the myth: Women's leadership in war and peace

## JOY DAMOUSI

'Never before in the world's history has the position of woman loomed so large and been more fraught with the ultimate destiny of the race', wrote the anti-conscriptionist Cecilia John in November 1916. John observed astutely that in Australia the women's vote in general was seen as 'an enlarged man's vote'. But in opposing conscription, she believed, 'women voters were more united as women than they have been on any other issue'. She called on women to stand against militarism 'lock, stock and barrel' and show 'the way to lasting peace'.[1]

By the end of the conscription plebiscites of 1916–17, women had worked tirelessly in committees and organisations on both the 'No' and the 'Yes' sides of the debate. Women led the charge for the No vote. They campaigned with courage, fortitude and conviction to defeat conscription. They pamphleteered, lectured, and endured violent attacks when they spoke publicly. On the Yes side, women were no less passionate and adamant in favour of conscription; they spared no effort in campaigning for Yes. This debate brought many women into the public spotlight in ways that were unprecedented until that time: this was the first time women had mobilised in such numbers. 'Probably never before', wrote 'Nance' on the women's page of *The Leader*, 'did so large a body of women give up everything else for the purpose of prosecuting a public campaign; and certainly never before was so much enthusiasm and high feeling engendered'.[2]

Attracting the votes of women, especially mothers, was central to the appeals of both sides. This made the campaign distinctive for women's activism – in the way that women took the lead, shaped the debates and, through their activism, inspired and moved the wider public. Women also clashed with each other; they fought, woman against woman, publicly and forcefully over this issue in a manner not seen previously in Australian history. Beginning this chapter with women's role in the conscription debate highlights several themes. The first is about women's leadership in wartime. While women's role in the conscription struggle has been acknowledged, I have framed this role here as political leadership. I do so to give weight not only to women's presence in the debate but also to their ability to develop arguments, to persuade, to show initiative and to mobilise. The conscription battle during the Great War is not always included in histories of women and leadership, but leadership is precisely what women displayed here. I also shift the focus from the way women voted – which is how much of the literature views the 'women question' and conscription – to how women led.

Secondly, framing women's contribution in this way forces us to raise the question of women and leadership in politics more broadly. Political leadership by women does not always conform to masculine ideas of leadership. This is especially the case with women during war. Because women are not in combat or on the front line, their leadership is often overlooked or devalued. Women could not make 'the ultimate sacrifice' but this does not mean they were unable to provide leadership in debates about war.

Scholars have also neglected women's humanitarian efforts after the Great War. Two leading women campaigners, Cecilia John and Jessie Webb, leaders not just during but also after the war, are the subject of this chapter. John and Webb, who led the No and Yes campaigns respectively, were involved in many post-war activities they believed would help to build a new world. Histories of the war and post-war period that have been framed exclusively or predominantly by the Anzac myth have marginalised the contribution of women such as John and Webb. Anzac has been a mostly male story; a nation that claims a mostly male story as its founding myth devalues women and their contribution to our history.

Finally, the broader question of women and leadership in political life continues to inform current behaviour and attitudes. While there have certainly been some significant shifts in this area, women remain underrepresented in our Parliament, in business and in other walks of life. There have been countless studies of why this is so. Political leadership continues to be defined in ways that value masculine traits. Perceptions have begun to shift, but gaining multiple understandings of leadership and how leadership can be exercised remains a challenge in contemporary times. If a nation's history has many strands, then the female strand of Australia's history needs to be strengthened.

## Leadership in wartime: women and conscription, 1916–17

Cecilia John was a leader in the thick of the battle against conscription. A member of the Women's Political Association and Women's Peace Army, John was a leading feminist and pacifist whose activism often found her in court. In December 1917, she was charged under the War Precautions Act for distributing a pamphlet, *Soldiers and Conscription: A Returned Soldier's View*, which contained 'a false statement of fact of a kind likely to affect the judgment of electors in relation to their votes'.[3] The offensive section of the pamphlet said that '88 of every 100 of the Australian troops' had voted against conscription. The pamphlet also included the words of one F Hower, a soldier who had recently returned from the front: 'Conscription was opposed to the spirit of the majority of Australian soldiers'. The accusations against John and the printer Fred Holland were dismissed on the grounds that the pamphlet was published before the regulations were applied.[4]

This was not the first time John had appeared in court to defy attempts to suppress her. Famously, she sang 'I didn't raise my son to be a soldier', a composition that was subsequently banned. The song became the anthem of the anti-war and anti-conscription cause. At a rally disrupted by returned soldiers, John tried to sing the same subversive song, only to be drowned out by soldiers singing such songs as 'Boys of the bulldog breed' and 'Australia will be there'.[5] Such scenes became commonplace as the song became the focus for garnering support and mobilising opposition.[6] The song succinctly encapsulated the No side's appeal to mothers: that mothers could not and should not send their sons to kill another mother's son. Through the Women's Peace Army, John and her fellow activist, the leading Victorian feminist Vida Goldstein, shaped the debate around women's interests; they especially framed conscription as a *mother's* concern.[7]

Women on the Yes side have received less attention but they also crafted and presented arguments. In her column 'Women to women' in *The Argus*, 'Vesta' (the journalist Stella Allan) wrote how she had tried 'by diligent talk' to discover the reasons for opposition to conscription (or 'the reinforcements campaign', as she called it). She offered counter-arguments. Conscription was 'undemocratic', the No side claimed. But we need to protect our freedoms and democracy, and this is what conscription was doing, Vesta argued. Men would leave and make our industries vulnerable, the anti-conscriptionists said. But Australian women could carry the 'country's business' and there was no danger of industrial collapse occurring, Vesta countered. These numbers of soldiers are not needed, it was asserted. But Australia needed to do its part! Every man should be sent to bring an end to the war more quickly, Vesta contended.[8]

Vesta proudly displayed the sacrifices of the mothers of men who had given up numbers of sons.[9] The pro-conscription case was driven very much by women who had sent their sons to war to sacrifice their lives. The Yes side saw this as the way mothers could participate fully in the war effort; it showed leadership by example. These women argued it was their patriotic duty to do this; others branded this attitude as irresponsible and murderous. But to the Yes side, mothers of fighting men were heroes, sending three or four sons at one time. The Sydney *Sun* ran a regular column throughout the war with such details as

> Mrs. M'Carthy, of 133 Redfern-street, Redfern, has given
> four boys to help in the great endeavor – Trooper Syd
> M'Carthy, went through the Gallipoli campaign, and is
> now in Egypt; Private John M'Carthy and Private Ernest
> M'Carthy, both in France; and Private Roy M'Carthy, at
> Salisbury Plains, England.[10]

In October 1916, a meeting of patriotic women was organised at the Melbourne Town Hall. Women who had relatives at the war were especially invited, and each woman was asked to wear a badge or ribbon connected to the regiment of their male relative.[11]

Among those who supported conscription were not only women who sent their sons to war. Jessie Webb, the classics lecturer at the University of Melbourne, led the pro-conscription cause within the university and beyond. Webb had no children; her arguments were based on liberty and freedom, and the need to uphold these values by defeating the German aggressor. She, her colleague William Harrison Moore and his wife, Edith, Webb's close friend, campaigned on the need to protect Australia's freedoms.[12]

There were those, too, who did not subscribe clearly to either view. Mary Darcey from Launceston wrote:

> I am neither a member of the I.W.W. [Industrial Workers
> of the World] nor a pro-German. Two of my sons have
> gone to the front voluntarily and with my whole-hearted
> approval. But I wish to say that while I am proud of
> them and of the thousands of other brave lads who have
> gone out to fight for God and freedom, I think it a blind
> and silly, as well as a cruel slander, to brand the men
> who stayed behind 'cowards, shirkers, etc.' though no
> doubt there are a few among them.[13]

Yet giving sons did not necessarily mean voting Yes for conscription. Darcey supported voting No because taking men to the front would mean cheap 'coloured' labour would flood Australia and threaten the cherished White Australia policy.

Two of the leading organisations in support of conscription were led by women: the Red Cross, with Lady Helen Munro Ferguson, wife of the Governor-General, at the helm; and the National Women's Council of Australia. As historians Melanie Oppenheimer, Marian Quartly and Judith Smart have shown, these women and their organisations showed exemplary leadership throughout the war years and after.[14]

The story of women's direct involvement in the conscription campaign – where they shaped many aspects of the debate – is invariably overshadowed by the emphasis on the Anzac military story. Similarly, as the ravages and legacy of war continued during the immediate post-war period, women did humanitarian work, but this too has been mostly lost behind the focus on military matters. Women's contribution was significant. After the war, two organisations formed that were at the centre of attempts to shape the new world: the League of Nations and the Save the Children

Fund (SCF). Australian women were actively involved in both organisations, but their roles have been under-researched. Both John and Webb continued to lead and contribute after the war, helping, nationally and internationally, to build what they hoped would be a peaceful new order.

## Leadership in peace: Cecilia John and Save the Children

Cecilia John continued her involvement in war-related matters when she became an active member of the SCF, from its inception in London in 1919. John established an Australian branch of the SCF after attending the Women's International Peace Congress in Zurich in 1919 with Vida Goldstein, where they witnessed the horror of images of starving children in Europe. John's efforts in the early years of the organisation were strenuous and challenging. She called a public meeting in Melbourne, formed a committee, and through the daily newspapers opened subscriptions to fund the SCF and its international activities.[15] While this fundraising was effective, the powerful images of children the SCF generated at the time garnered the most support. More than £8000 was raised after 60 000 copies of an SCF pamphlet were distributed by the committee. John travelled extensively during the 1920s in areas devastated by war and where children particularly were displaced. In 1923, she visited Austria, Hungary and Greece.[16] The Australian effort through the SCF was recognised as John's work:

> The Overseas propaganda of the Save the Children
> Fund may be said to have been cradled in Australia for

> it was in the Commonwealth, in the autumn of 1919,
> that extra-European interest in the work of the Save the
> Children Fund first developed, at the instance of Miss
> Cecilia John, a Melbourne citizen, who was in England
> at the time the Fund was founded.[17]

Humanitarian work in Australia attracted much attention. It included the efforts of the National Council of Women and religious groups, such as the Sydney Church of England kitchen and Methodist Church kitchens, as well as fundraising campaigns through the Adelaide *Advertiser*.[18] John exemplified women engaged in international affairs. She was a driving force nationally and internationally, as the SCF gave her a platform for assisting child refugees especially. But even in that more traditional area of humanitarian work that was perceived as acceptable to women, John's personality attracted attention. While she had feminine qualities of 'intense feeling and kindly humanity for all suffering peoples', her public engagement with this topic also brought out her 'masculinity'. *Stead's Review* noted that

> Miss John has, in curious contrast to her pity for the
> suffering, an impersonal detachment that is more
> masculine than feminine. Her quick grasp of an entire
> situation and her absolute genius for solving intricate
> problems leave her hearers in a state of profound
> admiration of her masterful grasp. She is essentially
> a leader, and would have been a stateswoman of no
> mean order had she not found her energies absorbed [in
> humanitarian causes].[19]

These supposedly masculine qualities did not overcome John's 'feminine' qualities, for her 'quality of mercy is essentially not strained, and her quick, ready sympathy for the suffering and infirm has a generous warmth that no calculating charity could ever inspire'.[20] Despite John's central contribution – or because of it – the ambivalent attitude towards women leaders certainly emerges from this commentary.

## Jessie Webb and the League of Nations

In 1923, Jessie Webb became the substitute Australian delegate to the League of Nations. The applications for her nomination set out her suitability for the task. The Victorian branch of the National Council of Women listed several qualities that were clear evidence of Webb's capacity to lead:

> Miss Webb has frequently lectured in public, and she is
> noted for her wit and readiness of apprehension, as well
> as for her learning, and the fresh and vivid manner in
> which she presents the most difficult subjects. Those who
> know Miss Webb best value her highest, not only for her
> personal charm, but for her clear and judicial brain.[21]

Webb's international travel also positioned her perfectly to undertake this role:

> Miss Webb made an extensive tour of Europe some years
> ago, and on her present trip she travelled through Africa
> from Cape to Cairo, and experienced … the greatest
> value to one so keenly interested in modern problems.

> She is now in Greece, where she intends to stay for
> some time. Miss Webb speaks French fluently and also
> modern Greek and Italian to a certain extent ... We feel
> that she understands European problems from the point
> of view of those who are most affected by the solution of
> them – she has an international mind.[22]

The announcement of Webb's appointment 'was received in academic circles with pleasure and gratification'.[23] She was even a favourite among conservatives, the *Farmers' Advocate* noting that her qualities and capacities as well her 'personal side' are 'bound to make her a success'.[24] Webb put this attribute into practice in the League of Nations Union, which was formed in Melbourne in 1921 and included Harrison Moore and other pro-conscriptionists such as John Latham. Webb spoke of the need for the league to undertake properly organised humanitarian work.[25] She expressed her support for Karen Jeppe, a member of the Commission on the Deportation of Armenian Women and Children, who began a colony for women and children who had survived the Armenian Genocide.[26] (Vicken Babkenian and Judith Crispin's chapter 3 in this book looks at the involvement of Australians, including women, with the Armenians.) Webb believed Jeppe was

> doing some of the noblest work with which I have ever
> come in contact ... It is a sad state of bondage that is
> endured by these Armenian women. Torn from homes
> and families, and I do wish a few hundreds of pounds
> could be promptly raised by the Australian States.[27]

Webb also defended the league's stand in the Greek island of Corfu in 1923 where, following the murder of some Italian diplomats in Greece, diplomatic relations between Greece and Italy deteriorated until the Italian Navy bombarded Corfu. Greece appealed to the League of Nations and, while the dispute was finally settled, the outcome was to the advantage of Mussolini's Italy. In the league's first test of averting a major crisis its actions were widely seen as weak and ineffectual.[28] Webb defended the league's role:

> Miss Webb dealt with the difficulties confronting the
> Assembly, and supported with logical reasons her claim
> that the League had handled the situation more adroitly
> and with better success than was generally understood.
> With less success than was achieved, she said, the world,
> probably, would have been plunged into war. Some thought
> that the League ought to have taken up a more aggressive
> stand … But the League had been created to secure justice
> to the smaller nations and to avoid war, and what Greece
> had wanted was not merely justice, but justice without war.

The incident, however, highlighted for Webb some of the shortcomings of the league, such as 'the fact that of the great nations America, Germany, and Russia were not included in the membership'. Fortunately, she believed, 'America to some extent was already co-operating with the League in its humanitarian activities'. She also supported the inclusion of Russia, whose current absence was based on its not having a capitalistic system. She argued that the presence of Russia would create a 'very much stronger League of Nations than you have to-day'.[29]

It was in the league's humanitarian work that Webb saw it making a difference and the best chance for Australia to offer a significant contribution. She argued in defence of the league and against claims that it was 'futile':

> [T]he League could not carry out the recommendations of its Humanitarian Committee without having some money at its disposal. Australia held an honoured place in the League, and the first thing to strike an Australian delegate upon returning home was the question whether Australia could not do more for the League than she was doing in the one department in respect of which all the nations were very ready to co-operate, namely its humanitarian work … [T]he failure to give financial support to the humanitarian activities would weaken the League and therefore indirectly weaken its power to fulfil its chief function.[30]

## Women in the lead

Focusing too intently on the military side of Australia's World War I takes our attention away from other key events such as conscription, where women shaped both sides of the debate. Women were not mere supporting actors, but were engaged fully in defining the arguments. Their involvement in public affairs became even more pronounced after the war. If we focus too much on the enduring Anzac story in understanding the post–Great War world and Australia's place within it, we lose sight of women's engagements in organisations such as the League of Nations and Save the Children that began to shape a new world.

Women's contribution to building peace internationally tends to be buried beneath the continuing emphasis on the nationalist Anzac narrative as the central story of war and peace in Australia.

How is this relevant today? The leadership that John and Webb showed overlapped – chronologically and in its objectives – the boundaries between a frightful war and an unsettled but hopeful peace. Their work addressed elements and consequences of war well beyond the battlefield and beyond Australia. It showed there is much more to war than military campaigns, that people who come through wars are looking above all for a richer, safer life afterwards, and that post-war problems are common to a world of nations. Their work also showed that skills appropriate to dealing with the scourge of war are transferable to peacetime.

A century after John and Webb were effective, influential and highly visible in the public arena, discussions still continue about how women assume leadership – even whether what they do *is* leadership – and how to broaden definitions of leadership itself so that the contributions of women are recognised. A historical perspective can identify the diversity of women's leadership and explore the social, historical and cultural context within which women's work has been done.[31] These questions remain as pertinent today as they were when Cecilia John and Jessie Webb took centre stage on issues of war and peace nationally and internationally.[32] Understanding and valuing the leadership contributions of women is something Australia has not done well and should do better.

# 16

# Settlement or invasion? The coloniser's quandary

LARISSA BEHRENDT

When the First Fleet sailed through the heads of what would become known as Sydney Harbour, the Cammeragal people on the south side of the harbour and the Eora on the north would have watched curiously. Their culture had been continuous for more than 60 000 years and, although ships had been spotted sailing up and down the coast before, they rarely stopped and always moved on. The idea that you would colonise someone else's land was unheard of for Aboriginal people. Indigenous connections to country run deep, and are a deeply personal and spiritual attachment. The Cammeragal and Eora may well have assumed that the people sailing into the harbour would need to return to their own country, wherever it was, to tend to their own obligations as custodians.

As the colonists landed and started unpacking, the Eora people avoided them. The concept of invasion was alien to the Eora, and they would only begin to understand the true situation as time passed, structures became permanent and the colonists asserted their authority. By then conflict had begun, but the biggest immediate impact on the Aboriginal population was not from firearms and force. It was from the introduction of diseases to which Aboriginal people had no immunity: smallpox, flu and other infectious diseases decimated families and clans, fundamentally unravelling the fabric of a close-knit hunter-gatherer community and its strong kinship ties and oral traditions. And while in the centuries to come Australians would debate whether these events were the beginning of settlement or of an invasion, for Indigenous people these unwanted, uninvited violators of land, cultural protocols and spiritual traditions clearly constituted an invasion. And this invasion was the beginning of a chain of continuing aggressive acts and misguided policies, a brutal and unrelenting colonisation process that has continued to the present day.

Some Aboriginal people in the Sydney Basin tried to find a way to negotiate with the colonists, to find a way to integrate into the society that had planted itself over theirs. Bennelong's initial contact with the colonists was forced – literally – when he and another man, Colebee, were captured by Governor Phillip in 1789. While Colebee escaped, Bennelong remained in the colony, adopting some habits and customs of the British, dressing in their clothes and learning their language. Although he returned to his own people, Bennelong was a frequent visitor to the colony once he was assured he would not be detained. In 1791, a hut was built for him in the place called Bennelong Point, today's site of the Sydney Opera House. When Phillip returned to England in 1792, Bennelong went with him, being presented to King George before returning to the colony in 1795 with Governor Hunter. He found it hard to fit back in with his own people but was never accepted by the colonists. He drank heavily and died in 1813, a symbol of being caught between two worlds.

While Bennelong sought to integrate, others clearly resisted. Pemulwuy was a member of the Bidgigal clan of the Dhurag nation to the south and west of Sydney Cove. Tension grew as the colonisers forced Indigenous people off their land and away from their food sources. European hunting and farming practices failed to recognise the complex cultivation and protection of ecosystems that Aboriginal societies maintained. Retaliating for incursions onto hunting grounds, Pemulwuy speared Governor Phillip's gamekeeper in 1790 and became an outlaw to the colonists but a symbol of resistance for the Aboriginal community. He led raids on pastoral runs, killing sheep and cattle and destroying crops. By 1801, Governor King had offered a reward for Pemulwuy's capture and ordered that Aboriginal people could be shot on sight. Although shot twice, Pemulwuy survived, creating the myth he could not be killed by bullets. He was eventually fatally wounded in 1802 and his head was sent back to England.[1]

There was strenuous resistance around Australia to the spread of colonies. It was led by Aboriginal heroes like Windradyne in the Bathurst region, Yagan near Perth and Multeggerah around Ipswich.[2] From the Indigenous perspective, this was a war against an invading force. To the colonists, Indigenous people were impediments to progress. Whether Indigenous people tried to become part of the life of the colony (like Bennelong) or to resist it (like Pemulwuy), the results were the same: there was no respect for Indigenous people, culture, knowledge, laws or customs. Colonists would make much of the fact that there was no initial violent resistance. Sesquicentennial re-enactments in 1938 of the landing of the First Fleet showed a flash of gunshot and Aboriginal people dispersing. By then the myth had been created that Aboriginal people had simply relinquished their land; already their tenacious struggle to maintain their cultural identity and to assert their sovereignty and proprietorship of their land was being written out by a colonial narrative built around the term 'settlement'. (Paul Daley's chapter 17 in this book discusses frontier conflicts.)

Actually, when Phillip planted the flag at Sydney Cove in 1788 he was not claiming the land for the British to take it away from the Aboriginal people but to make sure the French did not make the claim first. (Jean-François de Galaup, Comte de La Pérouse, was hanging around on an expedition with two ships.)[3] International law had developed a doctrine of discovery that dictated the rules by which European colonial powers could claim territory around the world.[4] Raising the flag was one of the acts recognised as an assertion of a prior claim against other colonial powers eyeing off the same land. Phillip did not consider the land *terra nullius* (nobody's land). He had instructions to deal with the 'natives' with 'amity and kindness'; everyone knew there were natives there. But Indigenous rights to land, systems of law and governance, customs and traditions were ignored and under-mined by the tenacious colonisation process. From an Indigenous perspective, this process continues today and is evidenced by the socioeconomic marginalisation of Indigenous communities. They have more unemployment and homelessness, are over-represented in the criminal justice system, and have less educ-ational attainment and lower incomes.[5]

## Since the 1970s: absorbing *Mabo*

Aboriginal people continued to resist and, when the bicen-tennial anniversary of the establishment of the colony came around in 1988, Indigenous presence was powerful and strong. There was no coercion into re-enacting the landing. Instead, Indigenous people travelled from all over the country to march in protest and to assert their sovereignty, their rights to land and their own version of 1788.[6] In 1988, there was still no recogni-tion of Indigenous land interests; Australian law had reasserted this lack of rights protection in 1971 and it was, after almost 20 years, clearly established law. The 1971 case would become known as the *Gove Land Rights Case (Milurrpum v Nabalco Pty Ltd).*[7] The Yolngu pursued their claim to their traditional land against the incursions of mining and their case came before Justice Blackburn of the Supreme Court of the Northern Territory. Blackburn knew that Aboriginal people had existed at the time Australia was claimed by the British and that they had their own laws and governance systems. He knew that the Indigenous people had a connection to their land – it just was not a claim that the British or the Australian legal system could recognise; the law treated the land as *terra nullius.*

The mining leases were upheld because Justice Blackburn was bound to apply existing law. The court reaffirmed that the Yolngu had no interest in their land because the 'doctrine of communal native title ... does not form, and never has formed, part of the law of any part of Australia'. This entrenched *terra nullius* into Australian law as a 'legal fiction'. Everyone knew there were Aboriginal and Torres Strait Islander people, and that they had laws and customs, but the law created a fiction that they did not. This fiction was consistent with attempts to write out any recognition of Indigenous resistance and Indigenous attachment to land. Justice Blackburn could not change any of that. But in 1982 a group of Torres Strait Islander men started a long legal journey that ended a decade later with the decision in the *Mabo Case*.[8] This time, the High Court did what Justice Blackburn could not and changed Australian law by overturning the doctrine of *terra nullius* and finding that there was a native title interest that could survive in certain circumstances. In the leading judgment, Justice Brennan eloquently set out the extent to which the Australian legal system could tolerate overturning longstanding traditions such as *terra nullius*. Brennan was a humanitarian with a deep sympathy for Indigenous Australians. He said there should not be unquestioning adherence to law if that offended 'the values of justice and human rights'. It was not the common law but the acts of government that had taken land from Indigenous people. The law was not wrong but it had been incorrectly applied. It should have acknowledged native title; it did not. *Mabo* put that right.

The imagery of Australian law is a striking one. The white scaffolding cannot be touched and Indigenous recognition is only permissible to the extent that this framework is left in place. As legal academic Sandra Berns wrote, Brennan navigated a thin line between making the law just and not undermining property rights.[9] He articulated how far the law would go while he warned how much institutional change could be tolerated. We can acknowledge the law, lore, culture and connection to country of Indigenous people, so long as the structural framework of white Australian law is not damaged. In fact, if native title conflicts with any other property right, it is extinguished. Every other (non-Indigenous) property right remains intact. But overturning the legal fiction of *terra nullius*, and assuming that Australia was settled, still refused to acknowledge the Indigenous perspective that what began in 1788 was an invasion. Australian institutions and legal frameworks still reflected popular – white – narratives.

Twenty-five years after *Mabo*, the word 'invasion' remains extremely contentious for Australians. In the lead-up to the 2016 election, the ABC conducted an online survey, Vote Compass, on several key issues.[10] Of the first 200 000 responses, 71 per cent agreed with Indigenous people being recognised in the Constitution. However, on whether school textbooks should refer to the arrival of European colonists in Australia as an invasion of Aboriginal lands, only 45 per cent agreed and 41 per cent disagreed. Tensions emerged as the question moved from the general – constitutional recognition – to specifics. These debates are not about history but about the national narrative non-Indigenous people want to follow about the Indigenous people they have colonised. The debate has been acrimonious and polarising – black armband and white blindfold – and it leaves no room for shades of grey or competing narratives.

# *Bringing Them Home*: 1995 and after

There was a time when the removal of Aboriginal children was not a well-known part of Australian history. It is no longer possible to say that. When I was at school in the 1970s and 1980s, my classmates had never heard of removal; they did not know the policy had existed nor that it was so prevalent and its legacy so damaging to so many people. This changed first with the *Bringing Them Home* report, commissioned in 1995 by the then Attorney-General Michael Lavarch.[11] Released in 1997, the report contained powerful personal accounts of how the policy impacted on the lives of the children who were taken away and the parents who lost their children. We read about the prolonged mourning by parents and the extraordinary lengths they went to, trying to recover their children from state care. We read of children who suffered psychological, mental and physical abuse within institutions, within adoptive families or in workplaces. The accounts were harrowing, and it is still impossible to read them and not be affected by them. They show that you can make all the pretty legal and ideological arguments you like about why a policy was wrong and cruel, but nothing is more persuasive in evaluating its impact than the legacy it has left on the people subjected to it.

Although the Keating government commissioned the report, the Howard government received it. The official response was to say dismissively that only one in ten children were taken away, many were removed for their own good or at least removed with the best of intentions, and that the report was too emotive, using inappropriate terms such as 'cultural genocide'. It seemed to me that much of the response to the report was designed to detract from the powerful personal narratives within it. Saying 'it was only one in ten' used statistics to lessen the power of personal experience. It seemed almost necessary to play down the lived Indigenous experience – which the report captured so powerfully – in order to save a non-Indigenous audience from feeling embarrassment or shame about the evidence presented.

Of course, not every person removed by the policy had a bad experience. Many of the children grew up in loving homes. Some of them had been rescued from neglect. But it should be a concern that *any* child was abused or mistreated while under the care and protection of the state; it is callous to be dismissive of such treatment. The *Bringing Them Home* report included accounts of continual sexual abuse, physical punishment akin to torture, and humiliating psychological abuse. Children were told their parents were dead or did not want them, when that simply was not true. These things should never have happened and we should be concerned that they did.

For Indigenous people, this debate about how Australian history deals with the policy of removing Aboriginal children from their families was so hotly contested because it goes to the heart of the story Australians tell about their past. It is a struggle between two competing narratives about the way we tell Australian history – do we romanticise our past or do we acknowledge the mistakes we have made? History is not a single story. It is competing narratives, brought to life by different groups whose experiences are diverse and often challenge the dominant story a country seeks to tell itself. There are no absolute truths in history. It is a process, a conversation, a constantly altering story. As Inga Clendinnen reminds us in her book *True Stories*, 'To consolidate good history made out of true stories we need time, and peace, and we need the will. We also need to keep in mind that truth is a direction and an aspiration, not a condition'.[12]

## William Dawes, Bungaree and Barangaroo

As the philosopher Michel Foucault observed, the central issue in constructing a discourse is 'to discover who does the speaking, the positions and viewpoints from which they speak, the institutions which prompt people to speak about it and which store and distribute the things that are said'.[13] History is much more shades of grey than black and white. Among those who arrived with the First Fleet in 1788 was Lieutenant William Dawes.[14] An astronomer by training, he came ashore as an engineer and surveyor to build the colony, construct streets and survey the surrounding countryside. But he maintained his interest in the skies and began to study the stars from what is now known as Dawes Point. Although Indigenous people were cautious about entering the colony, many of them came to Dawes's hut. It was seen as a welcoming place, a safe haven where knowledge and friendship were shared.

Dawes was curious about this country and its Aboriginal people. He was a man of science who wanted to understand his new surroundings. He engaged with the Aboriginal people, particularly a young girl, Patyegarang, from whom he learned the local language and about the tides, the food, the medicines, Aboriginal perspectives and stories about the stars.[15] We know this because he kept a diary. Kate Grenville's novel *The Lieutenant* is inspired by the relationship between William Dawes and Patyegarang.[16] Grenville's hero, Daniel Rooke, describes his anticipation of what he might learn from this strange new land and its mysterious, elusive inhabitants: 'He was watching one universe in the act of encountering another'. Rooke had a colleague, Silk, whose 'impulse was to make the strange familiar', where Rooke's instinct was to 'enter the strangeness and lose himself in it'.

Like Rooke, Dawes approached Indigenous people with curiosity and an interest in coexistence. Dawes's views were not the norm, and they were soon thrown into stark contrast with those of his fellow colonists. As conflict increased between the First Peoples and the new arrivals, it became increasingly evident to the Aboriginal people that the colonists intended to stay. When Pemulwuy speared Phillip's gamekeeper, Phillip ordered several marines, including Dawes, to capture two Aboriginal men and cut off the heads of ten more. After intervention from senior officers, Phillip reduced this to the capture of six Aboriginal men and, if they could not be captured, they should be shot. Dawes refused to participate. He was arrested but, after discussions with Reverend Richard Johnson, agreed to take part. Fortunately, the expedition was a failure. It found no Aboriginal people. Dawes then publicly declared that he regretted taking part, a stance that affected his relationship with Governor Phillip. Dawes, who had dreamed of finding a life in Australia for himself, applied to stay in the colony, perhaps to become a farmer. Phillip agreed, but subject to conditions, including that Dawes apologise for his public comments condemning the punitive expedition. Dawes refused.

Dawes left the colony in 1791 for England. He then went to Sierra Leone, served as Governor there and was involved with the international anti-slavery movement. In 1799, he gave evidence before a House of Lords committee considering legislation to limit the slave trade. In 1813, he went to Antigua, where he was a correspondent of the Church Missionary Society and established schools for the children of slaves.

Dawes offers another way not only of viewing first contacts but also of thinking about what might have been. Australia would still have been colonised, but the colonisers' relationships with the land and with the Aboriginal people could have been very different had Dawes' approach of mutual respect and knowledge exchange prevailed. For Dawes, being close to Indigenous people deepened his understanding both of the world around him and of a common humanity. His approach is rarely celebrated, yet it is an alternative that is neither black armband nor white blindfold. He related to the Indigenous people with curiosity, respect and an appreciation of the richness of their knowledge. He tried to grasp their understanding of the world because he knew it would help deepen his own. His was a humanitarian approach that valued Indigenous perspectives, culture and knowledge. It envisaged a very different relationship between Indigenous people and other Australians. Today, it offers a pathway to an Australia that is not 'us' and 'them' but instead sees Indigenous culture as a central part of Australian culture. It could lead to an inclusive nationalism that celebrates diverse perspectives and experiences. Such an inclusive approach would not only improve relationships with Indigenous people but also improve the way we understand multicultural communities and other marginalised groups, particularly asylum seekers. Within this inclusive nationalism we could acknowledge that there is no one dominant national narrative but many concurrent, competing and conflicting stories that reflect the diverse backgrounds and perspectives within Australian society.

The curiosity that Dawes had about Indigenous cultural practices and technologies was matched by that of Indigenous people, who were fascinated by the clothes, skills and tools the invaders brought with them. Another Aboriginal figure who became prominent in the early colony was Bungaree. From the Broken Bay area, he was just 13 years old when the tall ships of the First Fleet sailed into Port Jackson. He watched this apocalypse play out among the tribes around him and, as he grew into adulthood, had to make his own decisions about how to navigate this new world. He was curious, intelligent and had a sense of humour. He would mimic governors and other authority figures. A generation behind Pemulwuy and Bennelong, he befriended Governor Macquarie. Earlier, he had sailed with Matthew Flinders on the circumnavigation of the continent from 1801 to 1803, acting as an interpreter with Aboriginal nations around the country – an experience that would have been richer for him than for the colonists, whose main interest was in mapping the coastline. But, while Bungaree developed contacts and connections with the colonists, he also retained influence in his own community. He tried to adopt customs he thought useful and to use the invaders' technology and skill to understand his own world better. He tried to find a way to adapt to his new world without losing his sense of identity and his Aboriginal heritage.

Indigenous women also had to find ways to navigate their place in society, in the new world in which they found themselves. Patyegarang took on the role of patient teacher and gentle mediator in her relationship with Dawes. Bennelong's wife, Barangaroo, did not emulate her husband's conciliatory relationship with the colonists and was vocal about her opposition. She refused to drink wine and to wear European clothes, angering her husband. She would attend Government House with nothing more than a slim bone in her nose for decoration. But although she was defiant in her own way, Barangaroo was navigating a future for her own people. She died in childbirth in Government House. She had chosen it as the place to give birth with the intention that – as was the way in her culture – the place of birth would give her child special rights and obligations to that place. It was an intentional decision to give her child some claim over the spaces the colonists were claiming for their own.

## Where we are at in 2017

For Indigenous people, the perennial questions posed by that moment of invasion in 1788 are about the best strategies for surviving it and determining how to assert Indigenous identity, culture and sovereignty as it faces assaults from the dominant culture every day. These continuing, two-and-a-quarter-century-old tensions lie beneath policy questions (Closing the Gap, dealing with incarceration, education, domestic violence, drugs and alcohol) and constitutional options (Recognise or Treaty or both). For the rest of Australia, there is the challenge of how the dominant national narrative – the story the nation tells itself – deals with the invasion moment. This question has become bogged down in the emotions of the 'invasion' or 'settled' debate. The stand-off gets in the way of a more sophisticated, nuanced and inclusive narrative. Unless and until we get that part of the story straight – finally – the other parts matter less.

Surely what William Dawes shows is that there have always been those who – even though the dominant narrative was entrenched – still saw another way. In those places of curiosity and exchange that Dawes explored, there was little room for guilt or shame, just as there was little room for arrogance or an innate sense of cultural superiority. Until we bury the myth that

Australia was 'settled', we can never become a country where all Australians see Indigenous history and culture as a key part of the nation's history and culture – and until we do that we will never have found a way to truly share this colonised country.

# 17

# Our most important war: The legacy of frontier conflict

PAUL DALEY

I know the spirits are out here. And when the wind starts to howl across the plain in great booming gusts, it might just be the sound of them crying. I've visited many massacre sites in Australia. But usually I've been in the company of a local Indigenous custodian, someone who rubbed their scent on my face and hands and chanted to warn the spirits that this white man comes in peace. While it feels like I'm anything but alone, I'm by myself in the long grass that is blowing sideways. All around, the fields shimmer in kaleidoscopic gold, russet, black and India green as the sun strobes through the storm clouds scudding across the sky. The rain arrives horizontally in icy needles, stinging my bare legs and arms as I plod around looking for the creek I'm assured is here somewhere. I'm vigilant for the prolific black snakes. It's a spring Saturday.

## Names are important

In contemplating the creek, I'd had in my mind a treacherous torrent running through a great black ravine, so imbued is this place with malevolence, right down to its name, Butchers Creek. But it's scarcely a creek at all – more a gentle furrow padded with grass and lichen through which a stream trickles. A little ramshackle goldmining town once sprang up near the creek but it has long ago ceased to be. The town was named Boonjie, an Indigenous word, after the creek whose banks had been a meeting place for countless thousands of years for a tribe of the Ngadjon rainforest people. The Ngadjon were a physically diminutive mob, perhaps because they thrived mainly on native plants and nuts in a place where protein, mostly tree kangaroo, was tough to bag. Thanks to the rainforest canopy that sheltered them they were also lighter skinned than the tribal people of the coastal plains and continental centre.

In 1887 white miners and 'black police' (Indigenous recruits from elsewhere who had little compunction about killing other Aboriginal people at the behest of white so-called settlers) massacred a big group of Ngadjon camped near Boonjie. This was a reprisal for the murder of a Swedish goldminer, Frank Paaske. Among the tablelands mining and pastoral community there was much pioneer boasting (some of it apocryphal) about the massacre. One settler, Fred Brown, detailed a 'dispersal', including the stake-out of the Aboriginal camp overnight. He told of shooting a man with his 'old Schneider rifle' ('makes a bigger hole leaving the body than on entering it') and of 'protecting' a Ngadjon boy who survived. By some accounts the child's name was Poppin Jerri. The child was apparently snatched from the hands of a black tracker about to dash the child's brains out against a tree. A few days later the little boy was given to a Scottish-born zoologist, Robert Grant, and his wife Elizabeth. Grant worked for the Australian Museum in Sydney. The Grants took the boy home with them and raised him – apparently on equal terms with Henry, their natural child.[1]

This hints at a story that Australian history has scarcely addressed: the widespread theft of Aboriginal and Torres Strait Islander children from their families on the colonial and post-Federation frontier. (Shirleene Robinson's book *Something Like Slavery?* tells some of the story and is an invaluable exception.)[2] Many black children were stolen before the forced removal of Aboriginal children became a mainstay of assimilationist policy in the 20th century. At least one Indigenous man – an elder known to his people as Narcha but named by the miners as Barry Clarke because he had worked for a successful miner and pioneer, George Clarke – was also spared. Narcha had five wives and many children. Still, the child went to the Grants, who had been working in the area on a field trip, because Elizabeth had apparently wished 'to get a little black boy'. The 'little black boy' was renamed Douglas Grant and sent to school in Sydney.

Meanwhile, the killers replaced the name Boonjie with Butchers Creek. Today the name Butchers Creek applies to the creek itself and to the small, largely non-Indigenous community around it, with its modest hall and school. The renaming of Boonjie is disquieting enough. But dozens, perhaps hundreds, of places across the continent have been named or renamed, not to conceal but to commemorate terrible acts of violence against Indigenous people. There is a Skull Creek in each of Gippsland, the Northern Territory, Western Australia and Queensland. There's a Massacre Bay in Victoria, a Massacre Waterfall in Borroloola, a Slaughterhouse Creek in New South Wales and another Butchers Creek in Victoria. There were massacres in each of them. Twelve places in Queensland (where colonial and post-Federation violence against Indigenous people was most pronounced) are named Skeleton Creek but official records fail to reveal how many of these names commemorate massacres.[3]

But back to that little watercourse on the Atherton Tablelands, where in 1887 the boy survived to become Douglas Grant and his people's creek was renamed not to commemorate those murdered but the very act of murdering them. Douglas Grant's life draws together the competing historical elements of the Australian national narrative. As an Indigenous person, he was removed from his family with extreme violence, served in the 1st Australian Imperial Force (AIF) and became a prisoner of war in Berlin. He was later an Aboriginal rights activist and semi-vagrant in Sydney and Melbourne. Through him – or, at least, through the boy Poppin Jerri – we have a way in to the story of the first big conflicts, the Frontier Wars, that raged across this continent after the initial east coast European contact in 1770 and the invasion in 1788. For what happened to Poppin Jerri's people at Butchers Creek was replicated in an unknown number of battles, skirmishes, guerrilla attacks and reprisals as the pastoral and mining frontier crept further north and west. These conflicts killed countless – because uncounted – Indigenous people. The deaths of police, soldiers, settlers, shepherds and convict labourers are more quantifiable; they were quantified because those doing the counting thought these deaths mattered.

## Counting the uncountable

It is conservatively estimated that there were 20 000 violent deaths of Aboriginal and Torres Strait Islander people nationally from 1788 until Coniston in the Northern Territory in 1928. This figure is used consistently by historians such as Henry Reynolds and John Connor, who have been at the vanguard of promoting cultural awareness about frontier war since the 1980s.[4] Sceptical historians have contested this figure, though not that of 2000 non-Indigenous combatants and bystanders (a ratio of some 10 to one).[5] More recent academic research indicates, however, that the fatalities figure might have been at least three times higher than 20 000. Indeed, the evidence suggests the true black–white ratio of frontier war deaths in Australia might have been 44 to one. Historians Raymond Evans and Robert Ørsted-Jensen have concluded that in Queensland alone at least 65 180 Indigenous people were killed from the 1820s to the early 1900s.[6] Considering Evans and Ørsted-Jensen focus just on Queensland, their findings have implications for the number of Indigenous Australians killed continent-wide. If Evans and Ørsted-Jensen are to be taken seriously (and on the basis of their research, first made public at the 2014 Australian Historical Association conference, they ought to be) that is another reason why Australia should engage in a mature discussion about the conflicts that raged across the frontier and perhaps cost some 65 000 lives in Queensland alone – more than the 61 000 Australian deaths in World War I, the conflict that has so embedded itself in Australian consciousness. If settler Australia is ever to deal properly with frontier conflict and its continuing legacy, that body-count comparison would be a good place to start.

Evans and Ørsted-Jensen scoured the remaining records of the Queensland Native Police Force and studied the prevalence of 'black police' barracks from 1859 to 1898 to determine the approximate number of patrols, contacts and killings, based on reported body counts:

> [W]e arrive at the sobering total of 41 040 Aborigines killed during 3420 official frontier dispersals across almost forty years of conflict. This mortality figure … is a mathematical and statistical projection, produced by cautiously sampling the fragmentary evidence left to us about the severe degree of destruction accompanying the long project of land dispossession in colonial Queensland. It is not and can never be a precisely accurate figure, nor is it a confidently absolute or maximal one. That number will never be known … Furthermore, let us be entirely clear about what we are claiming here. The 41 040 death rate does not represent anywhere near a full quotient of those who fell on the Queensland frontier. It is merely a Native Police statistic that does not even cover, at this point, official dispersal activities across the prior decade of 1849–59. These may well have accounted for another 3000–4000 deaths.[7]

The 41 040 number also excludes actions against Indigenous people carried out not by police but by settlers. The authors calculate that these incidents accounted for 43 per cent of the total number of clashes or approximately 2580 clashes, giving a total of 6000 clashes, police and settler. Evans and Ørsted-Jensen conclude that their body counts for Native Police and settlers 'amount to no less than 61 680 in 6000 attacks'. They add another estimated minimum of 3500 Indigenous and 1500 settler deaths for the 1850s to 'arrive at an aggregate of 66 680 killed' between the 1820s and early 1900s.[8]

Evans and Ørsted-Jensen's research confronts the received view that the Australian wars that matter – or even the only ones that happened – are the ones that were fought overseas. The authors know their research makes some of us feel uncomfortable. Massacre denialism among some Australians and the mainstream media has driven the authors towards conservative calculations. Still, they want 'to return to history the full ledger of those who, long ago, died protecting their sovereignty, their cultures, their home-lands and their peoples but whose deaths were more often hidden than acknowledged by a society that made furtiveness its watch-word'.[9]

The Evans–Ørsted-Jensen research bears directly on the themes of this collection of essays. Of course war is important, as one of the many influences on making Australians what we are, but this is not war as most of us have known it in the last century. Because the research indicates a frontier conflict death rate in Queensland alone that eclipses Australian fatalities in World War I, the authors effectively argue that the Great War was never the greatest war in Australian history. They quote with approval Henry Reynolds, who says what happened on the domestic frontier 'was clearly one of the few significant wars in Australian history and arguably the single most important one. For Indigenous Australia, it was their Great War'.[10]

## The silence

In his 1968 Boyer Lectures, anthropologist WEH Stanner called it the 'great Australian silence'. He was referring to the failure of a number of books to substantively address Australian Indigenous history, including frontier violence:

> It is a structural matter, a view from a window which has been carefully placed to exclude a whole quadrant of the landscape. What may well have begun as a simple forgetting of other possible views turned under habit and over time into something like a cult of forgetfulness practised on a national scale.[11]

There has been lumbering progress since Stanner's lectures almost half a century ago, not least among historians, even of the Centre Right. Writers of novels, narrative non-fiction, popular history, plays and screenplays have increasingly addressed the extreme violence meted out to Aboriginal and Torres Strait Islanders on the colonial frontier and later, down to Coniston in 1928, which remained for some people until quite recently a part of living memory.[12]

Indigenous Australia's enduring culture of oral history (often reflected in music, visual art and dance) records the violence of the frontier (and corroborates what happened) in no less detail than the written words of the white perpetrators. In *One Blood:*

*200 Years of Aboriginal Encounter with Christianity,* John Harris recounts the description by early anthropologist EM Curr of the colonial violence involving Indigenous people and invaders.[13] Curr said it would usually take up to a decade after a settler's occupation of land before traditional owners were let back in as visitors or to hunt nearby, during which time 'the squatter's party and the tribe live in a state of warfare'. Settlers would shoot 'down a savage now and then when opportunity offers, and calling in the aid of black police from time to time to avenge in a wholesale way the killing or frightening of stock off the run by the tribe'. More cattle would be speared, more Indigenous men shot down. 'In revenge', Curr said, 'a shepherd or stock-man is speared'. The violence would escalate with the introduction of the 'black police', officially the Native Police, a tragic, little-explored phenomenon among white historians of frontier justice, whereby rival tribesmen would be enlisted and militarised to slaughter other blacks. Curr explained how these men would be 'enlisted, mounted, armed, liberally supplied with ball cartridges and despatched to the spot under the Sub-inspector of Police'.

> Hot for blood, the black troopers are laid on the trail of the tribe; then follow the careful tracking, the surprise, the shooting at a distance safe from spears, the deaths of many of the males, the capture of the women, who know that if they abstain from flight they will be spared; the gratified lust of the savage, and the Sub-inspector's report that the tribe has been 'dispersed', for such is the official term used to convey the occurrence of these proceedings.

> When the tribe has gone through several repetitions
> of this experience and the chief part of its young men
> been butchered, the women, the remnant of the men and
> such children as the black troopers have not troubled
> themselves to shoot, are let in or allowed to come to the
> settler's homestead and the war is at an end. Finally a
> shameful disease is introduced and finishes what the
> rifle began.[14]

The stories about the massacring (and other terrible abuses) of Indigenous people are easy to find in the archives of major cultural institutions in Australia and Great Britain. The personal journals, diaries, letters, memoirs and, indeed, the published works of colonial and post-Federation officials, troops, police, farmers, miners and pioneering frontiersmen (and -women) are replete with accounts of battles with – and all too often reprisal massacres of – 'natives' who are invariably referred to as 'marauding', 'troublesome' or 'threatening'. Through the National Library of Australia's Trove, very old government records and digitised newspapers can easily be found. They recount in detail the violence described by Curr. Little probing is needed to uncover biographies of the white men – such as Mounted Constable George Murray, former Light Horseman and Gallipoli hero, overseer of the murder of 31 Aboriginal men, women and children at Coniston – responsible for the slaughter.[15]

Sometimes the blacks were simply hunted for sport or for 'trophy-ing'. Little imagination is required to decipher this malignant euphemism. The body parts – especially skulls – of Indigenous people were highly sought after in early Australia. Indigenous body parts are still being surrendered to organisations, such as the repatriation unit of the National Museum of Australia, that are mandated to return them, where possible, to their 'country'. In recent years the museum has housed body parts of as many as 600 individuals; other state museums have their own collections that cannot, for various reasons (including a lack of detail about precise provenance) be returned to country. There is ample proof that some Aboriginals and Torres Strait Islanders were hunted and killed merely so that parts of their bodies could be kept as curios. Bodies left at massacre sites became part of the collections of museums, medical research institutions and universities. Meanwhile, the bodies of Indigenous people who died in institutions were, barely cold, stolen and sold or given to other institutions.[16] The head of Onyong, the Ngambri chief, was turned into a sugar bowl and kept for years at a Tuggeranong homestead near Canberra. Other bodies were ransacked from sacred burial sites by men like George Murray Black, a farmer from Gippsland, who supplied countless skeletons to the Australian Institute of Anatomy, the University of Melbourne Medical School and many institutions in Europe.[17]

Early newspapers offer concurring accounts (chilling in their candour and boastful detail) of the organised killings of black men, women and children on the frontier. In the journals and diaries of the frontiersmen, meanwhile, what is disquieting is the detachment of the perpetrators, the purpose that bleeds into their words as they describe the killing, the sense that they are involved merely in the extermination of subhumans. None more so than the memoir of Korah Halcombe Wills (1828–96), a former Mayor of Bowen and Mackay in Queensland, who reminisced at the end of his life about dispersing Aboriginal people in the mid-1860s.[18] His account makes difficult reading, as he boasts of massacring

Aboriginal people and chopping a man into pieces to keep as trophies. (Wills was a butcher by trade and later a publican.) He found this work to be 'a horrible repulsive thing' but he persisted because 'I was not going to be done out of any pet specimens of humanity'. He stuffed the body parts into his saddlebags to take home.

Wills fancied a live trophy as well, so 'from out of one of these mobs of Blacks I selected a little girl with the intention of civilising, and one of my friends thought he would select a boy for the same purpose'. Wills recalled that

> my little protégée of a girl ... rode on the front of my
> saddle [to Bowen] and crying nearly all the way ... I
> took compassion on her and decided to take her home
> and bring her up with my own children which I did, and
> even sent her to school with my own.

The child died. This saddened Wills, though not as much as the death of a favourite horse.[19]

The archives contain a story, too, of children stolen at the sites of Indigenous mass murders, from Appin in 1816 – during this operation Governor Lachlan Macquarie ordered that his troops 'select and secure' 18 children, aged between four and six, for his 'Native Institution at Parramatta' – to Boonjie, soon to become Butchers Creek in 1887, and well beyond to the stolen generations of the 20th century.[20] Which brings us back to Poppin Jerri, the little boy who survived the Butchers Creek massacre to grow up as Douglas Grant, an Aboriginal man who spoke with a Scottish burr, thanks to his adoptive parents and his education at Sydney's Scots College. Grant was conscious of his colour while growing up but, raised in a white adoptive family – although he never inherited and he ended up on the street – he lost all contact with his culture.[21] Grant enlisted in the AIF in mid-1916, just as Australian casualties on the Western Front were mounting. He was among 400 to 1000 Indigenous men accepted as volunteers, despite the regulations that recruits were to be of 'substantially European descent'.

## Belated recognition?

The Australian War Memorial embraces the war service of Indigenous Australians who bypassed the racist regulations and fought overseas for Australia.[22] Men like Douglas Grant have been used to support a theme that, in the army, many Aboriginal and Torres Strait Islander men experienced equality for the first time, although they were not treated as equals in civilian Australia, where most could not vote, were paid less than non-Indigenous workers, had been evicted from traditional lands, and were not yet counted as citizens. After demobilisation, though, many of these men returned home to find that their children, along with their wages, had been taken by the so-called protectors. Settler blocks for white veterans – blocks denied to the 'black Diggers' – were sometimes carved out of ancestral lands. Many returned servicemen's clubs would not admit black veterans, and some black returned men were also denied appropriate repatriation and medical support.

The War Memorial holds that Grant, whose life was partly the inspiration for the Wesley Enoch play *Black Diggers*, is an exemplar of such positive experience.[23] But that is far from true. Grant was adopted into a white European-Australian family, raised with a commensurate sense of entitlement and accepted, due to his adoptive parentage, as a citizen. It was not until he attempted to enlist that racism stung him. He was initially rejected because of his colour. In May 1917, when he was wounded at Bullecourt and captured, his colour once again determined his fate. He was imprisoned in Berlin with the black soldiers of the Empire – mostly men from Africa and the Indian subcontinent. The Germans, no less attracted than the British to the voodoo 'science' of eugenics and phrenology (whereby a man's intelligence and personality could supposedly be determined by his head shape) measured Grant's skull and fashioned a replica in alabaster. Grant, whose broad nose, distinctive brow and shiny skin distinguished him from all other prisoners, was given the run of the city. It was assumed, correctly, that he would be too conspicuous to attempt escape. This must have had an upside for Grant, a cultured man who loved music, art (he won competitions in Australia and was a fine draftsman) and, most of all, museums.

After the war, Grant returned to Australia disenchanted. He was in and out of work, often homeless and battling with alcoholism. He advocated for the rights of 'black Diggers' and he became, especially after Coniston in 1928, a vociferous campaigner for Indigenous rights generally, highlighting the history of massacres across the country and urging greater protection for Aboriginal and Torres Strait Islander people. He died in 1951 at La Perouse, on the northern headland of Botany Bay, land continuously occupied by the Kameygal for tens of thousands of years.

Black Diggers, the coloured warriors of the 1st AIF, make quite a story for the War Memorial. But the memorial, its Council heavy with former military personnel and writers of traditional military history, refuses to countenance telling the story of the warriors who died at the hands of soldiers, settlers, militias and black police after invasion in 1788.[24] The memorial has, I believe, occasionally used the black Diggers narrative as a fig leaf to distract from its intransigence on the Frontier Wars. Some years ago, when I put questions to the memorial on its refusal to commemorate frontier conflict, the response directed me to its detailed stories about Indigenous service personnel from all other Australian wars. The Australian Defence Force also uses the history of Indigenous service – in uniform – to attract new Indigenous recruits.[25] Many people officially associated with the memorial deny that frontier conflict was 'war', even though numerous settlers, as well as British commanders like Governor Macquarie, called it such.[26] The *Australian War Memorial Act 1980* clearly allows the memorial to tell the combat story of military forces of the Crown raised in Australia before and after the establishment of the Commonwealth, but it chooses not to do so.[27] Opponents of frontier war 'recognition' by the memorial – the current director, Brendan Nelson, included – argue that no Australian-raised army units waged war against black people. Prominent historians say this is wrong and point to, among other units, the Military Mounted Police, raised by the British Army in Sydney in 1825, which participated in numerous attacks on Indigenous people, including at Slaughterhouse Creek in 1838.[28]

And then, of course, there are the infamous black police – military units raised solely from men who were born and bred on this continent and whose antecedents can be traced back tens of thousands of years. They were the police involved in massacres like that in 1887 when Boonjie became Butchers Creek and Poppin Jerri became Douglas Grant. Narcha to his Ngadjon people (Barry Clarke to the killers) lived on after the massacre until 1903, surviving, it is said, another mass murder at Butchers Creek. Upon his death, he was mummified in a traditional manner and remained, unburied, with his rainforest people. In 1904–05 a German-born Darwinian anthropologist, Hermann Klaatsch, travelled the Atherton Tablelands to 'attack the problem of the origin of Australian blacks, and of their import in relation to the whole development of mankind'.[29] He stole Narcha and several other mummified adults and children. Klaatsch shipped Narcha to Berlin, where he was displayed prominently in a glass case at the Museum of Ethnology in the Prinz-Albrecht-Strasse. There is every chance that the distinctive captive Douglas Grant, once Poppin Jerri, free to roam Berlin, saw Narcha there behind glass, having been separated from him at a massacre at Butchers Creek 30 years earlier. If so, this reunion held a tragic poignancy. For Narcha, it is said, was in all likelihood Poppin Jerri's father.

# 18

# King, Queen and country: Will Anzac thwart republicanism?

MARK McKENNA

On the morning of 16 February 1954, Charles Bean and his wife Effie drove along Canberra's Anzac Parade towards the Australian War Memorial. As their official car approached the building, crowds of onlookers stood several lines deep on the roadside. Climbing the steps to the memorial, Bean 'could see the photographers and broadcasters above the entrance'. Inside, he walked past the solemn rows of 'widows, mothers, and children of men who had lost their lives'. Above him, the memorial cloisters were packed with 'veterans'. The significance of this moment was not lost, least of all on Bean. The memorial he had first imagined as a war correspondent on the Western Front in 1916 and that finally came to fruition in 1941 had never before been visited by a reigning British monarch. Now, having arrived half an hour early, he was to lead the Queen and Prince Philip through the memorial and introduce the royal couple to members of the memorial's Board of Management.[1]

Bean was apprehensive. Although he had rehearsed his lines and the appropriate protocol many times before – only when the previous couple had finished shaking hands with the Duke could he introduce the next couple – he was afraid he would embarrass himself. 'I had been very anxious about the task of presenting board members – in the fluster I would be likely to stumble or hesitate over the names, ranks, and titles or even forget them.' The waiting seemed interminable. Finally, a luminously pallid Queen, wearing 'a primrose frock with a small hat' and her reliably wooden consort, Prince Philip, conspicuously clad in 'naval white', stepped out into Canberra's glaring late summer light. 'They extended their hands', Bean wrote, 'and we remembered to shake, or rather hold, them lightly as the shaking of hands so many times is apt to bruise them. I did not see Eff make her curtsey as I had to get round to my position, but friends told us that she made it very well'.

> [Once the proceedings were underway] all trace of
> nervousness or self-consciousness vanished ... partly
> because [of] the girlish Queen standing beside me with
> her natural manner so like one or other of our own
> nieces, and partly because one's whole attention was
> concentrated upon making the visit interesting to her.

But I noticed that during the presentations, as soon as the lady of each couple had moved on from her to shake hands with the Duke, her little gloved hand came up as quickly as the arm of a railway signal to shake hands with the next board member.

Within a matter of minutes, Bean had gone from nervous colonial to father figure. He realised that the Queen had her own protocol anxieties to manage. Laying the wreath at the stone of remembrance, she asked him tentatively, 'How do I lay it? Do we just lay it against the stone?' Nor was she in need of Bean's tutoring. Approaching the Anzac galleries, he offered her some basic historical instruction: 'I suspect your Majesty knows that to us the landing at Anzac is regarded almost as the Battle of Hastings in England'. 'Yes I realise that', she replied bluntly. If Bean was sentimental – he described the 'grey headed diggers' waving to the Queen 'as if they were greeting a pal' – he was also conscious of the immense distance between them. 'The Queen always kept a slight reserve between me and herself – broken only by one or two flashes.' The reserve Bean felt from Her Majesty might equally have been expressed from his side. Although he was not a royalist – throughout his life he had repeatedly refused offers of a knighthood and his loyalty, first and foremost, was to those who had established the 'character of Australian men' in the eyes of the world – he had become a player in an episode of a particularly Australian ritual: linking fealty to the monarch with a national legend of death on foreign fields.

## 'Flesh of the British'

Although the imperial dimensions of the Anzac legend have largely been forgotten today, the presence of British royalty on Australian soil had long bolstered the foundational connection between Anzac and Empire. Even before Australian soldiers landed at Anzac Cove in 1915, the visit of Prince George, Duke of Cornwall and York (later King George V), and his wife Mary in 1901 had helped cement the bond between blood sacrifice to the Empire and fealty to the Crown. After opening Australia's first federal Parliament in Melbourne, the royal couple proceeded to Sydney, where the Duke presented medals to the officers and men of the New South Wales contingents who had returned from fighting in the Boer War. The 'Ode of Welcome', composed for the occasion and sung by a choir 4000-strong, proclaimed that Australia had 'fought for the Empire' and 'mingled [its] blood with the best'. 'We are flesh of the British', the choir proclaimed in unison, 'and bone of the British bone!'[2]

For a geographically isolated federation such as Australia, blooding in battle was the ultimate proof of the right to belong to a global British community. The script for Gallipoli was written decades before the event came to pass. And, when the war finally ended in 1918 with the loss of more than 61 000 Australian lives, the Anzac legend was quickly embedded in the fabric of Australia's commemorative culture through a succession of royal visits. Edward, Prince of Wales ('the Digger Prince') arrived to a dumbstruck Australian audience in 1920 and stayed for weeks. He spoke at Parliament House in Melbourne, proclaiming that Australia had finally 'won her spurs in the great ordeal of battle [and] taken her place in the councils of nations'. Everywhere

His Royal Highness travelled, returned men were prominently choreographed in public events. Reviewing 10 000 returned soldiers at Sydney's Centennial Park, the Prince was aware that among the crowd of onlookers were men who had fought in the Crimean War, the Indian Mutiny, the Sudan and the Boer War. Each commemoration flushed out the survivors from previous wars and implied that national communion could only truly occur through sacrifice on the battlefield. Journalists described Diggers, who remembered the Prince fraternising with the Australian Imperial Force on the Western Front, shouting out as he moved through Sydney's streets, 'How's this to the Somme?' A handful of crippled veterans reportedly waved their crutches in feverish adulation.[3] Throughout the carnival of the Prince's visit, in public speeches and press reports, the erection of a militarist national mythology mattered far more than learning from the folly of war. If the nation was 'born' in battle, implicitly it could only be reborn through participation in future conflicts; the democratic achievements of Australia before the war constantly gave way to sagas of blood sacrifice.

## Anzac Day and royalty

According to the speeches of visiting royals in the early 20th century, the foundation of the new Commonwealth's democracy was not to be found in the history of Federation but in the egalitarian ritual of the Anzac Day parade. During the 1927 royal tour, Prince Albert, Duke of York (later King George VI) and his wife Elizabeth (later the Queen Mother) presided over the Anzac Day ceremony in Melbourne, which was widely described as the high point of their visit. Nearly 30 000 ex-servicemen 'fell in' to march through the city's streets, with tram conductors marching along-side judges. As one observer remarked, the march was 'a vindication of democracy'. The 'rhythmically flowing column of men … were marching past a King's son, the son of the King for whom they had fought … and in so doing had made Australia a nation'. After Sir John Monash implored the crowd to 'Keep Anzac Day sacred', the Duke 'made one of the most emotional speeches of the tour'. 'They gave their all for their King and Empire', he declared, 'let us [emulate their example] and hand down to the children who come after us those traditions of loyalty, fortitude, and devotion to duty'.[4]

Little more than two weeks later, speaking after opening Parliament House in Canberra, Albert devoted scant time to the men and women who had forged Federation, preferring instead to beseech Australians to listen 'to the voices of the noble army of the dead' and 'march in step with them towards the … ideals for which they died'.[5] Departing the country from Fremantle, he returned to this well-worn theme in his farewell message: 'That loyalty to the British ideals for which Throne and Empire stand found its highest expression in the commemoration of Anzac Day, at which it was our privilege to be present'.[6]

To contemplate these words in the early 21st century is to be reminded of the dramatic change that has occurred in the meaning and significance of Anzac Day in recent years, one that has seen 25 April transformed from the highest expression of loyalty to the British Empire to a more inward-looking, nation-defining myth that reveals the country's 'sense of self' and occupies an 'eternal place in the Australian soul'.[7] Throughout World War II and well into the late 20th century, the Anzac legend remained tethered to the Empire through the reigning monarch's Anzac

Day message, which harped on imperial unity in the face of totalitarian aggression and stressed the longevity of the imperial connection and the depth of common feeling in the new British Commonwealth. As the term 'Anzac' was gradually extended to include those who fought not just in the Great War but in all our wars, Australian politicians, newspapers, and military and community leaders echoed the reigning monarch's sentiments on Anzac Day, extolling the 'indestructible strength of an Empire' and the 'military prowess' of Australia's 'muscular grim-faced veterans', and providing proof that 'this offshoot of Britain in the South Seas has a fighting tradition which it will strive desperately to uphold'.[8]

Pining for the presence of royal flesh and blood on Australian soil, state and federal governments occasionally invented the atmosphere of a royal tour in order to buttress the imperial theatre of Anzac Day. In 1948, when the British actor Sir Laurence Olivier visited Australia, he was astonished to find that he had taken on 'a quasi Royal role'. (His wife Vivien Leigh, Scarlett O'Hara in *Gone with the Wind*, took the part of consort.) Olivier's many appearances in kingly Shakespearean roles had seduced Australian officials into thinking he was blessed with the royal touch. Delivering speeches on official occasions, Olivier even took the salute at the Anzac Day march in Canberra and read Charles Bean's 'Anzac Requiem' (composed in 1944) at the War Memorial's dawn service.[9] The text Olivier read so eloquently that day referred specifically to the New Zealand, Indian and British divisions who had fought with the Australians at Anzac Cove, as well as at the more recent battles in the Middle East, North Africa, Malaya and Papua New Guinea, in which Australians had died with Americans and 'loving friends in our

Mother Country'. Bean's text highlighted the contribution of Australia's 'women's services' and concluded by remembering the 'peaceful millions in prostrated Europe, in defiant Greece, Russia and China ... [and] every man, woman and child who, in those crucial hours, died so that the lights of freedom and humanity might continue to shine'.

Bean's requiem was at once Australian, imperial and remarkably internationalist. In 2015, when a version of Bean's words was circulated by government authorities as part of a kit sent to schools in preparation for the Anzac centenary, they were suggested for use as 'an introduction to an Anzac ceremony'. By now, however, Bean's original text had been adapted. Aside from New Zealand, there was no mention of the contribution of any other nation's armed forces. Gone was specific mention of the Indians at Anzac Cove, our 'loyal friends among the people of New Guinea', and the American contribution during World War II. Russia and China politely disappeared. The British were nowhere to be found. All other nations were reduced to our 'staunch friends and allies'. The war dead were now imagined exclusively as Australian, servants of our 'splendid heritage' who 'adorn our nation's history'. What was originally Bean's powerful attempt to place Australia's military contributions in their full international context had by 2015 become a patriotic hymn.[10]

The point in the late 20th century at which the imperial foundations of the Anzac legend were dismantled is difficult to isolate because the process was slow and incremental. But reading the Queen's official speeches since her first visit in 1954 (a task which requires considerable perseverance) at least makes it possible to observe the long moment of the Empire's vanishing. When Queen Elizabeth II stepped ashore at Farm Cove in February 1954 it was clear that she saw her own family's connection with Australia primarily through the prism of the country's shared sacrifice in two world wars. The need to mesh the Anzac legend with loyalty to Britain was felt not only on Australia's side but from the monarch's perspective as well. Opening the new forecourt at Melbourne's Shrine of Remembrance, Elizabeth reminded her audience of her family's connection with the memorial. 'My grandfather, King George the Fifth, wrote these words in the King's book which is now in the Shrine: "Let their names be forever held in proud remembrance". My uncle, the Duke of Gloucester, dedicated the shrine itself on Armistice Day.' Time and again, she stressed that the bond between her and her Australian people – the loyalty that was 'not a mere form of words' – was given its most powerful expression through the 'grievous ordeal' of two world wars.

Visiting Australia four years later, the Queen Mother reinforced her daughter's sentiments by insisting that 'Australia first impressed the world at Anzac'. The monarchical connection and the Anzac legend walked hand in hand, repeatedly grounding the narrative of the nation's foundation in the performance of Australian soldiers on British battlefields overseas. As the Queen remarked during her visit in 1963, 'every ex-serviceman knows that when there is serious work to be done, Diggers stick together in a common loyalty'. Australians, it seemed, could only find their true identity by becoming Anzacs in civilian dress.

While the Queen's Anzac Day message appeared on the front page of many newspapers throughout the 50th anniversary of Gallipoli in 1965, by the 1970s this practice had declined. Throughout that decade and into the 1980s, the Queen continued to depict the Anzacs as 'the first to fight for freedom against tyranny and oppression', although, increasingly, the emphasis was on 'courage', 'duty' and 'values', which were now shorn of their earlier imperial baggage. 'Anzac', Elizabeth asserted in 1970, 'denotes valour in Europe and Africa, in the jungles and mountains and paddy fields of Asia'. Gradually, imperial themes became less prominent in her portrayal of Anzac at the same time as they disappeared more generally from her public addresses in Australia. As the idea of Australia as a British society slowly collapsed, the monarchical connection needed to find a new rhetoric of attachment and allegiance if it was to survive. Similarly, the Anzac legend, threatened as it was by the politics of the new social movements and the critique of an emerging generation with little direct experience of war, needed distance from traditional themes of imperial loyalty if it was to endure. Speaking in the Commonwealth Parliament in 1986, the Queen acknowledged this change herself:

> Whenever I am here ... I see a growing sense of identity and a fierce pride in being Australian. So it is right that the Australia Act has severed the last of the constitutional links between Australia and Britain ... [A]nachronistic constitutional arrangements have disappeared – but the friendship between two nations has been strengthened and will endure.[11]

Only one more anachronism remained to be removed. New themes had begun to emerge in the Queen's speeches – multiculturalism and immigration, Indigenous Australians and rural life – which for the most part blended seamlessly with old verities such as material progress to articulate a more contemporary conception of the monarchical bond. By the bicentenary of British settlement in 1988, the Queen's Anzac Day address, delivered in Hobart, prefigured many of the sentiments that would characterise the reinvention of the Anzac legend in the 1990s and beyond:

> [We should always remember] the debt we owe to the men and women who served their country in order that Australia could remain free from tyranny and oppression. They fought to preserve the things they valued most, their families, their future and their ideas of freedom, justice and fair play … Anzac Day does not seek to commemorate any material values. The costs of war cannot be counted in monetary terms alone. Nor does Anzac Day extol victories, or boast of conquests. Rather, it shines a light on the greatness of the human spirit … [E]ach Anzac Day when the Last Post sounds … it is a call of awakening and rededication, to remind us of the standards for which we should all strive when we are called upon to do our duty.

The specifics of imperial campaigns were omitted. No distinction was made between one war and the next. Laced in thinly veiled allusions to Christian teachings on love and redemption, the assumption of the Anzac legend into even more unearthly realms was almost complete. Over the next two decades, remembering war would increasingly become an exercise in spiritual nourishment. Bow the head. Be moved. Feel more Australian. And, touched by 'the Anzac spirit', walk on into the blinding light of the next war.

## Anzac takes on a nationalistic tinge

After a decade of fierce and largely unresolved debate over the dispossession of Indigenous Australians (in the lead-up to the bicentenary of settlement), the growing sense of pride 'in being Australian' that the Queen identified in 1986 had by the early 1990s turned to less problematic and more distant soil: Anzac Cove. The shedding of imperial baggage from the Anzac legend was given added force by Paul Keating's Unknown Australian Soldier speech in 1993.[12] ('He is all of them. And he is one of us … [R]eal nobility and grandeur belong not to empires and nations but to the people on whom they, in the last resort, always depend.') Keating's successor John Howard's decade-long crusade (1996–2007) to establish Anzac as the nation's core foundational narrative was also driven by the emergence of the Indigenous history and politics that had so effectively undermined the myth of peaceful British settlement from 1788.[13] The Empire, now tainted and inglorious, disappeared from Anzac at the same time as it was politely withdrawn from the rhetoric of national belonging more generally. The history of invasion and dispossession that had gnawed at the heart of the bicentenary celebrations and would later haunt the centenary of Federation in 2001 could not threaten the Anzacs. Unlike the illegitimate history of settlement or British constitution-making on Australian soil, stories of the Anzacs' courage and sacrifice could give birth to an *unblemished*, exclusively Australian nation.

Whether the all-pervasive nature of the new, Empire-free Anzac legend in contemporary Australia will have any bearing on the future prospect of an Australian republic is difficult to tell. The 2015 centenary of Anzac may well prove to be the legend's apogee. A culture saturated in Anzac mythology can only exist for so long before people recoil from its suffocating piety and begin to question the endless parade of speeches and media features that claim to pass for history. But at one profound level, Anzac's grip on *affective* expressions of Australian identity speaks directly of the challenges facing Australian republicans today. As Australians once found mystery and spiritual communion through their allegiance to the British monarch – a depth of attachment that was almost beyond human expression – they find similar virtues in Anzac today: something sacred, immaterial and gloriously irrational that binds them as a people and transports them beyond the everyday like no other national myth can. For the majority of Australia's history, it was only the birth, visit, marriage or death of a British monarch that witnessed similar outpourings of national emotion. When news of Edward VII's death reached Sydney in 1910, reports in the city's press described thousands of people united in their grief:

> Looking down and outwards from the top of one of the highest towers in the city, everywhere were limp and melancholy half-masted flags … The people everywhere seemed quieter, and … there appeared to be a tendency to cluster into groups. There was only one thing talked of. And there were no differences of opinion … Everyone was speaking of the dead King, and everyone was speaking solemnly, regretfully, and appreciatively.[14]

In Sydney, the Stock Exchange closed and the news of the King's death was written on the blackboard; men filed past silently, taking their hats off. On the street, many people wore black ties, shop windows were draped in strips of black cashmere and, on the day of the King's funeral, it appeared that the entire nation was in mourning. It was a time, said the Reverend WG Taylor, when 'silence was more eloquent than words'.[15]

The commemoration of Anzac today evinces similar moments of mass emotional resonance – the evocation of the sacred, the silent parades and the communion of millions through shared devotion to one national creed. As Dr Brendan Nelson, director of the Australian War Memorial, told the National Press Club in September 2013, 'the Australian War Memorial, in my view, represents the soul of our nation. Almost two million Australian men and women who've worn the uniform of our three services over 100 years, and 102,700 names on the bronze role [sic] of honour'.[16] The 'Anzac spirit' has effectively replaced Britishness as Australia's defining myth of civic attachment. It also represents the people's deepest expression of belonging to the nation. Ironically, the myth that began in blood sacrifice to the British Empire has become post-imperial Australia's national day. While members of the British royal family still troop through the Australian War Memorial, their visits captured in framed photographs – Prince Harry in uniform submitting cheerfully to 'selfies' with teenage girls – and on Facebook, Flickr and Instagram, they are treated as celebrities rather than royalty.[17]

## Weighing it up

Since the modern Australian republican movement began in 1991, the argument for a republic has been predominantly couched in terms of severance and minimal change – the removal of constitutional monarchy (the last 'anachronism') – and its replacement with an Australian head of state ('one of us'). Among the political class there is widespread consensus that the republic is a 'second-order issue'. The nation waits in vain for a political leader to champion the cause in the way Labor Prime Minister Paul Keating did in the early 1990s. Although a recent surge in the membership of the Australian Republican Movement is encouraging, a popular movement remains elusive. In simple terms, the republic does not cut deeply. It does not 'move' or 'connect' with a large enough number of people to force politicians to act. Instead, it waits in suspended animation for the Queen to die.

The questions raised for republicans by the recent rise of the Anzac legend are fundamental: can popular attachment to the idea of an Australian republic come from *severance* from the monarchy alone? Can a fully independent and republican Australia – a new 'sense of self' – emerge merely from the collapse of old loyalties? Or does the promise of a republic ask something more from us as citizens? Where is the republic's moral, civic and political compass? What does it have to say about the promise of a new settlement with Indigenous Australians? What of our attachment to the land and to one another? What new civic and national ideals will guide its implementation? And how is it possible to see the republic's promise of a shift in national consciousness when the arguments for its coming are targeted so narrowly? If Republic Day is ever to rival Anzac Day, Australians will need to discover a new way of speaking about the prospect of change, one that finds the courage to imagine that national dignity and constitutional renewal will come not from the removal of monarchy alone but from within.

# 19

# Australia's tug of war: Militarism versus independence

ALISON BROINOWSKI

Settler Australia had war in its genes. The colonies were founded by British military officers at a time when Britain was at war; a succession of these officers became governors. The Queen's subjects were expected to go to war for Britain and, when the Australian colonies were asked to supply troops to oppose Britain's enemies, individual volunteers and regiments obligingly did so. They fought in wars against Russians in Crimea, mutineers in India, Mahdists in the Sudan, Zulus and Boers in South Africa, Boxers in China, and Māori in New Zealand. As well, the colonists soon began waging their own Frontier Wars, in which more than 30000 – perhaps more than 60000 – Indigenous people were killed. (See Paul Daley's chapter 17 in this book.)

From Federation on, Australia sent troops to ten more wars, where the enemy was always decided by Britain or the United States, and in only one of which (World War II) Australia was directly threatened. Federation was not designed or intended to transform Australia into an independent nation with its own foreign and defence policies. Each state had a governor, and the governor-general was Commander-in-Chief. Although Britain encouraged the training of an Australian army, it resisted until 1909 Australia's wish to have its own navy.

Wars fought for Britain were a formative experience for the young nation, but not one that inclined it towards independence. A strand in our history labelled 'independent Australia' did exist in this period, although many settler Australians were what historian Henry Reynolds has called unquestioning 'adjunct imperialists'. Nonetheless, vigorous debates took place in the colonial parliaments about these early wars.[1] Plebiscites were held and protests occurred against conscription. Successive Australian leaders from John Dunmore Lang, Andrew Inglis Clark and HB Higgins to Gough Whitlam and Malcolm Fraser (after his retirement as prime minister) questioned the wisdom of military expeditions.[2] Some men and women who survived the wars marched with medals and pride while others muttered warnings to the young about repeating the mistake of going to war. Yet wars were so recurrent that, in spite of the loss of members of almost every family, schoolboys obediently joined cadet corps, youths did national service, and older men unquestioningly signed up as reservists.

War is often claimed – by those who applaud it – to have enabled Australia to 'come of age'. Just as childhood experiences condition individual adult behaviour, recurrent wars have been effective in shaping the attitudes of today's Australian nation. But considering the dismal results of most of our wars, successive Australian leaders seem not to have gained maturity or judgment from them. Instead of war contributing to our getting of wisdom, the Australian tendency to mutely accept armed conflict as inevitable or necessary has increased to the point where, in the 21st century, war's purpose and outcome is less vigorously questioned, and the value of the ANZUS alliance is almost unchallenged.

This chapter considers the lengthening list of Australia's wars. It suggests that Australia is increasingly disposed towards shaping the world with armed force – even as our leaders claim our country is a 'good global citizen' – and it asks how this militaristic trend can be reversed. It sees the fragile strand of independence in our history being overwhelmed by the militaristic strand, with the increasing support of both major political parties.

## British and American wars

Conservative Australian leaders have always preferred subservience to autonomy. Australia's British Empire loyalists endorsed their governments' devotion to Queen and country, particularly when war was imminent. Republicans and egalitarians, on the other hand, resented Australians being called up to fight for Britain; they agreed with Dunmore Lang that continental defence was paramount and that Australian foreign and defence policy should be 'national rather than imperial'.[3] The nascent Australian character was caught in a metaphorical tug of war between these two teams, representing imperialism and militarism on one side and nationalism and independence on the other. As soldiers were waved off with bands and flags and streamers to fight somewhere in the world, militarism progressively gained ascendancy over independence.

Questions – why and against whom Australians were going to fight – were swept aside by Empire loyalist politicians. Britain chose Australia's enemies and where we should fight them. Fortifications intended for defence against Germans, French and Russians still clutter Australia's coastline as derelict reminders of Britain's choices. Australia at the turn of the 20th century accepted that Boxers in China and Boers in South Africa were its enemies; the Japanese were allies before World War I but enemies in World War II; Russia at different times was ally and enemy. In the Kellogg–Briand Pact of 1928 all the major powers renounced the use of war for the settlement of disputes but by then the militarist habit was ingrained and Australia did not invoke the pact to avoid further wars. When Britain in 1931 offered its senior dominions the option, under the Statute of Westminster, to take control of their external affairs and defence, Australia declined. Despite Britain's manifest incapacity and unwillingness to defend Australia, our passports continued until 1984 to describe Australians as British subjects, more than ten years after Britain had stopped giving preference to the Commonwealth in trade and had joined the European Common Market.

In 1945, Australia was among 51 signatories to the United Nations Charter, which our External Affairs Minister, HV Evatt, helped draft and which prohibited the use of force in international relations, except for self-defence against imminent attack or in response to a resolution of the UN Security Council. But this did not eliminate what the charter's preamble called 'the scourge of war'. Rather, it helped do the opposite, leading to undeclared wars, including those in the Indian subcontinent, South-East Asia, Indochina, Korea, the Balkans, Africa and the Middle East. By not declaring wars, governments evaded the provisions of the charter and other rules and conventions that might constrain them. Certainly, the wars in Korea (1950–53), Kuwait (1990–91) and Afghanistan (2001–14) were the subject of Security Council resolutions. But now nations, including Australia, increasingly fight in undeclared wars waged by the United States or in wars against rebel militia. Australia's allies have used cluster bombs and drones to attack individuals and communities unaccountably and with impunity, oblivious to the prospect that, when similar attacks are made on the West in the future, none of us will be able to invoke our respect for international law or 'good international citizenship'.

The Australian government today, just as in 1901, can deploy military force without consulting Parliament, without any debate on the progress of a war or when the war should end. Constitutional or statutory provisions do not constrain the executive, giving a prime minister virtually free rein to exercise the 'privilege' that traditionally belonged to the sovereign.[4] The Constitution (section 61) empowers the governor-general to declare war, but only on the advice of the prime minister. The solicitor-general should certify to the governor-general that this advice is legally correct. Since 2003 prime ministers have bypassed this practice and convention, and committed Australian forces to several disastrous wars – because they can. In 2016, the Attorney-General was able to bypass the Solicitor-General.[5]

World War II was the last of Australia's declared wars and the last war the United States and Australia as allies can claim to have won (apart from Iraq War I in 1991, where Australia provided limited support for Kuwait against Iraq's invasion). This record shows ANZUS is an expensive insurance policy and a poor return on investment in national security. Faith in ANZUS simply ignores repeated statements by US leaders that America would defend Australia only in pursuit of its own interests.[6] But Australians have continued, whether out of sentiment, pious hope or years of conditioning, to support the American alliance; polls show an increase in our irrational confidence that America will protect us.[7]

## Australian wars

Australians have fought in 16 wars, half of them in Asia, but only once in defence of the continent itself against imminent invasion from Asia. This formative experience has meant that one Asian country after another has been identified as an enemy of Australia – China, Korea, Indonesia, Japan, Vietnam – but the identification has always been foisted on us by our allies. Another consequence has been Australia's bellicose image in parts of Asia. The first Australians many people in Asian countries over several generations saw or met were in military uniform. Early impressions formed in the region – which persist today and for good reason – are that Australia has a militaristic culture and has always been a compliant participant in its British or US allies' recurrent wars.[8] Asian countries voiced no dissent when Australia under the Howard government was described in *The Bulletin* in 1999 as the 'deputy sheriff' of the United States in the region.[9] No

Asian country felt so threatened by terrorism that it wanted to join Australia in sending armed forces to Afghanistan, Iraq or Syria, which are even more distant from Australia than from Asia.[10] When our public figures describe Australians as 'peace-loving' and 'law-abiding' their words do not resonate among our Asian neighbours. Australian claims about independence and sovereignty fail to impress those who remember colonial domination or revolutionary struggles in their own countries, who note that Australia has had no such struggles, and who observe Australia's servile compliance with US demands.

In the declared wars until 1939, Australia was at war because Britain was; Parliament debated but did not vote on these wars, and in none of them did Britain defend Australia. After World War II, Australia joined the conflicts in Korea, Kuwait, East Timor and Afghanistan in response to resolutions of the Security Council, all sponsored by the United States. In the Malayan Emergency, Indonesian Confrontation, Vietnam, Iraq (1990, 2003 and 2014) and Syria (2015), however, Australian troops were directly offered to, or were requested by, Australia's allies, Britain in the first two cases and the United States in the rest. By 1942, the United States had become Australia's dominant ally and Australia, having finally adopted the Statute of Westminster, could determine its own foreign and defence policies. After France left Vietnam in 1954 and the United States resumed the war against the Viet Minh and its successor, the Viet Cong, Australia provided civil aid, followed in the 1960s by an advisory training team and eventually by several military battalions, plus RAAF aircraft and RAN vessels. Australia's expanding deployment acquired a fig leaf of legitimacy after Prime Minister Robert Menzies contrived to receive a letter of invitation from the South

Vietnamese government in 1965. But none of it was put to a vote in Parliament. After widespread public protests against conscription, disaffection with the war and a change of government, Australia completed withdrawing its forces in 1973, in advance of the United States.

Together with the abandonment of the White Australia policy, the long peace that followed Vietnam opened the way for unprecedented engagement of many kinds with Asian countries. A supporter of ASEAN from its formation in 1974, Australia now takes part in many of its meetings and, as a signatory of the Treaty of Amity and Cooperation, has undertaken not to threaten or use force against its parties. Yet Asian countries, even those that are allies of the United States, have not joined America's wars in the Middle East. Australia, true to its militaristic form, has pressed to be involved.

In Iraq War I, Prime Minister Bob Hawke had Australia's limited involvement authorised by the Defence Minister under section 8 of the Defence Act (amended in 1975), which gives the minister 'general control and administration of the Defence Force' and requires the military to follow the directions of the minister.[11] A decade later, Prime Minister John Howard, having unilaterally invoked the ANZUS Treaty on his return from Washington in September 2001, used the same device to make a more significant deployment of Australian forces to Afghanistan in October. Their despatch was retrospectively authorised by a resolution of the UN Security Council. Then, for several months in 2002 and 2003, while Howard denied that war in Iraq was in prospect, he and his Foreign Minister repeatedly endorsed US and UK reports – widely regarded as false, even then – about Saddam Hussein's weapons of mass destruction.[12] Ignoring public demonstrations by many thousands of Australians in February 2003, Howard in March received a phone call from President George W Bush and at once informed the Parliament that Australian troops would be sent to Iraq, again using the Defence Act as Hawke had done. In the Parliament, Opposition Leader Simon Crean deplored this decision, as did the Greens, but no vote was taken. The Governor-General at the time, Reverend Peter Hollingworth, later said that Howard did not consult him.[13]

Before the wars in Afghanistan and Iraq and the deployment in Syria, Australian prime ministers urged the United States to accept military contributions. All these deployments then underwent 'mission creep', as had happened in Vietnam. Iraq Wars II and III and Syria lacked legitimising Security Council resolutions. The Geneva Conventions have been ignored with impunity on the ground that Islamic State (IS or ISIL or ISIS) is not a state but a militia movement.[14] These illegal wars potentially expose Australian leaders and participants to charges of war crimes. From 2017, when the International Criminal Court (ICC) is expected to acquire jurisdiction over the crime of aggression, if Australia does not adequately investigate or prosecute such an alleged crime, its leaders or their advisers who commit troops illegally could find themselves accused before the court. The United States under George W Bush adopted legislation authorising an invasion of the Netherlands if any US *or allied suspect* is brought to The Hague for trial before the ICC.[15] It would be even more demeaning if Australia (or indeed Britain) were to shelter behind such a provision.

When Prime Minister Abbott sought to redeploy the Australian Special Air Service Regiment (SAS) in Iraq in 2014, ostensibly at the behest of the United States but actually on his own initiative, he offered the vaguest of justifications for the SAS mission, set no time limit on the commitment and told the media a parliamentary debate would happen after the contingent's departure. In Parliament on 1 September, Abbott had said he had no plans for the deployment, which would occur only if Iraq requested it. Opposition Leader Shorten supported the deployment on certain weak conditions and a debate was held with more than 30 speakers but no vote. Exactly one month later, Abbott made a two-minute statement in the House, saying that forces had been despatched more than two weeks before and flights ('support operations') had begun. 'Final clearances' from the government of Iraq were still awaited. In March 2015, again after the event, Abbott revealed that the RAAF was already 'assisting' Allied (that is, US) combat operations in Syria (meaning bombing raids).

After IS publicised a series of gruesome executions, the United States and Australia announced in September 2015 that they would begin bombing IS targets in Syria. Foreign Minister Julie Bishop sought to justify this unilateral attack with the peculiar claim that, as IS was not a state and did not respect national boundaries, neither should Australia.[16] She did not say what the missions would achieve nor did she later report what they had achieved. Some 140 missions were flown in September, although, after Turnbull became prime minister on 15 September, the frequency of bombings reported on the Defence website fell off dramatically, again without explanation. Without explanation again, they resumed in later months, though not at the same level.

Australia spent several months of 2015 seeking an 'invitation' from the government of Iraq and a Status of Forces agreement. Abbott and Bishop repeatedly claimed that Australia had an invitation but none was tabled in Parliament or revealed in response to Freedom of Information requests.[17] Iraq's Prime Minister, Haider al-Abadi, made it clear that he wanted only Iranian troops and their Russian supporters on the ground in Iraq. Australian troops were reportedly confined to bases, on diplomatic passports, where they 'trained' Iranians while RAAF planes made bombing raids on Iraq from bases in the gulf. Abbott persuaded New Zealand Prime Minister John Key to send some 200 SAS to Iraq under similar restrictions, and continued to propose further deployments in the region for Australian troops. In July 2016, during a visit to Australia by US Vice President Joe Biden, Prime Minister Turnbull announced that Australian forces in Iraq would train Iraqi police. He followed this by stating that the SAS would operate on the ground in Syria.[18]

Public observers found it hard to obtain details about these plans, and former general Peter Leahy blamed the military, the government and the media for the silence. 'Along with Iraq, Afghanistan must be one of the most little reported wars in our military history', he said.[19] Leahy also deplored the fact that discussion of vision or strategy for these operations was lacking before the 2016 election. But what independent vision or strategy did Australia have to discuss? Australia has been at war since 2001, not because of any direct threat but because the United States has been continuously at war. Such vision and strategy as Australia has are inextricable from America's. None of these wars, in Afghanistan, Iraq and Syria, has been successful, whether measured against the objectives originally proposed, or the objectives that later replaced them, or the results achieved. By any measure, this is a negative return for the lives Australia, Iraq and Syria have lost and those we have ruined, the money we have spent, the countries we have devastated and the refugees we have created. As well, because the enemies in all cases are Muslims, the United States and its allies, including Australia, now face 'blowback' attacks at home from alienated Islamists who regard it as their duty to seek revenge for the invasion and bombing of Muslim countries or who have been prevented from going to fight in Syria.[20] There is clearly a lot wrong with the way Australia chooses wars and enemies or has them chosen for it.

## Choosing Australia's wars

Since 2001, when John Howard unilaterally extended the scope of ANZUS to cover any threat in the world, both major parties have been less prepared than ever to question the value or reliability of the American alliance. Howard, who had never retracted his claim that Saddam Hussein had weapons of mass destruction, later rationalised the war by claiming he had 'no choice' but to join Australia's British and American allies in the struggle against Islamic extremism.[21] Simon Crean, as Opposition Leader, objected to the illegal deployment in 2003, but in 2014 Bill Shorten, in the same job, proposed only the weak reservations mentioned above, which Abbott ignored.[22] As if competing with the Coalition to see who could display the most servility to the United States, Labor Prime Minister Julia Gillard was effusive in Washington; in Canberra she welcomed President Obama's 'pivot to Asia'; and then she gratuitously offered basing in the Northern Territory for US Marines.[23] In opposition, then foreign affairs spokesperson Tanya Plibersek endorsed bipartisanship, effectively shutting down debate on anything beyond minor details.[24] After the July 2016 election, the Coalition's hold on power weakened, and Senator Penny Wong as Labor foreign affairs spokesperson was a little bolder, calling the election of Donald Trump in the United States a 'change point' for Australia.[25] Greens leader Richard Di Natale called for a review of ANZUS.[26] But Australians continued to accept the stifling of discussion and the curbing of debate. Why? The answer is our increasing militarism, and four factors appear to be driving it, each of which succeeds by creating fear.

First, as suggested above, there has been a contest, a tug of war over Australian foreign and defence policy for more than a century, with militarism triumphing over independence in almost every round. Few Australians are sufficiently energised to compete in this contest, to demand such symbols of independence as a republic or a new flag, let alone an inquiry into Iraq Wars II and III. No Australian has mounted a challenge in the High Court to the way Howard and Abbott used the war powers to commit Australian forces to those wars and to Syria, perhaps for fear that the court's ruling would support the commitment. Public protest at the latest deployments has been muted in comparison to the nationwide 2003 demonstrations, which Prime Minister Howard ignored anyway. Malcolm Fraser's call for Australian 'strategic independence' failed to generate the outpouring of answers he sought from a cowed public.[27] Instead, as always, if Australians ask about wars at all, it is as if the wars were football games: we ask not what was gained and lost or why we went, but merely how well we fought.[28]

Second among the factors driving militarism, the dominant Murdoch mainstream media encourage war and support American policy rather than encouraging Australian independence. Letters editors selectively favour that policy line, while columnists use insulting epithets to bully and intimidate critics who advocate change. The resources available to the competing Fairfax media have shrunk to the point where such dissenting opinion as appears on foreign and defence policy can have little political impact. The ABC does what it can, also with dwindling capacity. Commercial media discussion of foreign and defence policy is thin and ill-informed. While media opinion does not necessarily represent what voters think – as successive elections have shown – public understanding about war and the American alliance cannot grow in a media desert such as Australia is becoming. In 2014, the Abbott government's national security legislation made it illegal, under threat of ten years in gaol, for journalists or their informants to report on 'special intelligence operations'. Reporting from the immigration detention centres on Manus Island or Nauru is also prohibited.[29] In both cases, some brave Australians have dared the authorities to arrest them; even to report their arrest and trial would be an offence.

The third factor promoting militarism is our obsession with national security. Always pointing to the bogeyman of terrorist attacks, national security has become a growth industry that demands rapidly rising public and private expenditure on intelligence, surveillance, propaganda, weaponry, military recruitment and deployment, and 'counter-terrorism'. Intimidated citizens, overlooking the fact that gun attacks at. home and violence against women kill many more Australians than terrorists do, opt for personal safety at the expense of their own or others' freedom to protest. In academia, 'National Security Studies' is a growth area; 'Peace Studies' is not. People who fear for their livelihoods in universities and research institutions have become suspicious of their colleagues and think twice before publishing controversial research. Aware that their institutional email is invigilated, they fear asking challenging questions and entering online searches that could put them on a watch list or even have them arrested. Powerful elites deliberately use fear, as Carmen Lawrence has pointed out, to justify their policies and deflect criticism of their failures.[30]

Fourthly, Anzackery aggrandises war and foments militarism, and has done so increasingly in this century, as others discuss in this book. The gulf is rapidly widening between the Australian national character presented by Charles Bean and his successors, and today's reality. Egalitarianism, fairness, courage and generosity are increasingly displaced by entitlement, selfishness, timidity and greed.[31] Those who draw attention to increasing inequality are attacked for advocating 'class warfare' and supporting 'leaners'. The fair go, if it ever existed, is not on the minds of football crowds who jeer Indigenous players or of monocultural bogans who form aggressive secret societies. If one of the characteristics of fascism is the falsification of history, there is nascent fascism inherent in the false history of Anzackery and the quasi-military, anti-multicultural movements it has spawned over the years, from the New and White Guards in the 1930s to today's Reclaim Australia and United Patriots Front.[32] The worse inequality becomes, the more this fascist tendency in Australia will revive and Anzackery will continue to nurture it.

So what can be done? It will not be easy to arrest or reverse a process that has taken a century to transform Australia from a wide, welcoming, prosperous land to the timid, hostile, selfish place it is now. Even if politicians could be persuaded to reduce their autonomy by reforming the war powers, militarism would still trump independence in foreign and defence policy. But do Australians, particularly the descendants of Anzacs, need to be so fearful? If Australians decide to, voters – the many – can make politicians – the few – fearful at election time, rather than the reverse. Australians do not have to fear everything and everyone we are told to fear, let alone invade their countries. If Franklin Delano Roosevelt was right about the Depression in 1933, all we have to fear now is fear itself. We can still say and write and find out things they do not want us to. We do not have to go on repeating past mistakes. But repeat them we will, if we wait another century to assert Australia's independence. Independence in foreign policy has been a very frayed strand in Australian history.

Times change, however. In 2017 the Trump presidency presents an unprecedented opportunity for Australia to reassess its foreign and defence policies. No certainty exists – if it ever did – that the United States will defend Australia against attack. It therefore becomes more necessary than ever for Australia to pursue its own interests independently, to build closer interaction with our Asian neighbours, and to negotiate ways to diffuse tensions, particularly with China. By withdrawing as soon as possible from the Middle East, and supporting the Paris Agreement on climate and a ban on nuclear weapons, Australia could demonstrate that our era of militarism has ended.[33] But if we make Darwin the beachhead for an American war in the South China Sea, we risk the end of everything.

# 20
# Conclusion

ALISON BROINOWSKI & DAVID STEPHENS

We began this book with the simple statement that honest history is interpretation robustly supported by evidence. The book has shown that the evidence supports many interpretations; Australian history is complex. We have presented evidence for a balanced history that puts Anzac in its proportionate place, explores other influences, confronts myths and fills silences. The Honest History coalition's mantra, 'Not only Anzac but also', is particularly relevant to Australia. The widely received view of Australian history has a special, disproportionate place for Anzac; honest Australian history means both downsizing Anzac and upsizing non-Anzac.

We also argued, particularly in chapter 9, against Anzackery, the excessive or misguided promotion of the Anzac legend. There should be no sacred cows in a free society. Anzackers, the peddlers of Anzackery, deserve and should receive trenchant criticism, whether they are jingoistic ministers of the Crown or sentimental directors of war memorials, gung-ho office-holders in the Returned and Services League or commercial shysters making money from the Anzac 'brand'. Anzackery – the extreme version – aside, Anzac may still be a secular religion for some Australians, but it is not the established church; other Australians have the right to be atheist or agnostic about it. In turn, Anzac atheists and agnostics should respect the adherents of the Anzac religion, but they should not in a democracy be required to worship at its altars.

There is still a place for Anzac, in the quieter, more reflective form described in chapter 9 of this book, and as a talisman for members of our defence forces, provided they have other values as well – professionalism, respect for the civil power and the rejection of misogyny, for example.[1] In a diverse society, there is room for this sort of Anzac, but it needs to get beyond sentimental stories of Australian men in khaki fighting and dying heroically. It also needs to look at why wars occur, how Australia enters them, whether they are worth it, what happens at home while the soldiers are fighting and what happens afterwards.

We also saw in the first part of this book how parochial and how bedevilled by myth is the way Australians relate to our war history. The chapters on the broader Great War and on the treatment of the Armenians should remind us that there was much more to that war than the alleged 'blooding' of Australia as a nation. Despite 61 000 deaths and many more people than that permanently affected, the impact of that war – and all our wars – on Australia pales beside the overall global impacts. Yet we act as if it does not – and that is national narcissism. If we are ever to value humanity as a whole, we need to cease 'setting Australian life and sense of loss above this common muddle of bones and blood'.[2]

The myths discussed in chapters 4 to 7 of the book should remind us again of the importance of evidence in history. The evidence is that Anzac has ebbed and flowed in our national consciousness over a century, that Charles Bean was but one man among many rather than the single founding father of Australian commemoration, that the story of men returning from Vietnam is not straightforward, and that the 'Atatürk words' are little more than a confidence trick, although they have become central to the Anzac legend. A national reluctance to further disseminate these words would be a great advance.

There are some other practical ways to change the balance of our history between Anzac and non-Anzac. First, we should 'level the playing field' between the institutions that promote Anzac (and flirt with Anzackery) and the other cultural institutions that deal with the broader spread of our history. At the federal level, the Australian War Memorial should be removed from the Veterans' Affairs portfolio (under the Defence umbrella) and returned to a cultural portfolio, from one of which it was excised more than 30 years ago.[3] The memorial would then have to compete directly for public money with institutions such as the National Gallery, the National Library and the National Museum, rather than continue its privileged funding of more and more buildings to house more and more military relics.[4] (It also needs a more representative governing Council.)[5] For similar reasons, the commemorative education function and staff of the Department of Veterans' Affairs should be moved into the Education portfolio and given a broader, less khaki-tinged role. Finally, the Commonwealth should abolish the requirement under the Parliament and Civics Education Rebate scheme that schools must visit the Australian War Memorial if they want their students to receive a subsidy for their trip to Canberra.[6] Mandating visits to a war memorial that has such a limited agenda should be anathema in a civil society that cherishes a peaceful future.[7]

Similar reforms are needed at state level. While some states have more balanced programs than others, the typical regime has an essay or project competition for children, with a question about the Anzac legend and prizes including a Gallipoli trip, supported by a website about 'the state at war' that emphasises the exploits of soldiers rather than the experience of a whole people, perhaps augmented by an online shop selling a range of Anzac knick-knacks.[8] Like their federal equivalents, state outlets of the commemoration industry simplify and sanitise war while claiming they do not glorify it. 'Yet', says historian Frank Bongiorno, 'a sense of sacred nationhood created through the blood sacrifice of young men remains at [the core of Anzac commemoration] today, as in 1916. Is this not to glorify war?'[9]

There is a need also for cultural change. Questioning Anzac should not be seen as disloyal. The late Inga Clendinnen said it was the job of historians like her to be 'the permanent spoil-sports of imaginative games played with the past'; Clendinnen's fellow historian Peter Cochrane reckoned history is 'a cautious, ever-questioning discipline'.[10] 'History is not a single story',

Larissa Behrendt writes in her chapter in this book. 'It is competing narratives, brought to life by different groups whose experiences are diverse and often challenge the dominant story
a country seeks to tell itself. There are no absolute truths in
history. It is a process, a conversation, a constantly altering
story.' Historians are not being true to their profession if they are
cowed by complaints that they are disturbing comforting myths
or removing security blankets. They – and their like-minded
supporters – need to be spoilsports, forever asking probing
questions, offering evidence-based answers, nailing myths and
distinguishing them from history.

Philosopher Raimond Gaita wrote recently that 'the capacity
to think critically requires also that we develop an ear for tone,
for what rings false, for what is sentimental, or has yielded to
pathos and so on'.[11] (All of these are skills particularly relevant to
targeting Anzackery.) In chapter 4 of this book Carolyn Holbrook
prioritises critical thinking skills for children. These skills should
also be more common among the journalists who write about our
wars. Critical reporting when a country is at war matters more
than at any other time, because the stakes and the costs are so
high. Critical thinking among politicians about our involvement
in wars would also be welcome; bipartisanship about the Anzac
legend, as described in Frank Bongiorno's chapter 8 of this book,
and support for serving soldiers should not mean an unquestioning acceptance of military adventures. (See Alison Broinowski's
chapter 19.)

Nevertheless, the best way of putting Anzac in its place
and seeing off Anzackery is by promoting the non-khaki side
of our national story. A century after Gallipoli, surely it is time
to pay more attention to the winding and fascinating tracks –

environmental, social, political, cultural, scientific, and so on – down which Australians have travelled to where we are now. In her chapter, Larissa Behrendt wrote of our need to 'acknowledge that there is no one dominant national narrative but many concurrent, competing and conflicting stories that reflect the diverse backgrounds and perspectives within Australian society'. This means looking at the many elements of the nation that has grown from the one the men of Anzac thought they were defending all those years ago. It means rejecting silly claims that a single, narrow story is 'our story'. It means trying to understand the history of our environment, of the multicultural country that immigrants from 200 countries have built, of the devastating effects of economic upheaval but the smugness that prosperity can breed. It means confronting the evidence of the growing gap between unequal 21st-century reality and our comforting national myth of egalitarianism. It means asking why leadership by women has not been recognised and promoted, so that our first is not our only female prime minister, and young women can aspire to and become leaders in all fields. It also means confronting – and ending – our continuing adolescent relationships with the monarchy, regardless of the 'star power' of its current representatives, and with great and powerful friends who take us for granted.

Most of all, upsizing our non-khaki side means facing up to what Larissa Behrendt calls 'the invasion moment', for 'until we do that we will never have found a way to truly share this colonised country'. That invasion of 1788 and its consequences deserve far more of our attention today than do the failed invasion of the Ottoman Empire in 1915 and our military ventures since. 'Not only Anzac but also' is shorthand for a complex history that deserves exploration, understanding, commemoration and even, sometimes, celebration. Australia is more than Anzac – and always has been.

# Notes

All websites cited in these endnotes were viewed on 14–16 November 2016. Most of the early Australian newspaper references were found using the National Library of Australia's Trove service.

## 1: Introduction

1     EH Carr, *What Is History?* Penguin, Harmondsworth, new edn, 1978, p. 23.
2     R Fathi, 'Is Australia spending too much on the "Anzac centenary"? A comparison with France', Honest History, 14 April 2016, <honesthistory.net. au/wp/fathi-romain-is-australia-spending-too-much-on-the-anzac-centenary-plus-hh-background-on-spending-politics>. By 'commemoration industry' we mean public and private bodies that specialise in – and often make money from – commemoration, as well as people who work for these bodies.
3     K Marks, 'Thomas Keneally: "I hope no one says Australia was born at Gallipoli"', *The Guardian* (Australia), 18 February 2014, <www.theguardian.com/culture/ australia-culture-blog/2014/feb/18/thomas-keneally-we-should-apologise-ghosts-wwi-soldiers-wronged>.
4     G Serle, 'Godzone: 6) Austerica unlimited', *Meanjin Quarterly*, vol. 26, no. 3, 1967, pp. 237, 244–45.
5     B Moore, A Laugesen, M Gwynn & J Robinson (eds), *Australian National Dictionary: Australian Words and Their Origins*, vol. 1, 2nd edn, Oxford University Press, Melbourne, 2016, p. 33.
6     P Cochrane, 'The past is not sacred', *Griffith Review*, no. 48, *Enduring Legacies*, 2015, <griffithreview.com/articles/past-sacred>.
7     'Themes', Honest History, <honesthistory.net.au/wp/themes>.
8     D Stephens, 'Two years of commentary on the Australian War Memorial: from the Honest History archives', Honest History, 11 November 2016, <honesthistory. net.au/wp/two-years-of-commentary-on-the-australian-war-memorial-from-the-honest-history-archives>.
9     On *Love and Sorrow*, see D Tout-Smith, 'Professional Historians Association Historically Speaking series, 5 April 2016: reflecting on the Anzac centenary and memorialisation', Honest History, 13 April 2016, <honesthistory.net.au/wp/tout-smith-deborah-anzac-centenary-and-memorialisation-speech-to-pha-vic>; on repatriation cases, see B Scates, R Wheatley & L James, *World War One: A History in 100 Stories*, Penguin, Melbourne, 2015.

10   T Abbott, 'Remarks at unveiling of the Sir John Monash Centre winning design, Villers-Bretonneux', 26 April 2015, PM Transcripts, <pmtranscripts.pmc.gov.au/release/transcript-24400>; B Nelson, 'Magna Carta and the Australian Defence Force', 14 June 2015, Australian War Memorial, <www.awm.gov.au/talks-speeches/magna-carta-and-australian-defence-force>.

11   'Honest History's Alternative Guide to the Australian War Memorial', Honest History, 26 April 2016, <honesthistory.net.au/wp/honest-history-honest-historys-alternative-guide-to-the-australian-war-memorial>.

12   D Watson, 'Enemy within: American politics in the time of Trump', *Quarterly Essay*, no. 63, 2016, p. 61.

13   'Australia's Vietnam War – and keeping it in context: an Honest History series', Honest History, 15 August 2016, <honesthistory.net.au/wp/australias-vietnam-war-and-keeping-it-in-context-honest-history-series>.

14   T Evans, Department of Veterans' Affairs, to Tour Operators, 'Re: Tour provider briefings – Australian government overseas commemorations – RSVP by 27 October 2016', 11 October 2016, <honesthistory.net.au/wp/wp-content/uploads/Doc1.pdf>. The original report to the Gillard government included a list of some 250 'key commemorative dates 2014–2018' with the caveat that the list is 'not all-inclusive'. The report is no longer available online but there is a summary at <honesthistory.net.au/wp/anzac-centenary-report-2011>.

15   P Daley, 'Why Australia Day and Anzac Day helped create a national "cult of forgetfulness"', *The Guardian* (Australia), 16 October 2016, <www.theguardian.com/australia-news/postcolonial-blog/2016/oct/16/why-australia-day-and-anzac-day-helped-create-a-national-cult-of-forgetfulness>.

16   For comment, see, for example, L Taylor, 'First Brexit, then Trump: can Australia be spared a similar voter backlash?', *The Guardian* (Australia), 12 November 2016, <www.theguardian.com/us-news/2016/nov/12/first-brexit-then-trump-can-australia-be-spared-a-similar-voter-backlash>.

17   'Every nation has its story. This is ours' or 'This is our story' has been a common refrain in the Australian War Memorial's marketing and in the speeches of its director, Brendan Nelson. For an example, see the beginning of chapter 9. Late in 2016 the memorial was market-testing a new slogan: 'For we are young and free'.

18   A Clark, *History's Children: History Wars in the Classroom*, NewSouth, Sydney, 2008, pp. 46, 62. Clark's later book has less detail on adolescent views about Anzac: see chapter 4 in A Clark, *Private Lives, Public History*, Melbourne University Press, Melbourne, 2016.

19   See, for example, from then Veterans' Affairs Minister Michael Ronaldson, 'Ministerial statement on the centenary of Anzac and Anzac Day 2015', 13 May 2015, Department of Veterans' Affairs, <minister.dva.gov.au/media_releases/2015/may/s02.htm>.

# Part 1: Putting Anzac in its place

## 2: Other people's war: The Great War in a world context

1   TW Wilson, 'An unpublished prolegomenon to a Peace Note', c. 25 November 1916, in AS Link (ed.), *The Papers of Woodrow Wilson*, vol. 40, Princeton University Press, Princeton, New Jersey, 1982, p. 67.

2   F Fischer, *Germany's Aims in the First World War*, Chatto & Windus, London, 1967, pp. 103–105.

3   M Erzberger, quoted in K Epstein, *Matthias Erzberger and the Dilemma of German Democracy*, Fertig, New York, 1971, p. 190.

4   Fischer, *Germany's Aims in the First World War*, p. x.

5   L Harcourt, 'The spoils', Cabinet Paper, 25 March 1915, National Archives, London, CAB 63/3, pp. 104–107.

6   Wilson to House, 21 July 1917, *The Papers of Woodrow Wilson*, vol. 43, p. 236. Italics original.

7   D Lloyd George, 'Speech to the trade unions, 5th January 1918', *War Memoirs of David Lloyd George*, vol. II, Odhams Press, London, 1936, pp. 1510–17.

8   Wilson, 'An address to a joint session of Congress', 8 January 1918, *The Papers of Woodrow Wilson*, vol. 45, pp. 534–39.

9   Wilson, 'A draft of an address', c. 8 February 1918, *The Papers of Woodrow Wilson*, vol. 46, pp. 274–79; 'An address in the Metropolitan Opera House', 27 September 1918, *The Papers of Woodrow Wilson*, vol. 51, pp. 127–33.

10  E Abraham, interviewed 25 January 2000, UNSW Australia: Australians at War Film Archive, no. 2541, <australiansatwarfilmarchive.unsw.edu.au/archive/2541-eric-abraham>.

11  J Graham, *Conscription and Conscience: A History, 1916–1919*, George Allen & Unwin, London, 1922, pp. 304, 309, 349, 351.

12  AW Wheen, 18 April 1929, quoted in T Crothers (ed.), *We Talked of Other Things: The Life and Letters of Arthur Wheen, 1897–1971*, Longueville Media, Sydney, 2012, p. 185.

13  *Daily Standard* (Brisbane), 11 January 1916, p. 4. The committee still existed a century later.

14  N Meaney, *Australia and World Crisis, 1914–1923*, Sydney University Press, Sydney, 2009, pp. 44, 59, 148, 247–48.

15  *Catholic Press* (Sydney), 31 January 1918, p. 23.

16  *Woman Voter* (Melbourne), 21 March 1918, p. 2.

17  T Abbott, 'Lone Pine address, Gallipoli (25 April 2015)', PM Transcripts, <pmtranscripts.dpmc.gov.au/release/transcript-24398>.

18  T Abbott, 'Remarks at the 1st Brigade welcome home reception, Parliament House, Darwin', 1 March 2014, PM Transcripts, <pmtranscripts.pmc.gov.au/release/transcript-23297>.

19  F Manning, *Her Privates We*, Readers Union, London, 1965, p. 9.

20  RL Outhwaite, *House of Commons Hansard*, 23 February 1916, <hansard.millbanksystems.com/commons/1916/feb/23/consolidated-fund-no-1-bill-S5CV0080P0_19160223_HOC_312>.

## 3: 24 April 1915: Australia's Armenian story over a century

1  V Babkenian & P Stanley, *Armenia, Australia and the Great War*, NewSouth, Sydney, 2016, p. 53.

2  T Akçam, *A Shameful Act: The Armenian Genocide and the Question of Turkish Responsibility*, Henry Holt, New York, 2006, p. 183. See also J Macleod & G Tongo, 'Between memory and history: remembering Johnnies, Mehmets and the Armenians', in R Frances & B Scates (eds), *Beyond Gallipoli: New Perspectives on Anzac*, Monash University Publishing, Melbourne, 2016, pp. 21–34.

3  Babkenian & Stanley, *Armenia, Australia and the Great War*, p. 70.

4  *The Mercury* (Hobart), 21 December 1915, p. 5.

5  Babkenian & Stanley, *Armenia, Australia and the Great War*, p. 83.

6  Babkenian & Stanley, *Armenia, Australia and the Great War*, pp. 70–71.

7  Babkenian & Stanley, *Armenia, Australia and the Great War*, p. 73.

8  Babkenian & Stanley, *Armenia, Australia and the Great War*, p. 91.

9  LH Luscombe, *The Story of Harold Earl: Australian*, WR Smith & Paterson, Brisbane, 1970, pp. 52–53.

10  DB Creedon, Diary, Australian War Memorial, 1DRL/0223. Creedon died in captivity a few months after this diary entry.

11  Babkenian & Stanley, *Armenia, Australia and the Great War*, p. 77.

12  Babkenian & Stanley, *Armenia, Australia and the Great War*, p. 133.

13  U Üngör & M Polatel, *Confiscation and Destruction: The Young Turk Seizure of Armenian Property*, Continuum, London, 2011, p. 65.

14  Babkenian & Stanley, *Armenia, Australia and the Great War*, p. 76.

15  Note the lack of Armenian material on the webpage of the Turkish Ministry of Culture and Tourism: <www.kultur.gov.tr/EN,98538/culture.html>.

16  Babkenian & Stanley, *Armenia, Australia and the Great War*, p. 111.

17  Babkenian & Stanley, *Armenia, Australia and the Great War*, p. 117.

18  *The Register* (Adelaide), 21 September 1923, p. 8; *The Armenian* (Armenian Relief Fund Committee, Adelaide), May 1923, pp. 4–5.

19  Babkenian & Stanley, *Armenia, Australia and the Great War*, p. 267.

20  Babkenian & Stanley, *Armenia, Australia and the Great War*, pp. 268–72.

21  M Brissenden, 'Turkey threatens to ban MPs from Gallipoli centenary over genocide vote', *ABC News*, 21 August 2013, <www.abc.net.au/news/2013-08-21/turkey-threatens-nsw-parliament-over-armenian-genocide-vote/4903444>; 'Turkey threatens to ban outspoken politicians from the Anzac Commemoration in 2015', *7.30*, ABC, 21 August 2013, <www.abc.net.au/7.30/content/2013/s3831003.htm>.

22  J Bishop to E Ozen, Australian-Turkish Advocacy Alliance, 4 June 2014, quoted in 'Australian FM: Armenian case not genocide', *Daily Sabah* (Istanbul), 23 July 2014, <www.dailysabah.com/politics/2014/07/23/australian-fm-armenian-case-not-genocide>.

23  C Simpson, 'From ruthless foe to national friend: Turkey, Gallipoli and Australian nationalism', *Media International Australia*, vol. 137, no. 1, 2010, p. 58.

24  Kemalist: deriving from the philosophy of Mustafa Kemal Atatürk, founder of the modern Turkish state: see M Tunçay, 'Kemalism', Oxford Islamic Studies Online, <www.oxfordislamicstudies.com/article/opr/t236/e0440>.

25    PA Shackel, 'Public memory and the search for power in American historical archaeology', *American Anthropologist*, vol. 103, no. 3, 2001, p. 656.

## 4: Adaptable Anzac: Past, present and future

1    T Swifte, *Gallipoli: The Incredible Campaign*, Magazine Promotions, Sydney, 1985, p. 2.

2    Chapter 7 of this book describes the events surrounding the installation of Atatürk memorials in Australia and Turkey.

3    M Lake & H Reynolds with M McKenna & J Damousi, *What's Wrong with Anzac? The Militarisation of Australian History*, NewSouth, Sydney, 2010, p. 137.

4    Australian Curriculum, Assessment and Reporting Authority (ACARA), '7–10 History', Australian Curriculum, <www.australiancurriculum.edu.au/ humanities-and-social-sciences/history/Curriculum/F-10>.

5    R Fathi, 'Is Australia spending too much on the "Anzac centenary"? A comparison with France', Honest History, 14 April 2016, <honesthistory.net.au/ wp/is-australia-spending-too-much-on-the-anzac-centenary-a-comparison-with-france>.

6    *The Argus* (Melbourne), 8 May 1915, p. 19; K Fewster, 'Ellis Ashmead Bartlett and the making of the Anzac legend', *Journal of Australian Studies*, vol. 6, no. 10, 1982, pp. 17–30; *The Mercury* (Hobart), 8 May 1915, p. 5.

7    *The Advertiser* (Adelaide), 2 February 1903, p. 6; *Sydney Morning Herald*, 20 February 1902, p. 8.

8    *The Argus* (Melbourne), 8 May 1915, p. 19; *The Mercury*, 8 May 1915, p. 5.

9    For example, WM Hughes, *Sydney Morning Herald*, 26 April 1918, p. 8.

10    P Deery & F Bongiorno, 'Labor, loyalty and peace: two Anzac controversies of the 1920s', *Labour History*, no. 106, May 2014, pp. 205–28.

11    *The Advertiser*, 22 October 1949, p. 4; *The Argus* (Melbourne), 21 June 1949, p. 6; *Warwick Daily News*, 6 June 1946, p. 4.

12    *Canberra Times*, 23 April 1960, p. 1; G Havers, 'Lest We Forget', *Honi Soit*, 24 April 1958, p. 4; Lake & Reynolds, *What's Wrong with Anzac?*, pp. 80–81.

13    A Seymour, *The One Day of the Year*, in A Seymour, D Stewart & H Porter, *Three Australian Plays*, rev. edn, Penguin, Melbourne, 1994, pp. 80, 86.

14    *Canberra Times*, 28 April 1967, p. 2.

15    Letter, RC Goldsworthy, public servant, to Prime Minister Gorton, 23 September 1968, quoted in J Curran & S Ward, *The Unknown Nation: Australia after Empire*, Melbourne University Press, Melbourne, 2010, p. 112.

16    J Gorton, *The Bulletin*, 5 October 1968, quoted in Curran & Ward, *The Unknown Nation*, p. 6.

17    Quoted in Curran & Ward, *The Unknown Nation*, p. 123.

18    B Gammage, *The Broken Years: Australian Soldiers in the Great War*, new edn, Melbourne University Press, Melbourne, 2010, p. 182.

19    A Simon, 'Peter Weir: the Hollywood interview', 15 December 2012, The Hollywood Interview, <thehollywoodinterview.blogspot.com.au/2008/03/peter-weir-hollywood-interview.html>.

20  C Twomey, 'Trauma and the reinvigoration of Anzac: an argument', *History Australia*, vol. 10, no. 3, 2013, p. 106.

21  K Inglis, 'Letters from a pilgrimage', Inside Story, 23 April 2015, <insidestory.org.au/letters-from-a-pilgrimage>.

22  *Canberra Times*, 26 April 1965, p. 1.

23  'The small print on Veterans' Affairs', Honest History, 23 October 2013, <honesthistory.net.au/wp/the-small-print-on-veterans-affairs>.

24  Department of Veterans' Affairs, 'Valuing our veterans: gathering Australia's war memories', Anzac Portal, <anzacportal.dva.gov.au/history/publications/valuing-our-veterans/gathering-australias-war-memories>.

25  'Education', Australian War Memorial, <www.awm.gov.au/education>. See also D Stephens, '"And the children went": hands-on history at the Australian War Memorial', Honest History, 4 August 2015, <honesthistory.net.au/wp/stephens-david-and-the-children-went-hands-on-history-at-the-war-memorial>.

26  'Online shop – children', Australian War Memorial, <www.awm.gov.au/shop/category/gifts/children>.

27  D Shanahan, 'Kevin Rudd rejects Paul Keating's view on Gallipoli', *The Australian*, 1 November 2008, <www.theaustralian.com.au/national-affairs/defence/rudd-rejects-keating-view-on-gallipoli/story-e6frg8yo-1111117915562>; 'Paul Keating's speech', *The Age*, 31 October 2008, <www.theage.com.au/national/paul-keatings-speech-20081031-5f1h.html>.

28  J Gillard, 'Transcript of doorstop interview, Singapore', 24 April 2012, PM Transcripts, <pmtranscripts.dpmc.gov.au/release/transcript-18531>.

29  J Gillard, 'Transcript of interview with Karina Carvalho, ABC Townsville, 25 April 2013', PM Transcripts, <pmtranscripts.pmc.gov.au/release/transcript-19271>.

30  R Peake, 'Gillard to fulfil Gallipoli pilgrimage dream', *Sydney Morning Herald*, 17 April 2012, <www.smh.com.au/national/gillard-to-fulfil-gallipoli-pilgrimage-dream-20120416-1x40f.html>.

31  D Stephens, 'Villers-Bretonneux boondoggle contract announced', Honest History, 23 December 2015, <honesthistory.net.au/wp/villers-bretonneux-boondoggle-construction-contract-announced>.

32  P Stanley, 'Do teachers have "patriotic" obligations? Address to ACT–NSW History Teachers' Associations conference, University of Canberra, 9 May 2014', Honest History, <honesthistory.net.au/wp/stanley-peter-patriotic-teachers>.

## 5: The Australian War Memorial: Beyond Bean

1  A Pegram, 'Charles Bean', in U Daniel et al. (eds), *International Encyclopedia of the First World War*, Freie Universität Berlin, 19 October 2016, <encyclopedia.1914-1918-online.net/article/charles_bean>.

2  'New director Brendan Nelson arrives at Memorial', media release, 17 December 2012, <www.awm.gov.au/media/releases/new-director-brendan-nelson-arrives-memorial>; R Peake, 'Role of honour for Nelson', *Canberra Times*, 15 December 2012, <www.canberratimes.com.au/act-news/role-of-honour-for-nelson-20121214-2bffg.html>.

3   C Spittel, 'Australia in the Great War', *reCollections*, vol. 10, no. 2, 2015, <recollections.nma.gov.au/issues/volume_10_number_2/exhibition_reviews/australia_in_the_great_war>.

4   CEW Bean, *Anzac to Amiens*, Australian War Memorial, Canberra, 1983; K Fewster (ed.), *Gallipoli Correspondent: The Frontline Diary of C.E.W. Bean*, Allen & Unwin, Sydney, 1983; D McCarthy, *Gallipoli to the Somme: The Story of C.E.W. Bean*, John Ferguson, Sydney, 1983; M Piggott, *A Guide to the Personal Family and Official Papers of C.E.W. Bean*, Australian War Memorial, Canberra, 1983.

5   R Gerster, *Big-noting: The Heroic Theme in Australian War Writing*, Melbourne University Press, Melbourne, 1987; DA Kent, '*The Anzac Book* and the Anzac legend: C.E.W. Bean as editor and image-maker', *Historical Studies*, vol. 21, no. 84, 1985, pp. 376–90; A Thomson, 'Steadfast until death? C.E.W. Bean and the representation of Australian military manhood', *Australian Historical Studies*, vol. 23, no. 93, 1989, pp. 462–90.

6   For example, C Holbrook, *Anzac: The Unauthorised Biography*, NewSouth, Sydney, 2014; M Lake & H Reynolds with M McKenna & J Damousi, *What's Wrong with Anzac? The Militarisation of Australian History*, NewSouth, Sydney, 2010; A Thomson, *Anzac Memories: Living with the Legend*, Monash University Publishing, Melbourne, 2013.

7   For the CEW Bean Foundation: 'Honouring the memory of Australian war correspondents', National Press Club, <npc.org.au/cew/about>.

8   F Anderson & R Trembath, *Witnesses to War: The History of Australian Conflict Reporting*, Melbourne University Press, Melbourne, 2011, pp. 73, 88–90.

9   Despatches from Gallipoli: Scenes from a Remote War, archived website, <pandora.nla.gov.au/pan/49545/20050730-0000/www.nla.gov.au/gallipolidespatches/index.html>.

10  G Lindsay, *Be Substantially Great in Thy Self: Getting to Know C.E.W. Bean; Barrister, Judge's Associate, Moral Philosopher*, Francis Forbes Society for Australian Legal History, Sydney, 2011, <www.forbessociety.org.au/?page_id=185>.

11  M Baker, 'Nelson faces a fight over roll of honour', *Sydney Morning Herald*, 27 January 2013, <www.smh.com.au/national/nelson-faces-a-fight-over-roll-of-honour-20130126-2ddi6.html>; M Green, 'Lest we remember: the Australian War Memorial and the Frontier Wars', Wheeler Centre, 23 February 2014, <www.wheelercentre.com/notes/f261bb085eb4>.

12  B Nelson, 'The 100th Anzac Day: war, politics and remembrance', The Strategist, 22 April 2015, <www.aspistrategist.org.au/the-100th-anzac-day-war-politics-and-remembrance>.

13  'Australian War Memorial and the Memorial Parade, Anzac Pde, Campbell, ACT, Australia', Australian Heritage Database, Department of the Environment and Energy, <www.environment.gov.au/cgi-bin/ahdb/search.pl?mode=place_detail;place_id=105889>; C Daley, *As I Recall: Reminiscences of Early Canberra*, Mulini Press with the Canberra and District Historical Society, Canberra, 1994 (ebook 2013), p. 119, <www.asirecall.org/Resources/As I Recall - Charles Daley - v1.0.pdf>; KS Inglis, 'A sacred place: the making of the Australian War Memorial', *War & Society*, vol. 3, no. 2, 1985, p. 104; M McKernan, *Here Is Their Spirit: A*

*History of the Australian War Memorial 1917–1990*, University of Queensland Press with the Australian War Memorial, Brisbane, 1991, pp. 94–95.

14 KS Inglis with J Brazier, *Sacred Places: War Memorials in the Australian Landscape*, Melbourne University Press, Melbourne, 2008, pp. 427–33; PJ Keating, 'Remembrance Day 1993', 11 November 1993, Australian War Memorial, <www.awm.gov.au/talks-speeches/keating-remembrance-day-1993>.

15 Holbrook, *Anzac*, pp. 187–89.

16 B Nelson, 'National Press Club address', 18 September 2013, Australian War Memorial, <www.awm.gov.au/talks-speeches/national-press-club-address>. In fact, Nelson mangled the second quote, saying, 'He is one of them, and he is all of us', but I have tidied it up. Compare this with 'Tomb of the Unknown Australian Soldier', Australian War Memorial, <www.awm.gov.au/visit/hall-of-memory/tomb>.

17 M Devine, 'Turning in their graves', *Daily Telegraph* (Sydney), 29 October 2013, <blogs.news.com.au/dailytelegraph/mirandadevine/index.php/dailytelegraph/comments/turning_in_their_graves>; 'War Memorial to keep "Known unto God" on tomb of Unknown Soldier', *ABC News*, 29 October 2013, <www.abc.net.au/news/2013-10-29/known-unto-god-to-remain-on-tomb-of-unknown-soldier/5051892>. The ABC report includes Nelson's mangled quote.

18 N Cater, 'Who are we to wage culture wars on heroes known only to God?' *The Australian*, 29 October 2013, <www.theaustralian.com.au/opinion/columnists/who-are-we-to-wage-culture-wars-on-heroes-known-only-to-god/story-fnhulhjj-1226748548630>.

19 KS Inglis with J Brazier, *Sacred Places*, pp. 318–19; Lindsay, *Be Substantially Great in Thy Self*.

20 Australian War Memorial, *Hall of Memory*, Australian War Memorial, Canberra, 2016.

21 See, for example, from his Press Club address in 2013, 'Our vision', Australian War Memorial, <www.awm.gov.au/1914-1918/our-vision>.

22 A-M Condé, 'A "gift to the nation": the diaries and notebooks of CEW Bean', *Archives and Manuscripts*, vol. 39, no. 2, 2011, pp. 43–64.

23 Quoted in P FitzSimons, *Gallipoli*, William Heinemann, Sydney, 2014, p. 685.

24 P Stanley, 'Ernie Bailey: "Founder" of Australian War Museum', *Wartime*, no. 28, 2004, pp. 34–35, <www.awm.gov.au/sites/default/files/ernie-bailey-stanley.pdf>. Bailey was accidentally killed in May 1918 while working for the AWRS.

25 CEW Bean, *Two Men I Knew: William Bridges and Brudenell White, Founders of the A.I.F.*, Angus & Robertson, Sydney, 1957, p. 149; CEW Bean, *Gallipoli Mission*, Australian War Memorial, Canberra, 1948, p. 5; A-M Condé, 'Imagining a collection: creating Australia's records of war', *reCollections*, vol. 2, no. 1, 2007, <recollections.nma.gov.au/issues/vol_2_no_1/papers/imagining_a_collection>; A-M Condé, 'John Treloar, official war art and the Australian War Memorial', *Australian Journal of Politics and History*, vol. 53, no. 3, 2007, pp. 451–64; McKernan, *Here Is Their Spirit*, chs 2–3; A Millar, 'Gallipoli to Melbourne: the Australian War Memorial, 1915–19', *Journal of the Australian War Memorial*, no. 10, 1987, pp. 33–42; M Piggott, 'The Australian War Records Section and its aftermath, 1917–1925', *Archives and Manuscripts*, vol. 8, no. 2, 1980, pp. 41–50.

26    G Windsor, 'Horrors clear in close-up are blurred in crowd scenes', *Weekend Australian*, 23–24 July 2016, pp. 20–21.

27    P Rees, *Bearing Witness: The Remarkable Life of Charles Bean, Australia's Greatest War Correspondent*, Allen & Unwin, Sydney, 2015, p. 490.

28    Rees, *Bearing Witness*, p. ix.

29    G Serle, *John Monash: A Biography*, Melbourne University Press, Melbourne, 1982, p. 328.

30    J Grey, 'War historian worthy of more attention', 'Panorama', *Canberra Times*, 22 November 2014, p. 23. For McCarthy's book, see note 4 above.

31    V Lindesay, 'Dyson, William Henry (Will) (1880–1938)', *Australian Dictionary of Biography*, National Centre of Biography, Australian National University, <adb. anu.edu.au/biography/dyson-william-henry-will-6074>.

32    Senator J Faulkner, Senate Hansard, 28 August 2001, Parliament of Australia, <parlinfo.aph.gov.au/parlInfo/search/display/display.w3p;db=CHAMBER;id=c hamber%2Fhansards%2F2001-08-28%2F0108;query=Id%3A"chamber%2Fhans ards%2F2001-08-28%2F0000>; R McMullin, 'Anzac Day 2016: Australia's finest war artist is missing in action', *Sydney Morning Herald*, 25 April 2016, <www. smh.com.au/comment/our-finest-war-artist-missing-in-action-20160422-goczgu. html>.

33    'Anzac auteur' is a coinage by Don Watson, in 'Digging: a moral equivalent to Anzac Day', *The Monthly*, May 2008, <www.themonthly.com.au/issue/2008/ may/1335251549/don-watson/digging>.

## 6: 'We too were Anzacs': Were Vietnam veterans ever truly excluded from the Anzac tradition?

1    Every Australian infantry battalion that fought in Vietnam produced at least one 'tour book', generally a pictorial record of their service. Seven of these volumes include the word 'Anzac' in the title. 'We too were Anzacs' commemorates 6RAR/ NZ's 1969–70 tour to South Vietnam. 'RAR' stands for Royal Australian Regiment and '1RAR' or '6RAR' stands for the battalion of the regiment.

2    'Mythbusting about Australians returned from Vietnam: Honest History highlights reel', Honest History, 9 June 2015, <honesthistory.net.au/wp/ mythbusting-about-vietnam-highlights-reel>.

3    J Grey, 'In every war but one? Myth, history and Vietnam', in C Stockings (ed.), *Zombie Myths of Australian Military History: The 10 Myths that Will Not Die*, NewSouth, Sydney, 2010, p. 211.

4    Nadine Jensen: *Canberra Times*, 10 June 1966, p. 3.

5    *The Age* (Melbourne), 26 April 1966, p. 1; *The Australian*, 26 April 1966, p. 1; *Canberra Times*, 23 April 1966, pp. 1, 3; *Sydney Morning Herald*, 26 April 1966, p. 1.

6    *Canberra Times*, 22 April 1967, p. 1, 26 April 1967, p. 3.

7    *Sydney Morning Herald*, 26 April 1968, p. 6.

8    *The Sun-Herald* (Sydney), 26 April 1970, p. 2.

9    *Sydney Morning Herald*, 26 April 1972, pp. 1, 15.

10   P Ham, *Vietnam: The Australian War*, HarperCollins, Sydney, 2007, p. 565.

11    *Canberra Times*, 26 October 1963, p. 2.
12    *The Age*, 31 January 1966, p. 9; *Canberra Times*, 28 April 1966, p. 8.
13    *Reveille*, vol. 41, no. 6, 1968, p. 5.
14    *Reveille*, vol. 43, no. 6, 1970, p. 23.
15    *Reveille*, vol. 43, no. 9, 1970, p. 3.
16    *Reveille*, vol. 45, no. 10, 1971, p. 3.
17    *Reveille*, vol. 46, no. 5, 1972, p. 6.
18    *Reveille*, vol. 46, no. 8, 1972, p. 4.
19    'Welcome home parade for 2nd Cavalry Regiment Task Group and Combined Team – Uruzgan Four and Five', Darwin, 1 March 2014, Australian Army, <www.army.gov.au/Our-work/Speeches-and-transcripts/Welcome-Home-Parade-for-2nd-Cavalry-Regiment-Task-Group-and-Combined-Team-Uruzgan-Four-and-Five>.
20    The term 'forgotten people' refers to the Australian middle class to whom RG Menzies appealed from 1943 onwards and who ensured his electoral success from 1949: J Brett, *Robert Menzies' Forgotten People*, Melbourne University Press, Melbourne, 2007.
21    *Reveille*, vol. 58, no. 1, 1983, p. 11.
22    J Bird, 'In the matter of Agent Orange: Vietnam veterans versus the Australian War Memorial', Honest History, 15 March 2016, <honesthistory.net.au/wp/in-the-matter-of-agent-orange-vietnam-veterans-versus-the-australian-war-memorial>.
23    *The Sun-Herald*, 26 April 1987, p. 5.
24    B Ruxton, quoted in A Blair, *Ruxton: A Biography*, Allen & Unwin, Sydney, 2004, p. 152.

## 7: Myth and history: The persistent 'Atatürk words'

1    Mustafa Kemal was not given the name 'Atatürk' ('Father Turk' or 'Ancestor Turk') until November 1934, but we will use the name throughout this article. For Honest History's research on the 'Atatürk words', see 'Talking Turkey', Honest History, <honesthistory.net.au/wp/talking-turkey>. See also M McKenna & S Ward, 'An Anzac myth: the creative memorialisation of Gallipoli', *The Monthly*, December 2015 – January 2016, <www.themonthly.com.au/issue/2015/december/1448888400/mark-mckenna-and-stuart-ward/anzac-myth>; J Macleod & G Tongo, 'Between memory and history: remembering Johnnies, Mehmets and the Armenians', in R Frances & B Scates (eds), *Beyond Gallipoli: New Perspectives on Anzac*, Monash University Publishing, Melbourne, 2016, pp. 21–34.
2    'Atatürk's words to the Anzac mothers, 03.10.2014', Turkish Embassy in Canberra, Ministry of Foreign Affairs, Republic of Turkey, <canberra.emb.mfa.gov.tr/ShowInfoNotes.aspx?ID=218750>.
3    C Özakıncı, 'The words "There is no difference between the Mehmets and the Johnnies" engraved on the 1915 Gallipoli monuments do not belong to Atatürk: Part I', *Bütün Dünya* (Ankara), March 2015 (trans. from Turkish by Baskent University of Ankara), at Honest History, 20 April 2015, <honesthistory.net.au/wp/wp-content/uploads/Part-1-March-article.pdf>.

4    D Stephens, 'Gold, rum but no sign of Ataturk's minister at Anzac, April–May
     1934', Honest History, 1 December 2015, <honesthistory.net.au/wp/no-sign-of-
     ataturks-minister-at-anzac-april-may-1934>.
5    U İğdemir, *Atatürk ve Anzaklar (Atatürk and the Anzacs)*, Turkish Historical
     Society Printing House, Ankara, 1978. We have a copy of the *Dünya* article.
6    'Atatürk's words to the Anzac mothers, 03.10.2014'; D Stephens, 'Martyrs' Day in
     Turkey and what probably did not happen on 18 March 1934: recent research from
     Cengiz Özakıncı', Honest History, 15 March 2016, <honesthistory.net.au/wp/
     martyrs-day-in-turkey-and-what-probably-did-not-happen-on-18-march-1934>.
7    S Kaya & E Ergüven, *Şükrü Kaya: Sözleri – Yazıları 1927–1937 (Şükrü Kaya: Words
     – Writings 1927–1937)*, Republic Print, Istanbul, 1937; Stephens, 'Martyrs' Day in
     Turkey'.
8    P Daley, 'Ataturk's "Johnnies and Mehmets" words about the Anzacs are shrouded
     in doubt', *The Guardian* (Australia), 20 April 2015, <www.theguardian.com/
     news/2015/apr/20/ataturks-johnnies-and-mehmets-words-about-the-anzacs-
     are-shrouded-in-doubt>; S Hope, *Gallipoli Revisited*, WE Stanton Hope, London,
     1934.
9    Özakıncı, 'The words "There is no difference between the Mehmets and the
     Johnnies"'.
10   *The Advertiser* (Adelaide), 11 November 1938, p. 28; GF Davis, 'Anzac Day
     meanings and memories: New Zealand, Australian and Turkish perspectives
     on a day of commemoration in the twentieth century', PhD thesis, University
     of Otago, Dunedin, New Zealand, 2008, p. 213, <ourarchive.otago.ac.nz/
     handle/10523/342>; İğdemir, *Atatürk and the Anzacs*, p. 40; *Sydney Morning
     Herald*, 11 November 1938, p. 13; *The Times* (London), 11 November 1938, p. 15.
11   *Daily Mail* (Brisbane), 25 April 1931, p. 13.
12   C Özakıncı, 'Old tales of Greece, the Anzacs and Atatürk', *Bütün Dünya*
     (Ankara), July 2015 (trans. from Turkish by Baskent University of Ankara),
     Honest History, 12 August 2015, <honesthistory.net.au/wp/wp-content/uploads/
     July-2015-R.pdf>.
13   İğdemir, *Atatürk and the Anzacs*, pp. 36–37.
14   See the references in D Stephens, 'Tracking Atatürk: Honest History research
     note', Honest History, 20 April 2015, sections 3 and 12, <honesthistory.net.au/wp/
     tracking-ataturk-honest-history-research-note>.
15   Özakıncı, 'Old tales of Greece'; email from EJ Zürcher, March 2016; EJ Zürcher,
     *Turkey: A Modern History*, IB Tauris, London & New York, 2004, p. 235.
16   To illustrate Önen's Kemalism, Özakıncı supplied (and Çakır read) a number of
     articles on Önen from the *Milliyet* newspaper 1950–60.
17   D Stephens, 'More on the Australian pilgrimages to Gallipoli, 1960 and 1965',
     Honest History, 26 April 2016, <honesthistory.net.au/wp/more-on-the-
     australian-pilgrimages-to-gallipoli-1960-and-1965>. The emphasis is ours. The
     anecdote about Captain Akomer appeared in Mrs Eileen Yeo's 'Anzac Day at
     Anzac' in the June 1960 issue of *Reveille* (RSSAILA NSW Branch), vol. 33, no. 11,
     pp. 5–6.
18   Stephens, 'More on the Australian pilgrimages'.

19    Preamble, Article 134, Constitution of the Republic of Turkey, Grand National
      Assembly of Turkey, <global.tbmm.gov.tr/docs/constitution_en.pdf>; İğdemir,
      *Atatürk and the Anzacs*; 'Türk Tarih Kurumu'nu tanıyalım (Short history of the
      Turkish Historical Society)', <www.ttk.gov.tr/index.php?Page=Sayfa&No=1>.
      'Türk Tarih Kurumu' can also be translated as 'Turkish History Institution'.
20    D Stephens, 'Turks did the heavy lifting: a longer look at the story of the Atatürk
      Memorial, Canberra, 1984– 85, Part I' and 'Part II', Honest History, 11 October
      2016, <honesthistory.net.au/wp/stephens-david-turks-did-the-heavy-lifting-a-
      longer-look-at-the-story-of-the-ataturk-memorial-canberra-1984-85-part-i>, and
      25 October 2016, <honesthistory.net.au/wp/stephens-david-turks-did-the-heavy-
      lifting-a-longer-look-at-the-building-of-the-ataturk-memorial-in-anzac-parade-
      canberra-1984-85-part-ii>; Stephens, 'More on the Australian pilgrimages'.
21    BN Şimşir, '*Kanberra'da Atatürk aniti tasarısı* (The Atatürk memorial project in
      Canberra)', *Journal of the Atatürk Research Center*, vol. XVII, no. 51, 2001, pp.
      698–702.
22    General references in English for the following paragraphs are: F Ahmad, *The
      Making of Modern Turkey*, Routledge, London & New York, 1993, ch. 9; Davis,
      'Anzac Day meanings and memories', ch. 7; K Öktem, *Angry Nation: Turkey since
      1989*, Zed Books, London & New York, 2011, ch. 2; Zürcher, *Turkey*, ch. 15.
23    Stephens, 'Turks did the heavy lifting, Part I' and 'Part II'.
24    D Stephens, 'How some Turks would rather that Johnnies and Mehmets were not
      equal: research report', Honest History, 19 July 2016, <honesthistory.net.au/wp/
      stephens-david-how-some-turks-would-rather-that-johnnies-and-mehmets-were-
      not-equal>.
25    A Aktar, 'Mustafa Kemal at Gallipoli: the making of a saga, 1921–1932', in MJK
      Walsh & A Varnava (eds), *Australia and the Great War: Identity, Memory and
      Mythology*, MUP Academic, Melbourne, 2016, pp. 149–71.
26    *Maryborough Chronicle* (Queensland), 25 April 1930, p. 6; İğdemir, *Atatürk and
      the Anzacs*, pp. 33, 60; Stephens, 'More on the Australian pilgrimages'; *Daily Mail*,
      25 April 1931, p. 13.
27    McKenna & Ward, 'An Anzac myth'.
28    P Stanley, 'Gallipoli 1915: a century on – conference report', Honest History,
      14 April 2015, <honesthistory.net.au/wp/gallipoli-1915-a-century-on-conference-
      report>.
29    P Stanley, 'Gallipoli – 98 years on: Professor Peter Stanley's speech to Gallipoli
      Memorial Club symposium, 7 August 2013', Honest History, 28 October 2013,
      <honesthistory.net.au/wp/gallipoli-club-peter-stanley>.
30    M Polatel, 'Social engineer: Şükrü Kaya', *Agos*, 27 March 2015, <www.agos.
      com.tr/en/article/11045/social-engineer-sukru-kaya>; R Silverman, 'The Şükrü
      Kaya problem', 19 April 2015, Reuben Silverman blog, <reubensilverman.
      wordpress.com/2015/04/19/the-sukru-kaya-problem>; 'Şükrü Kaya 1882–
      1959', Imprescriptible: base documentaire sur le génocide arménien, <www.
      imprescriptible.fr/turquie-memoire/Sukru_Kaya.html>.
31    The Commonwealth War Graves Commission pays local Turks as caretakers
      (Stanley, 'Gallipoli – 98 years on').

32  'Ataturk in the City of Hume, Victoria: Honest History factsheet', Honest History, 9 June 2015, <honesthistory.net.au/wp/ataturk-in-the-city-of-hume-victoria-honest-history-factsheet>.

33  A Pym, 'On the passage of transcendent messages: Johnnies and Mehmets', 28 September 2015', <usuaris.tinet.cat/apym/on-line/translation/2015_transcendent.pdf>, p. 21.

## 8: A century of bipartisan commemoration: Is Anzac politically inevitable?

1   D Newton, *Hell-bent: Australia's Leap into the Great War*, Scribe, Melbourne, 2014, p. 107.

2   C Holbrook, 'Commemorators-in-chief', in T Frame (ed.), *Anzac Day Then and Now*, NewSouth, Sydney, 2016, pp. 214–31. See also Holbrook's chapter 4 above.

3   E Andrews, '25 April 1916: first Anzac Day in Australia and Britain', *Journal of the Australian War Memorial*, no. 23, 1993, pp. 13–20; J Moses & GF Davis, *Anzac Day Origins: Canon DJ Garland and Trans-Tasman Commemoration*, Barton Books, Canberra, 2013, p. 158.

4   C Bridge, *William Hughes: Australia*, Haus, London, 2011, p. 84.

5   W Angwin to SM Bruce, 21 March 1925, quoted in P Deery & F Bongiorno, 'Labor, loyalty and peace: two Anzac controversies of the 1920s', *Labour History*, no. 106, 2014, p. 224; D Lee, *Stanley Melbourne Bruce: Australian Internationalist*, Continuum, London & New York, 2010, pp. 12–13; *The Sun* (Sydney), 24 April 1925, p. 8; *West Australian*, 17 May 1923, p. 8.

6   *The Argus* (Melbourne), 25 April 1942, p. 3.

7   AW Martin, *Robert Menzies: A Life*, vol. 1, *1894–1943*, Melbourne University Press, Melbourne, 1993, pp. 29–30, 274–80; Menzies diary entry, 26 April 1941, in AW Martin & P Hardy (eds), *Dark and Hurrying Days: Menzies' 1941 Diary*, National Library of Australia, Canberra, 1993, p. 118; *The Times* (London), 26 April 1941, p. 5.

8   *The Age* (Melbourne), 26 April 1957, p. 3; Holbrook, 'Commemorators-in-chief', pp. 218–19; *Sydney Morning Herald*, 22 April 1955, p. 3.

9   *The Age*, 7 March 1973, p. 9; *Sydney Morning Herald*, 26 April 1968, p. 6.

10  *Canberra Times*, 26 April 1969, p. 3; *Sydney Morning Herald*, 26 April 1968, p. 1; *The Times* (London), 26 April 1968, p. 2; *West Australian*, 26 April 1969, p. 1.

11  *The Australian*, 26 April 1984, p. 3; J Curran & S Ward, *The Unknown Nation: Australia after Empire*, Melbourne University Press, Melbourne, 2010, pp. 172–73; *Sydney Morning Herald*, 20 April 1973, p. 8, 26 April 1974, pp. 1, 2.

12  *The Age*, 26 April 1989, p. 5; *The Australian*, 26 April 1983, p. 3; F Bongiorno, *The Eighties: The Decade that Transformed Australia*, Black Inc., Melbourne, 2015, pp. 259–61.

13  *The Australian*, 25 April 1990, p. 11; N Bromfield, 'Welcome home: reconciliation, Vietnam veterans, and the reconstruction of Anzac under the Hawke government', Australian Political Studies Association, n.d. 2012? <www.auspsa.org.au/sites/default/files/welcome_home_nicholas_bromfield.pdf>; R Hawke, 'Speech by Bob Hawke at the Anzac Day ceremony, Athens', 25 April 1986, Bob

Hawke Prime Ministerial Library, University of South Australia, <archives.
library.unisa.edu.au/record/UNISA_ALMA51117413380001831>; Holbrook,
'Commemorators-in-chief', pp. 221–22; 'Kaching! Australia's Anzac centenary
spend hits $A562 million', Honest History, 11 January 2016 <honesthistory.net.
au/wp/kaching-australias-anzac-centenary-spend-hits-a562-million>.

14    Holbrook, 'Commemorators-in-chief'.

15    *The Age*, 26 April 1990, p. 2; *The Australian*, 26 April 1990, p. 2; Bongiorno, *The
Eighties*, pp. 104–05, 109–12.

16    P Keating, 'Funeral service of the Unknown Soldier', 11 November 1993, PM
Transcripts, <pmtranscripts.pmc.gov.au/release/transcript-9035>.

17    J Howard, 'Transcript of the Prime Minister the Hon John Howard MP address
at the State Funeral Service of Alec William Campbell the Cathedral Church of
St David, Hobart', 24 May 2002, PM Transcripts, <pmtranscripts.pmc.gov.au/
release/transcript-12946>. See also J Brett, *Australian Liberals and the Moral
Middle Class: From Alfred Deakin to John Howard*, Cambridge University Press,
Melbourne, 2003, pp. 204–205.

18    For example, K Rudd, 'Prime Minister speech at the ANZAC Day national
ceremony, Australian War Memorial, Canberra, on the commemoration of the
centenary of ANZAC', 25 April 2010, PM Transcripts, <pmtranscripts.pmc.gov.
au/release/transcript-17247>.

19    Holbrook, 'Commemorators-in-chief', p. 227; K Rudd, 'Nation shows its courage
and compassion', *Sydney Morning Herald*, 23 February 2009, <www.smh.com.au/
national/nation-shows-its-courage-and-compassion-20090222-8eq0.html>.

20    J Gillard, 'We remember them with our silence: speech at the Anzac Day service,
Seoul', 25 April 2011, PM Transcripts, <pmtranscripts.pmc.gov.au/release/
transcript-17811>.

21    T Abbott, '2015 Dawn Service, Gallipoli', 25 April 2015, PM Transcripts,
<pmtranscripts.pmc.gov.au/release/transcript-24397>.

22    J Howard, 'Address at Lone Pine, Gallipoli, Turkey – ANZAC Day', 25 April 2000,
PM Transcripts, <pmtranscripts.pmc.gov.au/release/transcript-22689>.

23    J Power, 'Outrage as Lone Pine ceremony at Gallipoli axed', *Sydney Morning
Herald*, 13 February 2016, <www.smh.com.au/national/outrage-as-lone-pine-
ceremony-at-gallipoli-axed-20160213-gmt8ba.html>.

24    JB Hirst, 'The pioneer legend', *Historical Studies*, vol. 18, no. 71, 1978, pp. 316–37.

## 9: Anzac and Anzackery: Useful future or sentimental dream?

1    B Nelson, 'Welcome address: official opening of First World War galleries',
22 February 2015, Australian War Memorial, <www.awm.gov.au/talks-speeches/
welcome-address-official-opening-first-world-war-galleries>.

2    B Moore, A Laugesen, M Gwynn & J Robinson (eds), *The Australian National
Dictionary: Australian Words and Their Origins*, vol. 1, 2nd edn, Oxford
University Press, Melbourne, 2016, p. 33.

3    For a discussion of statistics, see D Stephens, ' "Visitation" numbers at the
Australian War Memorial since 1991: is this joint really jumpin'?', Honest History,

2 February 2016, <honesthistory.net.au/wp/visitation-numbers-at-the-australian-war-memorial-since-1991-is-this-joint-really-jumpin>.

4   M McGirr, *Bypass: The Story of a Road*, Picador, Sydney, 2004, p. 246.

5   DG Faust, *This Republic of Suffering: Death and the American Civil War*, Vintage, New York, 2009, p. 268.

6   K Aubusson, 'Why my generation grew up thinking it was un-Australian to question Anzac', *Sydney Morning Herald*, 17 April 2015, <www.smh.com.au/comment/why-my-generation-grew-up-thinking-it-was-unaustralian-to-question-anzac-20150416-1mmee6>.

7   J Valentine, 'Gallipoli: the story we all grew up with', *The Age* (Melbourne), 26 April 2015, <www.theage.com.au/comment/gallipoli-the-story-we-all-grew-up-with-20150421-1mpsew>.

8   M Stipe, 'Are we that warlike, that childish, that afraid?', *The Guardian* (Australia), 11 September 2014, <www.theguardian.com/artanddesign/2014/sep/10/michael-stipe-rem-douglas-coupland-artwork-haunt-us>.

9   McGirr, *Bypass*, p. 246.

10  P Stanley, *Lost Boys of Anzac*, NewSouth, Sydney, 2014.

11  E Toller, *I Was a German: The Autobiography of Ernst Toller* (1934), quoted in K Vondung, *The Apocalypse in Germany*, trans. S Ricks, University of Missouri Press, Columbia & London, 2000, p. 11.

12  See, for example, M Turnbull, 'Anzac Day National Commemorative Address', 25 April 2016, Prime Minister of Australia website, <www.pm.gov.au/media/2016-04-25/anzac-day-national-ceremony-commemorative-address>.

13  M Larsson, *Shattered Anzacs: Living with the Scars of War*, UNSW Press, Sydney, 2009.

14  'Media release: National Archives exposes the ongoing impact of war', 10 June 2015, National Archives of Australia, <www.naa.gov.au/about-us/media/media-releases/2015/14.aspx>; B Scates, R Wheatley & L James, *World War One: A History in 100 Stories*, Penguin, Melbourne, 2015.

15  M Lake, *The Limits of Hope: Soldier Settlement in Victoria, 1915–38*, Oxford University Press, Melbourne, 1987; B Scates & M Oppenheimer, *The Last Battle: Soldier Settlement in Australia, 1916–1939*, Cambridge University Press, Melbourne, 2016.

16  B Scates, 'Professor Bruce Scates', transcript of speech at Anzac Centenary Peace Coalition Forum, Melbourne, 16 March 2015, Peace Coalition Anzac Centenary, <georgiapeacecoalition.wordpress.com/forums-2/federation-to-the-aftermath-of-wwi/professor-bruce-scates>.

17  R Fathi, 'Is Australia spending too much on the "Anzac centenary"? A comparison with France', Honest History, 14 April 2016, <honesthistory.net.au/wp/fathi-romain-is-australia-spending-too-much-on-the-anzac-centenary-plus-hh-background-on-spending-politics>.

18  J Lack, *No Lost Battalion: An Oral History of the 2/29th Battalion AIF*, Slouch Hat Publications, Melbourne, 2005, p. 300.

19  R Hamond, *A Fearful Freedom: The Story of One Man's Survival behind the Lines in Japanese-occupied Territory 1942–1945*, Secker & Warburg, London, 1984.

20  P Stanley, *Bad Characters: Sex, Crime, Mutiny, Murder and the Australian Imperial Force*, Allen & Unwin, Sydney, 2010.

21  P FitzSimons, *Gallipoli*, Random House, Sydney, 2014, p. 687; B Nelson, quoted in S Heanue & E Pianegonda, 'Australian War Memorial opens newly refurbished World War I galleries', *ABC News*, 9 December 2014, <www.abc.net.au/news/2014-11-30/australian-war-memorial-unveils-newly-refurbished-wwi-gallery/5929306>.

22  F Bongiorno, 'Anzac and the politics of inclusion', in S Sumartojo & B Wellings (eds), *Nation, Memory and Great War Commemoration* (2014), quoted in P Cochrane, 'The past is not sacred', *Griffith Review*, no 48, *Enduring Legacies*, 2015, <griffithreview.com/articles/past-sacred>.

23  A welcome development at the Australian War Memorial is the opening of a permanent exhibition on the Holocaust (B Nelson, 'Witnesses and survivors Holocaust exhibition', 29 November 2016, Australian War Memorial, <www.awm.gov.au/talks-speeches/witnesses-and-survivors-holocaust-exhibition>).

24  M Leitenberg, 'Deaths in wars and conflicts in the 20th century', Cornell University Peace Studies Program, occasional paper no. 29, 3rd edn, Centre for International Security Studies at Maryland, School of Public Policy, University of Maryland, College Park, 2006, <www.clingendael.nl/sites/default/files/20060800_cdsp_occ_leitenberg.pdf>.

25  J Beaumont, *Broken Nation: Australians in the Great War*, Allen & Unwin, Sydney, 2013.

26  J Rose, 'Here's looking at us #1 – the Australian War Memorial', Crikey, 13 August 2013, <blogs.crikey.com.au/truthtotell/2013/08/13/heres-looking-at-us-1-the-australian-war-memorial>; D Stephens, 'Ministers tell future generations: there will be blood, your blood', *Sydney Morning Herald*, 9 September 2015, <www.smh.com.au/comment/ministers-tell-future-generations-there-will-be-blood-your-blood-20150908-gjhwhd.html>.

27  E Samet, 'Can an American soldier ever die in vain?' *Foreign Policy*, 9 May 2014, <foreignpolicy.com/2014/05/09/can-an-american-soldier-ever-die-in-vain>.

# Part 2: Australian stories and silences

## 10: Fires, droughts and flooding rains: Environmental influences on Australian history

1  Extracts from J O'Brien (PJ Hartigan), 'Said Hanrahan', originally published in *Around the Boree Log and Other Verses*, Angus & Robertson, Sydney, 1921.

2  See, for example, *The Forerunner*, made by John Heyer in 1958 for the Shell Film Unit, 'about the threats of floods in Australia, the special water schemes devised and the forerunner of these projects, the Snowy Mountains scheme', BFI Film Forever, <www.bfi.org.uk/films-tv-people/4ce2b6a2797b5>.

3     On the naming of fires, see C Gough-Brady, 'Fire words', *Griffith Review*, no. 35, *Surviving*, 2012, <griffithreview.com/articles/fire-words>.

4     S Macintyre, *The Oxford History of Australia: The Succeeding Age 1901–1942*, Oxford University Press, Melbourne, 1993, p. 209.

5     T Griffiths, 'We have still not lived long enough', Inside Story, 16 February 2009, <insidestory.org.au/we-have-still-not-lived-long-enough>.

6     Griffiths, 'We have still not lived long enough'.

7     S Pyne, *Burning Bush: A Fire History of Australia*, Henry Holt & Company, New York, 1999, p. 205. See also B Gammage, *The Biggest Estate on Earth: How Aborigines Made Australia*, Allen & Unwin, Sydney, 2011; K Hancock, *Discovering Monaro: A Study of Man's Impact on His Environment*, Cambridge University Press, Cambridge, 1972.

8     CW Coote, Diaries and papers, 1896–1955, University of Melbourne Archives, A.1964.0005.

9     J Hirst, *Adelaide and the Country, 1870–1917: Their Social and Political Relationship*, Monash University Press, Melbourne, 1973, pp. 2, 6; DW Meinig, *On the Margins of the Good Earth: The South Australian Wheat Frontier, 1869–1884*, South Australian Government Printer, Adelaide, 1988, p. 91.

10    TLP Bettison, Diaries and Papers, 1927–1962, State Library of South Australia, PRG1484.

11    EA Cornish, 'Yield trends in the wheat belt of South Australia during 1896–1941', *Australian Journal of Scientific Research*, series B, vol. 2, no. 2, 1949, p. 84.

12    Department of Community Safety, Queensland, *Risk Frontiers, State-wide Natural Hazard Risk Assessment: Report 8: Major Historical Flash Flooding in Queensland*, Brisbane, 2011, pp. 3–10.

13    E O'Gorman, *Flood Country: An Environmental History of the Murray Darling Basin*, CSIRO Publishing, Melbourne, 2012, pp. 10–11, 228.

14    LR East, *Water in the Mallee*, State Rivers and Water Supply Commission, Melbourne, 1965, p. 31.

15    T Sherratt, 'The weather prophets: the Charleville rainmaker', 1 July 2001, Discontents blog, <discontents.com.au/the-weather-prophets>. See also 'Federation and meteorology', Australian Science and Technology Heritage Centre, University of Melbourne, August 2001, <www.austehc.unimelb.edu.au/fam>.

16    PE Charman & BW Murphy, *Soils: Their Properties and Management*, Oxford University Press, Melbourne, 2000, pp. 265–66.

17    A Holt, *Wheat Farms of Victoria: A Sociological Survey*, School of Agriculture, University of Melbourne, 1947, p. 146.

18    Griffiths, 'We have still not lived long enough'.

19    Bureau of Meteorology and CSIRO, Climate Change in Australia, <www.climatechangeinaustralia.gov.au/en>; P Holper, *Climate Change, Science Information Paper: Australian Rainfall – Past, Present and Future*, CSIRO and Bureau of Meteorology, Melbourne, 2011; Intergovernmental Panel on Climate Change, *Climate Change 2014: Synthesis Report*, IPCC, Geneva, 2014.

## 11: From those who've come across the seas: Immigration and multiculturalism

1   By 'Anglo-nativism' I mean an excessive belief in the racial and cultural superiority of Australian-born people of British descent.

2   Australian Bureau of Statistics, *3412.0 - Migration, Australia, 2014–15*, ABS, Canberra, 30 March 2016, <www.abs.gov.au/ausstats/abs@.nsf/mf/3412.0>.

3   K Neumann & G Tavan (eds), *Does History Matter? Making and Debating Citizenship, Immigration and Refugee Policy in Australia and New Zealand*, ANU E Press, Canberra, 2009, <press-files.anu.edu.au/downloads/press/p109651/pdf/prelims4.pdf>.

4   J Jupp, *From White Australia to Woomera: The Story of Australian Immigration*, Cambridge University Press, Melbourne, 2002; A Markus, J Jupp & P McDonald, *Australia's Immigration Revolution*, Allen & Unwin, Sydney, 2009; E Richards, *Destination Australia: Migration to Australia since 1901*, UNSW Press, Sydney, 2008.

5   G Megalogenis, *Australia's Second Chance: What Our History Tells Us about Our Future*, Hamish Hamilton, Melbourne, 2015.

6   Department of Immigration and Border Protection, *Australian Citizenship: Our Common Bond*, DIBP, Canberra, 2014, <www.border.gov.au/Citizenship/Documents/our-common-bond-2014.pdf>.

7   DIBP, *Australian Citizenship*, p. 14.

8   DIBP, *Australian Citizenship*, p. 14.

9   Prime Minister Gillard's office required that focus groups be repeated to obtain evidence that non-Anglo-Celtic Australians identified with Anzac, while a recent children's publication from the Department of Veterans' Affairs includes Samir from the Sudan watching an Anzac Day march so he can become familiar with Australian customs. See R Peake, 'Move "soon" on Anzac centenary', *Canberra Times*, 17 April 2013, <www.canberratimes.com.au/national/move-soon-on-anzac-centenary-20130416-2hytr.html>; J Cole-Adams & J Gauld, *Here They Come: A Day to Remember*, Department of Veterans' Affairs, Canberra, 2016, at Anzac Portal, <anzacportal.dva.gov.au/sites/default/files/publication-attachments/Here They Come FINAL.pdf>.

10  W K Hancock, *Australia*, Ernest Benn, London, 1930, p. 55.

11  Commonwealth Bureau of Census and Statistics, *Official Year Book of the Commonwealth of Australia, No. 9, 1916*, ABS, <www.ausstats.abs.gov.au/ausstats/free.nsf/0/D07DF68BB3EB332FCA257AEE00161CEC/$File/13010_1901_1915 section 4.pdf>.

12  For how the dictation test worked, see 'Immigration Restriction Act', Journeys to Australia, Museums Victoria, <museumvictoria.com.au/discoverycentre/websites-mini/journeys-australia/1900s20s/immigration-restriction-act>. Very few people passed the test.

13  Markus, Jupp & McDonald, *Australia's Immigration Revolution*.

14  J Phillips & J Simon-Davies, 'Migration to Australia: a quick guide to the statistics', in Parliament of Australia, *Parliamentary Library Research Paper Series, 2015–16* (2016), Department of Pariamentary Services, Canberra, p. 3,

<parlinfo.aph.gov.au/parlInfo/download/library/prspub/3165114/upload_binary/3165114.pdf;fileType=application/pdf>.

15 P Mares, *Not Quite Australian: How Temporary Migration Is Changing the Nation*, Text Publishing, Melbourne, 2016.

16 G Tavan, 'No going back? Australian multiculturalism as a path-dependent process', *Australian Journal of Political Science*, vol. 47, no. 4, 2012, pp. 547–61.

17 Permanent migration increased from 73 900 in 1996–97 to 148 200 in 2006–07 and then to 189 097 in 2014–15 (Phillips & Simon-Davies, 'Migration to Australia', p. 3). See also H Sherrell & P Mares, 'How many migrants come to Australia each year?', Inside Story, 14 October 2016, <insidestory.org.au/how-many-migrants-come-to-australia-each-year>.

18 M Saville, *The Battle for Bennelong: The Adventures of Maxine McKew, Aged 50something*, Melbourne University Press, Melbourne, 2007.

19 Megalogenis, *Australia's Second Chance*, p. xi.

## 12: Bust and boom: What economic lessons has Australia learned?

1 W Vamplew (ed.), *Australians: Historical Statistics*, Fairfax, Syme & Weldon Associates, Sydney, 1987, p. 152.

2 S Macintyre, *Australia's Boldest Experiment: War and Reconstruction in the 1940s*, NewSouth, Sydney, 2015, p. 66.

3 HC Coombs, 'Seven million pairs of hands', ABC radio transcript, 4 December 1942, White Paper on Full Employment, National Archives of Australia, NAA: M448, 101.

4 J Furphy, *Such Is Life: Being Certain Extracts from the Diary of Tom Collins*, Bulletin Library, Sydney, 1903, p. 1.

5 D Potts, *The Myth of the Great Depression*, Scribe, Melbourne, 2006, p. 31.

6 J Schumpeter, *Capitalism, Socialism and Democracy*, Routledge, London, 1942, pp. 82–83.

7 R Skidelsky, *John Maynard Keynes*, vol. 3, *Fighting for Britain 1937–1946*, Macmillan, London, 2000, p. 385.

8 R Garnaut, *Dog Days: Australia after the Boom*, Black Inc., Melbourne, 2013, pp. 1, 60.

9 The standard accounts are EA Boehm, *Prosperity and Depression in Australia, 1887–1897*, Clarendon Press, Oxford, 1971; and CB Schedvin, *Australia and the Great Depression: A Study of Economic Development and Policy in the 1920s and 1930s*, Sydney University Press, Sydney, 1970.

10 J Cranfield & K Inwood, 'A tale of two armies: comparative growth in the mirror of the First World War', *Australian Economic History Review*, vol. 55, no. 2, 2015, pp. 212–33.

11 S Macintyre, *The Labour Experiment*, McPhee Gribble, Melbourne, 1989.

12 C White, *Mastering Risk: Environment, Markets and Politics in Australian Economic History*, Oxford University Press, Melbourne, 1992, p. 223.

13 IW McLean & JJ Pincus, 'Did Australian living standards stagnate between 1890 and 1940?', *Journal of Economic History*, vol. 43, no. 1, 1983, pp. 193–202.

14   P Kelly, *The End of Certainty: The Story of the 1980s*, Allen & Unwin, Sydney, 1992, p. 13.

15   I McLean, *Why Australia Prospered: The Shifting Sources of Economic Growth*, Princeton University Press, Princeton, New Jersey, 2013, pp. 144–57.

16   Macintyre, *Australia's Boldest Experiment*.

17   G Davison with S Yelland, *Car Wars: How the Car Won Our Hearts and Conquered Our Cities*, Allen & Unwin, Sydney, 2004, p. 15; S Marginson, *Educating Australia: Government, Economy and Citizen since 1960*, Cambridge University Press, Melbourne, 1997, p. 22; P Troy, *Accommodating Australians: Commonwealth Government Involvement in Housing*, Federation Press, Sydney, 2012, p. 251; Vamplew (ed.), *Australians*, p. 53.

18   A Leigh, *Battlers and Billionaires: The Story of Inequality in Australia*, Black Inc., Melbourne, 2013, pp. 35, 41.

19   The historical Human Development Index calculations are based on statistics for population and real GDP in S Ville & G Withers (eds), *The Cambridge Economic History of Australia*, Cambridge University Press, Melbourne, 2015, pp. 557, 560, 565, 569.

20   R Tiffen & R Gittins, *How Australia Compares*, Cambridge University Press, Melbourne, 2009, p. 8.

21   Australian Bureau of Statistics, 'Explanatory notes', *6227.0 – Education and Work, Australia, May 2011*, ABS, <www.abs.gov.au/AUSSTATS/abs@.nsf/Lookup/6227.0Explanatory Notes1May 2011>.

22   Tiffen & Gittins, *How Australia Compares*, pp. 80, 82.

23   Tiffen & Gittins, *How Australia Compares*, p. 210.

24   G Whitwell & S Nicholas, 'Weight and welfare of Australians, 1890–1940', *Australian Economic History Review*, vol. 41, no. 2, 2001, p. 169.

25   Ville & Withers (eds), *The Cambridge Economic History of Australia*, pp. 593–94.

26   Leigh, *Battlers and Billionaires*, p. 35.

27   C Sheil & F Stilwell, *The Wealth of the Nation: Current Data on the Distribution of Wealth in Australia*, Evatt Foundation, Sydney, 2016, p. 10, <evatt.org.au/files/files/The Wealth of the Nation.pdf>.

28   Organisation for Economic Cooperation and Development, 'Focus on inequality and growth', OECD, December 2014, <www.oecd.org/social/Focus-Inequality-and-Growth-2014.pdf>.

29   For a collection of recent survey and research material on inequality, see the Honest History website: 'Inequality in Australia', Honest History, <honesthistory.net.au/wp/inequality-in-australia>.

## 13: 'Fair go' nation? Egalitarian myth and reality in Australia

1   J Howard, 'Four distinct and enduring Australian values', transcript of speech to the Melbourne Press Club, *Australian Politics*, 22 November 2000, <australianpolitics.com/2000/11/22/john-howard-distinct-enduring-australian-values.html>.

2   'Australian values statement', Department of Immigration and Border Protection, <www.border.gov.au/Trav/Life/Aust/living-in-australia-values-statement-long>.

3     F Argy, 'Equality of opportunity in Australia: myth and reality', Australia
      Institute Discussion Paper, no. 85, April 2006, Australia Institute, <www.tai.
      org.au/sites/defualt/files/DP85_8.pdf>. See also 'Inequality in Australia', Honest
      History, <honesthistory.net.au/wp/inequality-in-australia>.

4     H Mackay, 'The pleasing myth of egalitarian Australia: Ninth Mitchell Oration',
      10 October 1997, Equal Opportunity Commission, <www.eoc.sa.gov.au/eo-
      resources/events/mitchell-oration-1997>.

5     Argy, 'Equality of opportunity in Australia', p. 1.

6     Argy, 'Equality of opportunity in Australia', p. 1; Equal Opportunity
      Commission, Western Australia, 'The policy framework for substantive equality:
      1', November 2004, p. 4, EOC WA, <www.eoc.wa.gov.au/substantive-equality/
      resources>.

7     EOC WA, 'The policy framework for substantive equality', 2004, p. 1.

8     Quoted in 'Affirmative action', The Leadership Conference, <www.civilrights.org/
      resources/civilrights101/affirmaction.html>.

9     Australian Council of Social Service, A Fair Go for All Australians: International
      Comparisons, 2007: 10 Essentials, Australia Fair, Sydney, 2007.

10    Department of Education, Employment and Workplace Relations, Review of
      Funding for Schooling – Final Report, Canberra, 2011. I was a member of the
      Gonski Expert Panel.

11    G Meagher & S Wilson, 'Richer, but more unequal: perceptions of inequality in
      Australia 1987–2005', Journal of Australian Political Economy, no. 61, June 2008,
      pp. 220–43.

12    A Markus, Mapping Social Cohesion: The Scanlon Foundation Surveys, 2016,
      Australian Centre for Jewish Civilisation, Monash University, Melbourne,
      2016, pp. 16–17, <scanlonfoundation.org.au/wp-content/uploads/2016/11/2016-
      Mapping-Social-Cohesion-Report-FINAL-with-covers.pdf>.

13    B Douglas, S Friel, R Denniss & S Morawetz, Advance Australia Fair?
      What to Do about Growing Inequality in Australia, Australia21 with
      the Australia Institute, Canberra, 2014, <www.tai.org.au/sites/defualt/
      files/50497Aus21InequalityinAustraliaReportComplete_FA3LoRes-1.pdfh>.

14    D Hetherington, 'Per Capita tax survey, 2016', Per Capita, April 2016, <percapita.
      org.au/research/per-capita-tax-survey-2016>.

15    A Pedersen, P Dudgeon, S Watt & B Griffiths, 'Attitudes toward Indigenous
      Australians: the issue of "special treatment"', Australian Psychologist, vol. 41,
      no. 2, 2011, pp. 85–94.

16    JR Kluegel, G Csepeli, T Kolosi, A Orkeny & M Nemenyi, 'Accounting for the rich
      and the poor: existential justice in comparative perspective', in JR Kluegel, DS
      Mason & B Wegener (eds), Social Justice and Political Change: Public Opinion in
      Capitalist and Post-Communist States, De Gruyter, Berlin & New York, 1995,
      pp. 179–203.

17    L Osberg & TM Smeeding, '"Fair" inequality? Attitudes toward pay differentials:
      the United States in comparative perspective', American Sociological Review,
      vol. 71, no. 3, 2006, pp. 450–73.

18    SH Schwartz, 'Are there universal aspects in the content and structure of values?',
      Journal of Social Issues, vol. 50, no. 4, 1994, pp. 19–45.

19 'Living in Norway: Norwegian society', Study in Norway, <www.studyinnorway. no/Living-in-Norway/Norwegian-society>.
20 Osberg & Smeeding, '"Fair" inequality?'.
21 United Nations Development Programme, *Humanity Divided: Confronting Inequality in Developing Countries*, UNDP, New York, 2014, <www.undp.org/ content/undp/en/home/librarypage/poverty-reduction/humanity-divided-- confronting-inequality-in-developing-countries.html>.
22 'Inequality', OECD, <www.oecd.org/social/inequality.htm>. Simply defined, 'income' is earnings; 'wealth' is assets that may produce income or other benefits.
23 Australian Council of Social Service, *Inequality in Australia: A Nation Divided*, ACOSS, Sydney, 2015, <www.acoss.org.au/wp-content/uploads/2015/06/ Inequality_in_Australia_FINAL.pdf>.
24 'Ending poverty requires more than growth, says WBG', media release, World Bank, 10 April 2014, <www.worldbank.org/en/news/press-release/2014/04/10/ ending-poverty-requires-more-than-growth-says-wbg>.
25 RG Wilkinson & K Pickett, 'The problems of relative deprivation: why some societies do better than others', *Social Science and Medicine*, vol. 65, no. 9, 2007, pp. 1965–78.
26 R Wilkinson & K Pickett, *The Spirit Level: Why Equality Is Better for Everyone*, Penguin, London, 2010.
27 EM Uslaner, *The Moral Foundations of Trust*, Cambridge University Press, Cambridge, 2002; EM Uslaner & M Brown, 'Inequality, trust, and civic engagement', *American Politics Research*, vol. 33, no. 6, 2005, pp. 868–94.
28 N Breznau, 'Economic equality and social welfare: policy preferences in five nations', *International Journal of Public Opinion Research*, vol. 22, no. 4, 2010, pp. 458–84.
29 G Arikan, 'Economic individualism and government spending', *World Values Research*, vol. 4, no. 3, 2011, pp. 73–95.
30 C Ronzio, E Pamuk & G Squires, 'The politics of preventable deaths: local spending, income inequality, and premature mortality in US cities', *Journal of Epidemiology and Community Health*, vol. 58, no. 3, 2004, pp. 175–79.
31 A Sakamoto & C Kim, 'Is rising earnings inequality associated with increased exploitation? Evidence for U.S. manufacturing industries, 1971–1996', *Sociological Perspectives*, vol. 53, no. 1, 2010, p. 20.
32 P Krugman, 'Oligarchy, American style', *New York Times*, 3 November 2011, <www.nytimes.com/2011/11/04/opinion/oligarchy-american-style.html?_r=0>.
33 F Solt, 'Economic inequality and democratic political engagement', Luxembourg Income Study Working Paper Series, no. 385, July 2004, <www.lisdatacenter.org/ wps/liswps/385.pdf>.
34 JK Galbraith, 'With economic inequality for all', National Jobs for All Coalition, September 1998, <02d9ed5.netsolhost.com/gal-ineq.htm>.
35 J Stiglitz, *The Price of Inequality: How Today's Divided Society Endangers Our Future*, Norton, New York, 2012, p. 28.

## 14: Australian heroes: Some military mates are more equal than others

This chapter is partly based on an essay, 'A hundred in a million', published in *Griffith Review*, no. 48, *Enduring Legacies*, 2015.

1   B Rule, 'The greatest of all – our 50 top Australians', *The Australian*, 27 January 2013, <www.theaustralian.com.au/news/the-greatest-of-all-our-50-top-australians/story-e6frg6n6-1226562801398>.

2   'Enlist in the Sportsmen's Thousand', recruitment poster, 1917, Australian War Memorial, <www.awm.gov.au/collection/ARTV00026>.

3   N Dyrenfurth, *Mateship: A Very Australian History*, Scribe, Melbourne, 2015, especially Introduction, chs 1, 7, 9.

4   P Rees, *Bearing Witness: The Remarkable Life of Charles Bean, Australia's Greatest War Correspondent*, Allen & Unwin, Sydney, 2015, pp. xvii, 488.

5   Australian Imperial Force Records Section, *Australian Imperial Force: Statistics of Casualties, etc. Compiled to 30th June, 1919*, AIF Records Section, London, 1919, p. 23.

6   V D'Alton, 'Behind the valour: a technical, administrative and bureaucratic analysis of the Victoria Cross and the AIF on the Western Front, 1916–1918', MA thesis, UNSW Canberra, Australian Defence Force Academy, 2011.

7   'Valour: Inquiry into unresolved recognition for past acts of naval and military gallantry and valour (Valour Inquiry)', Australian Government Defence Honours and Awards Appeal Tribunal, 2013, <defence-honours-tribunal.gov.au/inquiries/completed-inquiries/valour>.

8   R Macklin, *Bravest: How Some of Australia's Greatest War Heroes Won Their Medals*, Allen & Unwin, Sydney, 2008, p. 3.

9   Quoted in Rees, *Bearing Witness*, p. 249.

10  G Kieza, *Monash: The Soldier Who Shaped Australia*, ABC Books, Sydney, 2015; PA Pedersen, *Monash as Military Commander*, Melbourne University Press, Melbourne, 1988; R Perry, *Monash: The Outsider Who Won a War*, Random House, Sydney, 2004; G Serle, *John Monash: A Biography*, Melbourne University Press & Monash University, Melbourne, 1982.

11  *Monash: The Forgotten Anzac*, 360 Degree Films, Screen Australia, Screen Victoria and the ABC, 2008, see: <www.youtube.com/watch?v=AGkRJHJ5juI>.

12  T Fischer, *Maestro John Monash: Australia's Greatest Citizen General*, Monash University Publishing, Melbourne, 2014.

13  D Stephens, 'Minister defends Abbott's wasteful war museum boondoggle', Independent Australia, 21 January 2016, <independentaustralia.net/politics/politics-display/minister-defends-abbotts-wasteful-war-museum-boondoggle,8596>.

14  ABC Television & Screen West, 'Invitation to pitch: Sir John Monash documentary', 9 May 2016, at Honest History, <honesthistory.net.au/wp/wp-content/uploads/Invitation-To-Pitch-Sir-John-Monash-Documentary-1.pdf>.

15  Senate Foreign Affairs, Defence and Trade Legislation Committee, 'Estimates', Official Committee Hansard, 19 October 2016, p. 141.

16   ANZAC Heroes Great War 1914–1918: Bunbury–Wellington District, Western
     Australia, <anzacheroes.com.au>; 'Australia's favourite hero', Anzac, <www.
     anzacs.net/Simpson.htm>; 'Commemorating our heroes on Anzac Day', Find My
     Past, <www.findmypast.com.au/anzacday>; M Gill, *Anzac Heroes*, Scholastic,
     Auckland, 2016; 'Topic 8: What makes a hero? Worksheet 8E: Websearch for
     World War II heroes', Gallipoli and the Anzacs, <www.gallipoli.gov.au/teaching-
     about-gallipoli/operation-click/pdf/Topic_08/8E_WS_ww2hero.pdf>; B Nelson,
     'Celebrating all our heroes', Australian War Memorial, 14 March 2013, <www.
     awm.gov.au/blog/2013/03/14/celebrating-all-our-heroes>.
17   I McPhedran, 'Camp Gallipoli honours sacrifice of all fallen soldiers',
     *Herald Sun* (Melbourne), 14 February 2015, <www.news.com.au/national/
     camp-gallipoli-honours-sacrifice-of-all-fallen-soldiers/news-story/
     e6b36b2ea708c30ec3e340a764b2294f>; A Webster, 'Aussie VC winner Ben
     Roberts-Smith to deliver Anzac Cup for clash between Roosters and Dragons',
     *Daily Telegraph* (Sydney), 7 April 2011, <www.dailytelegraph.com.au/sport/nrl/
     aussie-vc-winner-ben-roberts-smith-to-deliver-anzac-cup-for-clash-between-
     roosters-and-dragons/story-e6frexnr-1226034998899>.

## 15: Hidden by the myth: Women's leadership in war and peace

1    *Woman Voter* (Melbourne), 23 November 1916, p. 2.
2    *The Leader* (Melbourne), 21 October 1916, p. 46.
3    *The Age* (Melbourne), 5 December 1917, p. 10.
4    *Barrier Miner* (Broken Hill), 6 December 1917, p. 4.
5    *Farmer and Settler* (Sydney), 21 December 1915, p. 3.
6    *Daily News* (Perth), 4 January 1916, p. 4.
7    *Woman Voter*, 29 November 1917, p. 2.
8    *The Argus* (Melbourne), 28 November 1917, p. 12.
9    *The Argus*, 10 May 1916, p. 12.
10   *The Sun* (Sydney), 5 November 1916, p. 16.
11   *The Leader*, 21 October 2016, p. 46.
12   J Damousi, 'Universities and conscription: the "Yes" campaigns and the
     University of Melbourne', in R Archer, J Damousi, M Goot & S Scalmer (eds),
     *The Conscription Conflict and the Great War*, Monash University Publishing,
     Melbourne, pp. 92–110.
13   *Daily Telegraph* (Launceston), 27 October 1916, p. 7.
14   M Oppenheimer, 'Lady Helen Munro Ferguson and the Australian Red Cross:
     vice-regal leader and internationalist in the early twentieth century', in F Davis,
     N Musgrove & J Smart (eds), *Founders, Firsts and Feminists: Women Leaders in
     Twentieth Century Australia*, University of Melbourne eScholarship Research
     Centre, Melbourne, 2011, pp. 274–91, <www.womenaustralia.info/leaders/fff/
     index.html>; M Quartly & J Smart, *Respectable Radicals: A History of the National
     Council of Women in Australia, 1896–2006*, Monash University Publishing,
     Melbourne, 2015.
15   C John, 'How Australia helped', *The Record of the Save the Children Fund*, vol. 1,
     no. 16, 1 July 1921, p. 252, SCF Archive, Birmingham, Box A0670.

16   SCF Council Minutes, 21 September 1923, SCF Archive, Birmingham, A/1/1/2, 16 January 1922 – 26 October 1923.

17   *The Record of the Save the Children Fund*, vol. 111, no. 1, third quarter 1922, p. 45.

18   *The Record of the Save the Children Fund*, vol. 111, no. 1, third quarter 1922, p. 45.

19   *Stead's Review*, 14 June 1924, p. 20.

20   *Stead's Review*, 14 June 1924, p. 20.

21   E Burrett, Hon. Home Secretary, National Council of Women in Victoria, to the Hon. Prime Minister, 29 May 1923, National Archives of Australia, NAA: A981/1, League of Nations 4th Assembly 1.

22   E Burrett to Prime Minister, 29 May 1923.

23   *The Argus*, 12 July 1923, p. 9.

24   *Farmers' Advocate* (Melbourne), 19 July 1921, p. 10.

25   *The Argus*, 29 March 1924, p. 36.

26   *The Age*, 1 March 1924, p. 17; B Cabanes, *The Great War and the Origins of Humanitarianism, 1918–1924*, Cambridge University Press, Cambridge, 2014, p. 250; *The News* (Adelaide), 19 July 1924, p. 1.

27   *The Register* (Adelaide), 4 March 1924, p. 6. See also *The Argus*, 6 August 1924, p. 6; *Evening News* (Sydney), 3 June 1924, p. 11.

28   PJ Yearwood, ' "Consistently with honour": Great Britain, the League of Nations and the Corfu crisis of 1923', *Journal of Contemporary History*, vol. 21, no. 4, 1986, pp. 559–79.

29   *West Australian*, 23 February 1924, p. 9.

30   *West Australian*, 23 February 1924, p. 9, 26 February 1924, p. 8.

31   J Damousi & M Tomsic, 'Introduction', in J Damousi, K Rubenstein & M Tomsic (eds), *Diversity in Leadership: Australian Women, Past and Present*, ANU Press, Canberra, p. 13.

32   A Sinclair, 'A feminist case for leadership', in Damousi, Rubinstein & Tomsic (eds), *Diversity in Leadership*, pp. 17–35.

## 16  Settlement or invasion? The coloniser's quandary

1   JL Kohen, 'Pemulwuy (1750–1802)', *Australian Dictionary of Biography*, National Centre of Biography, Australian National University, <adb.anu.edu.au/biography/pemulwuy-13147>.

2   DA Roberts, 'Windradyne (1800–1829)', *Australian Dictionary of Biography*, <adb.anu.edu.au/biography/windradyne-13251>.

3   LR Marchant, 'La Pérouse, Jean-François de Galaup (1741–1788)', *Australian Dictionary of Biography*, <adb.anu.edu.au/biography/la-perouse-jean-francois-de-galaup-2329>.

4   R Miller, J Ruru, L Behrendt & T Lindberg, *Discovering Indigenous Lands: The Doctrine of Discovery in the English Colonies*, Oxford University Press, Oxford, 2012.

5   Australian Human Rights Commission, *Close the Gap: Progress and Priorities Report 2016*, Close the Gap Campaign Steering Committee, Sydney, 2016, <www.humanrights.gov.au/our-work/aboriginal-and-torres-strait-islander-social-justice/publications/close-gap-progress>.

6   *88*, television film, Pursekey Productions, Screen Australia, ABC TV and Screen NSW, 2014, <www.pursekey.com.au/88>.

7   *Milirrpum v Nabalco Pty Ltd* (1971) 17 FLR 141.

8   *Mabo v Queensland (No. 2)* (1992) 175 CLR 1.

9   S Berns, *To Speak as a Judge: Difference, Voice and Power*, Ashgate, Aldershot, UK, 1999, pp. 64–67.

10  M Ford & C Blumer, 'Vote Compass: most Australians back constitutional recognition for Indigenous Australians', *ABC News*, 20 May 2016, <www.abc.net.au/news/2016-05-20/vote-compass-indigenous-recognition/7428030>; M Liddy, 'Vote Compass: Australians split on teaching kids about "invasion"', *ABC News*, 23 May 2016, <www.abc.net.au/news/2016-05-23/vote-compass-australians-split-on-teaching-kids-about-invasion/7431906>.

11  Australian Human Rights and Equal Opportunity Commission, *Bringing Them Home: Report of the National Inquiry into the Separation of Aboriginal and Torres Strait Islander Children from Their Families (April 1997)*, HREOC, Sydney, 1997, <www.humanrights.gov.au/publications/bringing-them-home-report-1997>.

12  I Clendinnen, *True Stories: History, Politics and Aboriginality*, Text Publishing, Melbourne, 2010, p. 13.

13  M Foucault, *The History of Sexuality*, vol. 1, *The Will to Knowledge*, Pantheon Books, New York, 1978, p. 11.

14  P Mander-Jones, 'Dawes, William (1762–1836)', *Australian Dictionary of Biography*, <adb.anu.edu.au/biography/dawes-william-1968>; 'William Dawes (1762–1836)', Trove, National Library of Australia, <trove.nla.gov.au/people/616869?c=people>.

15  The Notebooks of William Dawes on the Aboriginal Language of Sydney, <www.williamdawes.org/refs.html>.

16  K Grenville, *The Lieutenant*, Text Publishing, Melbourne, 2008.

## 17: Our most important war: The legacy of frontier conflict

1   P Daley, 'From Butchers Creek to Berlin: did Douglas Grant see the body of an Indigenous relative in Germany?' *The Guardian* (Australia), 16 October 2015, <www.theguardian.com/australia-news/postcolonial-blog/2015/oct/16/from-butchers-creek-to-berlin-did-douglas-grant-see-the-body-of-an-indigenous-relative-in-germany>.

2   S Robinson, *Something Like Slavery? Queensland's Aboriginal Child Workers, 1842–1945*, Australian Scholarly Publishing, Melbourne, 2008.

3   J Richards, '"Many were killed from falling over the cliffs": the naming of Mount Wheeler, Central Queensland', in ID Clark, L Hercus & L Kostanski (eds), *Indigenous and Minority Placenames: Australian and International Perspectives*, ANU Press, Canberra, 2014, pp. 147–61, <press-files.anu.edu.au/downloads/press/p286811/pdf/ch081.pdf>; state geographical names board websites, particularly 'Queensland place names search', Queensland Department of Natural Resources and Mines, <https://www.dnrm.qld.gov.au/qld/environment/land/place-names/search>; Wikipedia references for each name.

4    J Connor, *The Australian Frontier Wars, 1788–1838*, UNSW Press, Sydney, 2014;
     H Reynolds, *Forgotten War*, NewSouth, Sydney, 2013.

5    K Windschuttle, *The Fabrication of Aboriginal History*, vol. 1, *Van Diemen's Land,
     1803–1847* and vol. 3, *The Stolen Generations, 1881–2008*, Macleay Press, Sydney,
     2009.

6    R Evans & R Ørsted-Jensen, ' "I cannot say the numbers that were killed":
     assessing violent mortality on the Queensland frontier', Social Science Research
     Network, 19 July 2014, pp. 1–10, <papers.ssrn.com/sol3/papers.cfm?abstract_
     id=2467836>.

7    Evans & Ørsted-Jensen, ' "I cannot say the numbers that were killed" ', p. 4.

8    Evans & Ørsted-Jensen, ' "I cannot say the numbers that were killed" ', p. 5.

9    Evans & Ørsted-Jensen, ' "I cannot say the numbers that were killed" ', p. 6.

10   Evans & Ørsted-Jensen, ' "I cannot say the numbers that were killed" ', p. 6,
     quoting Reynolds, *Forgotten War*, p. 248.

11   Stanner, quoted in A Curthoys, 'WEH Stanner and the historians', in M Hinkson
     & J Beckett (ed.), *An Appreciation of Difference: WEH Stanner and Aboriginal
     Australia*, Aboriginal Studies Press, Canberra, 2008, p. 233.

12   K Finnane, 'Coniston: survivors and descendants recall the massacre in a new
     film', *Alice Springs News*, 19 September 2012, <www.alicespringsnews.com.
     au/2012/09/19/coniston-survivors-and-descendants-recall-the-massacre-in-a-
     new-film>.

13   J Harris, *One Blood: 200 Years of Aboriginal Encounter with Christianity*,
     Albatross Books, Sydney, 1994, pp. 481–82.

14   EM Curr, quoted in Harris, *One Blood*, p. 482.

15   E Hill, 'Murray – scourge of the Myalls', *Northern Standard* (Darwin), 3 March
     1933, p. 5.

16   P Daley, 'Restless Indigenous remains', *Meanjin Quarterly*, vol. 73, no. 1, 2014,
     <meanjin.com.au/essays/restless-indigenous-remains>.

17   Daley, 'Restless Indigenous remains'.

18   K Wills, 'Reminiscence', Brandon Papers, John Oxley Memorial Library,
     Brisbane, OM 75–75/3; 'Korah Halcombe Wills, 1876, 1877', Mackay Mayors,
     Mackay Historical Society, <www.mackayhistory.org/research/mayors/004_wills.
     html>.

19   Wills, quoted in Daley, 'Restless Indigenous remains'.

20   For Macquarie, see P Daley, 'Lachlan Macquarie was no humanitarian: his own
     words show he was a terrorist', *The Guardian* (Australia), 5 April 2016, <www.
     theguardian.com/australia-news/postcolonial-blog/2016/apr/05/lachlan-
     macquarie-was-no-humanitarian-his-own-words-show-he-was-a-terrorist>.

21   P Daley, 'Black Anzac: the life and death of an Aboriginal man who fought for
     king and country', *The Guardian* (Australia), 25 March 2016, <www.theguardian.
     com/australia-news/2015/mar/25/black-anzac-the-life-and-death-of-an-
     aboriginal-man-who-fought-for-king-and-country>.

22   'Aboriginal and Torres Strait Islander peoples in the Australian Defence Force',
     Australian War Memorial, <www.awm.gov.au/encyclopedia/aborigines>.

23   'Douglas Grant', Australian War Memorial, <www.awm.gov.au/education/
     schools/resources/private-douglas-grant>.

24 'Members of Council', Australian War Memorial, <www.awm.gov.au/about/council>. See also D Stephens, 'Keepers of the flame: why do the people who control our war memorials look so different from the rest of us and why does this matter?', Honest History, 7 June 2016, <honesthistory.net.au/wp/keepers-of-the-flame-making-war-memorial-councils-more-representative>.

25 *Indigenous Pre-recruitment Course*, pamphlet, Australian Defence Force, at Young Diggers, <www.youngdiggers.com.au/sites/default/files/IPRC brochure.pdf>.

26 Daley, 'Lachlan Macquarie'; Reynolds, *Forgotten War*, chs 2–3.

27 See section 3 of the *Australian War Memorial Act 1980*, particularly the definition of 'Defence Force' and the lack of any restriction to 'wars' or 'warlike operations' fought outside Australia: <www.austlii.edu.au/au/legis/cth/consol_act/awma1980244/s3.html - active_service>.

28 P Stanley, 'NAIDOC Week 2014 address at Australian Defence Force Academy, 10 July 2014', Honest History, 10 July 2014, <honesthistory.net.au/wp/stanley-peter-naidoc-week-2014-adfa-address>.

29 Daley, 'From Butchers Creek to Berlin'; J Robertson, ' "Blatant war and genocide": memories of Native Police haunt Indigenous Queensland', *The Guardian* (Australia), 3 September 2016, <www.theguardian.com/australia-news/2016/sep/03/blatant-war-and-genocide-memories-of-native-police-haunt-indigenous-queensland>.

## 18: King, Queen and country: Will Anzac thwart republicanism?

1 Quotes from Bean's 'simple notes': 'Reminiscences – Royal Visit 1954', Australian War Memorial Archives, File 275/019/002. See also KS Inglis, 'Bean, Charles Edwin (1879–1968)', Australian *Dictionary of Biography*, Natonal Centre of Biography, Australian National University, <adb.anu.edu.au/biography/bean-charles-edwin-5166>; M McKernan, *Here Is Their Spirit: A History of the Australian War Memorial 1917–1990*, University of Queensland Press & Australian War Memorial, Brisbane, 1991, pp. 224–25.

2 DM Wallace, *The Web of Empire: A Diary of the Imperial Tour of their Royal Highnesses, the Duke and Duchess of Cornwall in 1901*, Macmillan, London, 1902, pp. 201–202.

3 *Evening News* (Sydney), 16 June 1920, p.7; *Sydney Morning Herald*, 23 March 1920, p. 6, 28 May 1920, p. 9, 18 June 1920, p. 7, 23 June 1920, p. 11. See also AG Holman, *Our Digger Prince with the Australian Kiddies*, John L Bennett, London, c. 1921.

4 T Derbyshire, *The Royal Tour of the Duke and Duchess of York*, Edward Arnold, London, 1927, pp.184–86; *Sydney Morning Herald*, 26 April 1927, p. 11.

5 Derbyshire, *The Royal Tour of the Duke and Duchess of York*, p. 244.

6 M Whitington (ed.), *The Decades of Royalty: Western Australia's Unique Relationship with the House of Windsor*, WA Newspapers, Perth, 1995, p. 17.

7 'Howard says Anzac legend defines nation', *The Age* (Melbourne), 24 April 2005, <www.theage.com.au/news/National/Howard-says-Anzac-legend-defines-nation/2005/04/24/1114281441799.html>; J Howard, 'Address at Anzac Dawn Service Gallipoli', 25 April 2005, PM Transcripts, <pmtranscripts.dpmc.gov.au/release/transcript-21719>.

8    *Sydney Morning Herald*, 26 April 1940, p. 9.
9    *Canberra Times*, 26 April 1948, p. 4; Whitington (ed.), *The Decades of Royalty*, p. 43.
10   For Bean's original requiem, see *Portland Guardian*, 1 May 1944, p. 2; for amended version, see *Their Spirit, Our History*, Department of Veterans' Affairs and Australian War Memorial, Canberra, 2007, p. 36, Anzac Portal, Department of Veterans' Affairs, <anzacportal.dva.gov.au/sites/default/files/publication-attachments/theirspirit.pdf>.
11   Speeches presented by Her Majesty Queen Elizabeth II in Australia, 1954–1992, National Library of Australia, MS 9174. See also: *Canberra Times*, 26 April 1965, p. 1 (Duke of Gloucester reads Queen's message); *Daily Telegraph* (Sydney), 21 February 1958, p. 13 (Queen Mother); *Sydney Morning Herald*, 25 April 1940, p. 1 (King George VI).
12   PJ Keating, 'Remembrance Day 1993', 11 November 1993, Australian War Memorial, <www.awm.gov.au/talks-speeches/keating-remembrance-day-1993>.
13   For example, Howard, 'Address at Anzac Dawn Service Gallipoli', 2005.
14   *Daily Telegraph*, 9 May 1910, pp. 10–11.
15   *National Advocate* (Bathurst), 10 May 1910, p. 3.
16   B Nelson, 'National Press Club address', 18 September 2013, Australian War Memorial, <www.awm.gov.au/talks-speeches/national-press-club-address>.
17   For example, 'Prince Harry lands in Australia to begin his Australian tour of duty', News Corp, 7 April 2015, <www.news.com.au/national/prince-harry-lands-in-australia-to-begin-his-australian-tour-of-duty/news-story/bc68c9e3bc14c431424dc1c84e98f6d7>. See also, for a number of visits (including 1954), 'Royal visit to the Australian War Memorial, 25 October 2011', Australian War Memorial, <www.awm.gov.au/events/royal-visit-2011>.

## 19: Australia's tug of war: Militarism versus independence

1    H Reynolds, *Unnecessary Wars*, NewSouth, Sydney, 2016, p. 234.
2    M Fraser with C Roberts, *Dangerous Allies*, Melbourne University Press, Melbourne, 2014.
3    Reynolds, *Unnecessary Wars*, p. 235.
4    G Appleby, 'What say do our elected representatives have in going to war?', The Conversation, 10 December 2015, <theconversation.com/what-say-do-our-elected-representatives-have-in-going-to-war-51860>.
5    H Belot & A McGhee, 'Solicitor-General resigns over "broken" relationship with Attorney-General George Brandis', *ABC News*, 24 October 2016, <www.abc.net.au/news/2016-10-24/justin-gleeson-resigns-as-solicitor-general/7960632>.
6    A Broinowski, *Allied and Addicted*, Scribe, Melbourne, 2007.
7    'The Lowy Institute poll: The US alliance', Lowy Institute, <lowyinstitute.org/lowyinstitutepollinteractive/the-us-alliance>.
8    A Broinowski, *About Face: Asian Accounts of Australia*, Scribe, Melbourne, 2003.
9    'Australia as regional police doctrine puts Howard in damage control', *7.30 Report*, ABC TV, 27 September 1999, <www.abc.net.au/7.30/stories/s55116.htm>.

10  T Kevin, '"We go to war when our cousins do": the countries Australia consults', in A Broinowski (ed.), *How Does Australia Go to War? A Call for Accountability and Change*, Australians for War Powers Reform, Melbourne, 2015, pp. 45–49.

11  C Sampford, 'Issues and options: changing the Constitution and complying with international law', in Broinowski (ed.), *How Does Australia Go to War?*, pp. 40–44.

12  A Broinowski, *Howard's War*, Scribe, Melbourne, 2003.

13  C Sampford, 'A better Westminster way to war?', in A Broinowski (ed.), *Why Did We Go to War in Iraq? A Call for an Australian Inquiry*, Iraq War Inquiry Group, Melbourne, 2012, pp. 57–58.

14  O Stone & P Kuznick, *The Untold History of the United States*, Random House, London, 2012, p. 507.

15  K Roth, 'A case against America', review of Noam Chomsky's *Who Rules the World?*, *New York Review of Books*, 9 June 2016, <www.nybooks.com/articles/2016/06/09/a-case-against-america>.

16  J O'Neill, 'Australia and the war in Syria: continuing obfuscation', *New Eastern Outlook*, 19 January 2016, <journal-neo.org/2016/01/19/australia-and-the-war-in-syria-continuing-obfuscation>.

17  O'Neill, 'Australia and the war in Syria'.

18  M Grattan, 'Abbott denies "mission creep" as more Australian troops committed to Iraq', The Conversation, 3 March 2015, <theconversation.com/abbott-denies-mission-creep-as-more-australian-troops-committed-to-iraq-38304>; A Henderson, 'Joe Biden, Malcolm Turnbull agree to expand Iraq training commitment to police operations', *ABC News*, 19 July 2016, <www.abc.net.au/news/2016-07-19/joe-biden-malcolm-turnbull-agree-to-iraq-police-training/7642572>; 'Joint press conference – The Syrian and Iraqi humanitarian crisis; Australia to extend air operations against Daesh into Syria', Department of Defence Ministers, 9 September 2015, <www.minister.defence.gov.au/2015/09/09/joint-press-conference-the-syrian-and-iraqi-humanitarian-crisis-australia-to-extend-air-operations-against-daesh-into-syria>; F Keany, 'Tony Abbott would have "considered" sending special forces to fight Islamic State in Iraq', *ABC News*, 21 July 2016, <www.abc.net.au/news/2016-07-21/tony-abbott-says-he-would-have-'considered'-deploying-troops/7648368>; 'Press conference: Parliament House – two years of Tony Abbott, Syrian Refugee Crisis', Bill Shorten, ALP, 7 September 2015, <www.billshorten.com.au/press-conference-parliament-house-two-years-of-tony-abbott-syrian-refugee-crisis>; 'Turnbull government expands Australian military powers at home and abroad', World Socialist Web Site, 12 September 2016, <www.wsws.org/en/articles/2016/09/12/mili-s12.html>.

19  P Leahy, 'Afghanistan: we had no strategy in this war and the details were kept from us', *Sydney Morning Herald*, 22 February 2016, <www.smh.com.au/comment/australian-armys-afghanistan-experience-finally-revealed-in-documentary-20160221-gmzumr.html>.

20  C Johnson, *Blowback: The Costs and Consequences of American Empire*, Metropolitan Books, New York, 2000; J Todenhöfer, *My Journey into the Heart of Terror: Ten Days in the Islamic State*, Scribe, Melbourne, 2016.

21  J Howard, *Lazarus Rising: A Personal and Political Autobiography*, HarperCollins, Sydney, 2010, pp. 423–63.

22  M Swieringa, 'Can parliamentary conventions limit executive privilege?', in Broinowski (ed.), *How Does Australia Go to War?*, pp. 59–64.

23  J Gillard, 'Address to the Congress of the United States, Washington', 9 March 2011, PM Transcripts, <pmtranscripts.pmc.gov.au/release/transcript-17726>; J Gillard, 'Australia-United States force posture initiatives', media release, 16 November 2011, PM Transcripts, <pmtranscripts.pmc.gov.au/release/transcript-18272>; J Gillard, 'Speech to the joint sitting of Australian Parliament in honour of President Obama, Canberra', 17 November 2011, PM Transcripts, <pmtranscripts.pmc.gov.au/release/transcript-18274>.

24  'The Hon Tanya Plibersek MP on how Australia can be a better international citizen', 31 May 2016, Lowy Institute, <www.lowyinstitute.org/news-and-media/multimedia/audio/hon-tanya-plibersek-mp-how-australia-can-be-better-international>.

25  P Wong, 'Trump's election is a turning point for Australian foreign policy', *Sydney Morning Herald*, 15 November 2016, <www.smh.com.au/comment/trumps-election-is-a-turning-point-for-australian-foreign-policy-20161114-gsp5kd.html>.

26  R Di Natale, Senate Hansard, 4 May 2016, <parlinfo.aph.gov.au/parlInfo/genpdf/chamber/hansards/c59815f1-0832-42c3-b73b-d3ee21b57955/0318/hansard_frag.pdf;fileType=application%2Fpdf>.

27  Fraser with Roberts, *Dangerous Allies*, p. 278.

28  Reynolds, *Unnecessary Wars*, p. 209.

29  J Wilson, 'Chasing Asylum review: Eva Orner's documentary makes concrete the horrors of Australia's immigration detention centres', *Sydney Morning Herald*, 26 May 2016, <www.smh.com.au/entertainment/movies/chasing-asylum-review-eva-orners-documentary-makes-concrete-the-horrors-of-australias-immigration-detention-centres-20160525-gp3csl.html>.

30  C Lawrence, *Fear and Politics*, Scribe, Melbourne, 2006.

31  A Leigh, *Battlers and Billionaires: The Story of Inequality in Australia*, Black Inc., Melbourne, 2013.

32  On the New and White Guards, see S Cahill, '"This fascist mob"', *Overland*, no. 189, 2007, <overland.org.au/previous-issues/issue-189/feature-shane-cahill>; M Cathcart, *Defending the National Tuckshop: Australia's Secret Army Intrigue of 1931*, McPhee Gribble, Melbourne, 1988.

33  A Broinowski, 'Trump: seize the moment', John Menadue – Pearls and Irritations blog, 28 November 2016, <johnmenadue.com/blog/?p=8455>.

## 20: Conclusion

1  Australian of the Year 2016 and former Chief of Army General David Morrison made a number of speeches in which he linked the Anzac legend to misogyny within the Australian Defence Force. See, for example, 'Lieutenant General David Morrison, AO, Chief of the Australian Army: Chief of Army address to the White Ribbon Breakfast, Adelaide, Tuesday 25 November 2014', Australian Army, <www.army.gov.au/~/media/Files/Speeches/CA_WhiteRibbonAddress_25NOV2014.pdf>.

2    J Green, 'Why must a war define us?', The Drum, ABC TV, 24 April 2014, <www.abc.net.au/news/2014-04-24/green-why-must-a-war-define-us/5408046>.

3    M McKernan, *Here Is Their Spirit: A History of the Australian War Memorial, 1917–1990*, University of Queensland Press with the Australian War Memorial, Brisbane, 1991, pp. 328–31. Prime Minister Hawke made the change after discussion with the then national president of the RSL, Sir William Keys.

4    Director Nelson of the memorial has foreshadowed an approach to the government for capital funds to build new galleries. See Senate Foreign Affairs, Defence and Trade Legislation Committee, 'Estimates', Official Committee Hansard, 19 October 2016, pp. 144, 146.

5    D Stephens, 'Keepers of the flame: why do the people who control our war memorials look so different from the rest of us and why does this matter?', Honest History, 7 June 2016, <honesthistory.net.au/wp/keepers-of-the-flame-making-war-memorial-councils-more-representative>.

6    Parliament and Civics Education Rebate (PACER), <www.pacer.org.au>. The other mandated PACER visits are Parliament House, the Museum of Australian Democracy at Old Parliament House and/or the National Electoral Education Centre. Not the National Film and Sound Archive, the National Gallery, the National Library, the National Museum or the National Portrait Gallery, the cultural institutions that between them present a broad view of Australia, and not Questacon, which is about education in science and technology, the central planks of an agile and innovative future society.

7    *Honest History's Alternative Guide to the Australian War Memorial* suggests different priorities for the Memorial. See Honest History, 26 April 2016, <honesthistory.net.au/wp/honest-history-honest-historys-alternative-guide-to-the-australian-war-memorial>.

8    For example, in Queensland see Anzac Centenary Queensland, <anzac100.initiatives.qld.gov.au>; Anzac Day Commemoration Committee, <anzacday.org.au/home>.

9    F Bongiorno, 'A legend with class', *Griffith Review*, no. 48, *Enduring Legacies*, 2015, <griffithreview.com/articles/legend-class>.

10    I Clendinnen, 'The history question: who owns the past?', *Quarterly Essay*, no. 23, 2006, p. 20; P Cochrane, 'The past is not sacred', *Griffith Review*, no. 48, *Enduring Legacies*, 2015, <griffithreview.com/articles/past-sacred>.

11    R Gaita, 'Raimond Gaita on Donald Trump's America: a cloud cuckoo land devoid of fact, evidence and argument', The Conversation, 15 November 2016, <theconversation.com/raimond-gaita-on-donald-trumps-america-a-cloud-cuckoo-land-devoid-of-fact-evidence-and-argument-68752>.

# Acknowledgments

onest History – the coalition – is based upon Honest History Incorporated, an association set up under the law of the Australian Capital Territory. Details about Honest History can be found on the Honest History website (honesthistory.net.au). The association has office-bearers and a committee but no formal membership arrangements. It welcomes support and donations.

Many people have helped with this book (and the whole Honest History project), some of them perhaps without realising it. We particularly thank Derek Abbott, Kristen Alexander, Kathy Bail, Joan Beaumont, Diane Bell, John Bowan, James Brown, Pamela Burton, Christine Chappell, Sebastian Clark, Stephen Clarke, Judith Crispin, Paul Daley, David Donovan, Emma Driver, Matt Esterman, Margaret Fanning, Steve Flora, Ian Gollings, Anne Gripton, Steve Hurren, Greg Keith, Paul Kiem, Marilyn Lake, Greg Longney, Phillipa McGuinness, Harriet McInerney, David McKinlay, John Menadue, Graham Mills, John Myrtle, Douglas Newton, Rod Olsen, Cengiz Özakıncı, Philip Peters, Tony Powell, John Robertson, Gerry Schulz, Brad Snell, Straker Translations, Tom Tescher, Richard Thwaites, Sue Wareham, Carole Wigg, Geoffrey Winter, Tony Wright (Aotearoa New Zealand), Nicola Young, Louise Zarmati and Erik-Jan Zürcher. And our families. And lots of supporters of Honest History – including the historians and others who agreed to their names being listed on our website as 'distinguished supporters' – and followers on Twitter and friends on Facebook.

Thank you also to each of our authors. It should go without saying that not every author agrees with every word in the book.

David Stephens

Alison Broinowski

# Index